BERKELEY DAZE

Memoir of a Frat Boy

By
Allan Brown

ISBN 978-0-6151-3950-0

DISCLAIMER

BERKELEY DAZE is a memoir. It is not history. However, there are historical references and events throughout. It is my recalled account of attending the University of California at Berkeley in the late 1950s and early 1960s. Most names have been changed. Dialogue has been reconstructed with the goal of conveying the spirit of the conversation if not the exact words. Certain events have been rearranged, and a few individuals have been combined into composite characters. If I had to guess, this work is 90% perceived reality and 10% fiction. I hope you enjoy reading *BERKELEY DAZE: Memoir of a Frat Boy.*

Dedicated to the Class of 1963 and UC Berkeley
for opening up new worlds

CHAPTERS

1. NORTHSIDE

Jutting up from the Berkeley hills, Indian Rock offers a spectacular view of the San Francisco Bay Area. This massive chunk of granite is made for sitting and contemplating the panorama of water, bridges, islands and the far-off towers of San Francisco itself. There are several well-worn paths up to the craggy summit, but I usually follow my own route and make a minor climbing expedition out of it. In my college days, Indian Rock was a favorite spot for fraternity boys to hang out with a six-pack of beer in the late afternoon. Often, someone would bring along the house dog, usually a brute of a beast such as a St. Bernard or a Great Dane. The frat boys would feed the hound potato chips and let it lick spilt beer off the rock. Today, no sign of the frat boys. Instead, the rock is full of young women in hiking shorts with firm tan legs who compete with the view.

After a half hour or so of gazing out over the sparkling bay, I climb back down Indian Rock and continue my tour of my old Northside haunts from the time I was a student at the University of California many long years ago.

I drive by the corner of Hearst Avenue and Gayley Road and pull up before a hulking, shake-shingled apartment building that fills the entire block. My fraternity house, Alpha Kappa Lambda, once stood here. It was an elegant three-story, craftsman styled Tudor house that the university took over in the late 1960s and demolished to make way for this university owned apartment monstrosity that has none of the elegance of our long-vanished house. It's sad to see so I don't linger.

Down the hill, I stop for a beer and a slice of pizza at La Vals on Euclid Avenue. The place is seedy now, the beer flat and the pizza soggy. A Mexican fast-food joint shares La Vals' patio, adding an element of congestion and trash. The Northgate Theater that had once shown underground films such as Kenneth Anger's *Fireworks* is long gone. Also gone from the Northside is Cody's Bookstore, one of the first great counter-culture bookstores in Berkeley, with rack after rack of the left-wing newspapers and magazines. I used to prowl its aisles and skim the latest edition of the *Daily Worker* or the most recent Zen work by Alan Watts. Cody's is now located on Telegraph Avenue on the south side of campus.

Across the street from La Vals is a sedate little coffee and pastry shop. Once this was a jazz café that featured Afro-Cuban jazz on the weekends. We frat boys would dance away the night to the beat of the bongo drums and saxophones with the local beatnik chicks. They said they liked fraternity boys because they had good bodies and loved to turn them on.

Later, I stroll along Solano Avenue on the border of Berkeley and Albany, checking out the shops and bookstores while I sip on a coffee-to-go from Peets. This area is home to many longtime Berkeley-ites most of whom had gone to Cal in the sixties and couldn't bear to leave the university setting. Now, well past middle age, they live a comfortable life in their remodeled bungalows and still groove on the Berkeley scene.

My old friends, Gerard and Marie, fall into this category. Gerard, tall and slim with grizzled blonde hair graduated from Cal two years ahead of me in 1961. They bought a bungalow off Solano Avenue in the early 1970s, raised two sons and have been in the same house ever since. Now, Gerard runs his own printing company, owns a country home in France and appears to be doing well. In recent years, Marie, a fiery brunette with dark, flashing eyes, has been active in a variety of causes including South Africa's anti-apartheid movement and women's rights issues.

I drop by and stay a couple of nights. Their bungalow is a combination of Mother Jones and Euro-modern décor. Marie is radical-chic now, always challenging, always arguing, always lambasting the news media, of which I am a member.

"The news does nothing but parrot the corporate line," she declares as she sips on her Chardonnay

"That's funny," I respond. "Most of the time we're accused of being so liberal."

"Oh, come on, Al. You know you people are all bought and sold. It's all about selling papers or ratings. There's always some fat, old

Republican pulling the strings in the news business."

I glance back over my shoulder. "No strings there."

"No. Just a paycheck," she laughs.

"Yes. That's right, a paycheck that pays the bills," I say, slightly annoyed. "After I retire, then maybe I can afford to be a radical like you."

"Ha, fat chance!" She smiles and gives me a kiss on the forehead.

The next evening, we attend a photo exhibit in Berkeley given by a friend of theirs. Richard is an advertising photographer and does travel photography on the side. The exhibit is on Bali, mostly tourist shots, yet done with grace and professionalism. A small Balinese gamelan orchestra playing in the background adds to the exotic atmosphere. The Berkeley crowd is here in full force. Some are indistinguishable from the Hyde Park or the Old Town crowd in Chicago where I live—a few beards, a couple of unrepentant hippies and one homeless person who Richard wants to throw out, but is persuaded not to. More common are the sleek, Euro-dressed yuppies in black, including a young, fresh-faced babe in a low-cut blouse and tight jeans. She is apparently a newcomer to the scene and attracting much attention. Gerard, an admirer of young women, smiles at her, but is unable to make a move because of the proximity of Marie.

After the exhibit, we go to Spenger's, a seafood restaurant on the Berkeley waterfront. Marie protests that it's too touristy. Still, I like it with its jaunty nautical décor, its teak bar and its sense of history. Most of its bric-a-brac is authentic, ripped right off the sailing ships that used to ply the Bay. The place is also full of personal memories for me. My family used to eat here on Sundays with my grandmother, who lived nearby on Ninth Street in what was then a shabby industrial section of Berkeley.

While we sip rum punches, Marie waxes eloquent on how great Berkeley is.

"I mean, this place is unique in the world! Where else do you find such a cool collection of people, Al?"

"Actually, you can find interesting people everywhere—Chicago, New York, Colorado," I answer. "You ought to get out more and explore your own country."

"For sure," she replies.

I am always struck by the provincialism of the Berkeley-ites. As far as they are concerned, if you live in Berkeley, there is little else worth visiting. Only Europe and New York, with an occasional foray into Latin America or maybe Southeast Asia. The Midwest is the great fly over region, Chicago only a change of planes at O'Hare Airport.

When we return to their house, I bid Gerard and Marie adieu, all the time wondering if Berkeley is still relevant to my life; wondering what it meant to have lived here and gone to Cal so many years ago.

2. BERKELEY BOUND

Eighteen miles east of Berkeley, nestled in the rolling hills of Contra Costa County, on the shores of the Carquinez Strait, is my hometown, Martinez, California. Although a world apart, Martinez has long felt the impact of Berkeley. Many teachers who taught at my high school had graduated from the University of California at Berkeley. As a county seat, Martinez was home to lawyers and judges who had gone to UC's Boalt Law School. Several civil engineers who worked for the county had graduated from UC's School of Engineering. All touted the glories of Berkeley, calling it the Harvard of the West.

My father was a civil engineer who earned his degree through correspondence schools, later becoming a registered civil engineer. He regretted not going to college, but as he always said, "If you are at all interested in engineering, Allan, get trained at the best. The best around here is Berkeley."

Thus, from an early age I was indoctrinated about Berkeley. Because I was good in science and math at high school, I naturally thought about going into engineering at Berkeley. I realized there were other good engineering schools around such as Cal Poly, San Jose State and the University of Nevada at Reno. However, Berkeley was the one. I ignored the advice of my high school counselor, Mr. McBride, who warned me in his world-weary voice, "Berkeley engineering is a tough nut to crack, Allan. They take only the best and your competition comes from around the country and the world."

"I've heard that," I said, "but my dad says I should at least give it a try."

"Sure, Allan, give it a try; however, also consider applying to other engineering schools."

"I'll think about it," I replied.

But, in the end, I applied only to Berkeley.

Early May of 1958, I found myself sitting in a large auditorium at Cal about to take the engineering entrance test, a test that could determine the rest my life. Many of my fellow test takers were Asians—Japanese, Chinese and a scattering of East Indians. Mostly though, they were regular American high school seniors like me who thought they had a chance at Berkeley engineering.

A balding professor in a rumpled suit walked to the podium and made a little speech to the effect that this was the test that separated the men from the boys.

"Look around you," he said with a sweeping arm gesture. "Two out of three of you will not pass this test. That doesn't mean you're not engineering material. It simply means that you're not engineering material for Berkeley. We take only the best. Good luck."

The test was a bitch. I had tried to study for it with some review books, but it was still tough. Many algebra and trig questions, some plane geometry questions. There were a few chemistry questions, but the killer was the physics section. I had thought physics was easy in high school, but these problems required a lot of thought. Worse, the test consisted of timed sections and it was impossible for me to finish the physics section.

By the second hour of the three-hour test, I had a splitting headache, and I sensed that I was not doing well. I was guessing too much, even though educated guessing was encouraged. Finally, it was over. I got up glassy-eyed and made my way out of the auditorium. As we filed out, the proctor wished us good luck and told us we should have our scores in three weeks.

Three long weeks later, I received a short letter saying that I hadn't scored high enough to be admitted to the College of Engineering at Berkeley for the fall. I was stunned. Didn't pass? What did they mean I didn't pass? I took a close look at the breakdown of my scores and saw that I missed the cutoff point by one percentile point. I had ranked in the 76th percentile. The 77th percentile was the cutoff point. One measly percentile!

My father thought there was some mistake. He telephoned one of the engineering professors that he knew to find out what was going on. It turned out, had I scored the same on the test last year, I might have gotten in. Every year the cutoff point was different. The group this year was either smarter or better test takers than last year. The professor told my father that if I were determined to go to the College of Engineering at Berkeley, I would have to take the test in the fall for the spring semester, which would probably be less competitive. However, he strongly recommended that I enroll in the two-year engineering program at Mt. Diablo Junior College and then transfer to Berkeley as a junior. He said students who transferred to Berkeley in their junior year usually did well.

Ugh! Junior college! As far as I was concerned, that was simply a big playground for students who couldn't make it into a four-year college. I didn't want to go to junior college, and I didn't want to go to another engineering school such as Cal Poly or the University of Nevada. Those schools were second-rate compared to Berkeley. Instead, I looked over the college course catalog for Berkeley and noticed that chemical engineering was in the College of Liberal Arts and Sciences, not in the School of Engineering. Since I had been admitted to the College of Liberal Arts and Sciences, I could theoretically major in chemical engineering. The only hang-up was I would have to take a bunch of liberal arts courses to fulfill distribution requirements that would make earning a degree in chemical engineering at least a four-and-a-half-year project.

Then there was the question: did I really want to be a chemical engineer? I took a look at the engineering career book that my dad had given me and noticed that one subdivision of chemical engineering was petroleum engineering.

'Hmm,' I thought, 'Petroleum engineers build refineries around the world. Well, maybe that's O.K. too. Traveling around the world and building oil refineries.'

My father seemed happy with my decision to go into chemical engineering at Berkeley; although, he did say Cal Poly wasn't a bad option if I still wanted to pursue civil engineering. I stuck with my decision. I was Berkeley bound. However, there were other factors at play as well.

***

Berkeley was a portal into a brave new world of politics and social movements that I found intriguing thanks to my high school Spanish teacher, Mr. Thompson, who was an escapee from years of graduate work at Berkeley.

Mr. Thompson, a tall, balding, bespectacled man was also the coach of the tennis team that I had played on for three years. In the spring of my junior year, Mr. Thompson took me and three other players to the

Berkeley Tennis Club to call lines at a local tennis tournament. The club was located right next to The Claremont Hotel, a sprawling, white European-styled hotel in the Berkeley hills on the border of Oakland. The Claremont was a watering hole for the East Bay elite. Sleek Jaguars and Mercedes filled its parking lot.

Unlike our rundown courts at Alhambra Union High School, the courts at the Berkeley Tennis Club were perfect— smooth green asphalt with freshly painted white lines and nets pulled taut to the precise height. The players sported the latest in tennis fashion with tailored shirts and shorts. They wore the newest Converse tennis shoes with the proper arch support. Their racquets were handcrafted with the finest catgut. Cool under pressure, graceful in their serves, these players had skills that were probably the result of years of private lessons.

My teammates and I sat on little stools on either side of the courts, our eyes focused on the white lines, ready to pronounce a ball in or out. Our word was law. No arguments at all. We were simply sharp-eyed young men with no interest in who won or lost. It was, however, mind-numbing work with the sun beating down for hours. We had to concentrate on those lines, hardly taking a breath and only occasionally taking a drink from the water-cooler.

"Line umpire, your call. Was the ball in or out?" the chief umpire asked from his perch on a high observation chair in mid-court.

"Out, sir," I responded.

"Very good. Forty-love."

Finally, the matches ended and we regrouped. Mr. Thompson was pleased with our performance. To celebrate, he was going to take us to a Chinese restaurant down on Shattuck Avenue.

As we made our way to his car in the hotel parking lot, we were greeted by one of Thompson's old friends. His name was Alex and he was dressed like a seventeenth century buccaneer in a flowing white silk shirt with black pantaloons tucked into the tops of knee-high boots. He had shoulder length hair, a full bushy mustache and a gold earring in one ear. All that was missing was an eye patch.

"Thompson, you bald fuck, I haven't seen you for ages. You don't hang around Berkeley much any more," said Alex in a thick Russian accent.

"Hey, Alex, you old fake. I see you're still up to your same old tricks."

"Only trying to make an honest living in this capitalist society. What about you?"

"Oh, I'm busy with these young lads and school and whatnot over in Martinez," replied Thompson, defensively.

"Oh yes, Martinez, the end of nowhere and teaching Spanish too. Such a shame." Turning to us, Alex said, "You know boys, Thompson speaks perfect Russian. He has a doctorate in it. Spanish is a waste of his talents."

"Spanish is the most important language you can learn in California," retorted Thompson.

"Yes, yes, but enough talk. Come, I want you all to be my guests for some refreshments at the Med." Alex led us over to his car, a hot cinnamon red Cadillac convertible hardtop. Inside we could see a rack of clothes, all fancy shirts and pants hanging from a bar. "Pardon my haberdashery, but I am in the midst of moving. Two of you can ride with me. Thompson can take the rest."

My teammate Ken and I piled in the Caddy and Alex drove off followed by Thompson down towards Telegraph Avenue, the main college drag in Berkeley.

Alex took us to the Mediterraneum Café, a scruffy place full of creaky tables and chairs, cigarette smoke and various beatnik types. Posters of Marx, Lenin and Trotsky lined one wall; nude paintings by local artists lined the other. Loud talk was of how the Russian Revolution had gone off track, had gone bourgeois and had betrayed the working-man.

No one paid much attention to us, even though we were conspicuous in our tennis whites and short hair in the midst of beards and long, stringy hair.

Alex and Thompson appeared to know everyone in the place. "Fellow graduate students in Russian studies at Berkeley," Thompson explained to us. "They talk big, but they're harmless. Unless you work for the military or the government or teach at the university level, there are no jobs for Russian speakers and some of these clowns couldn't hold a job anyway because of their political affiliations."

Thompson had an espresso while we had Cokes. His friends rapped on:

"McCarthyism is just another Salem witch-hunt. Arthur Miller had it right in *The Crucible*."

One said he offered a daily prayer giving thanks for Berkeley as "an island of sanity in a sea of insane Cold War politics."

"Maybe you have the right idea," said Alex turning to Mr. Thompson. "Sell out and educate the sons and daughters of the bourgeoisie."

Of course I was wondering just how socialist or communist Alex really was. He apparently had enough money to buy that cinnamon red Cadillac.

We finally said goodbye to Alex and his buddies, and Thompson took us to his favorite Chinese restaurant on Shattuck Avenue. As we dined on tasty, yet mysterious dishes, I mulled over the contrasts of the day: the money world of tennis and the scruffy world of espresso cafes, socialists and revolution, both coexisting right here in Berkeley, worlds away from Martinez.

***

The capper in my decision to go to Berkeley was the lure of fraternity life with its promise of endless partying and willing women. My friend Gerard, who had graduated ahead of me at Alhambra High, had joined Alpha Kappa Lambda at Berkeley. Gerard was the son of our high school French teacher. He was a cool looking dude—thin, with long blond hair and a vaguely French look that girls found attractive.

One evening in June, he came over in his black MG sports car to give me some material on fraternity life at Cal. I glanced at it and told him I would think about it. Later we drove to the local drive-in for a hamburger while he continued to pitch the glories of Greek life at Berkeley.

"Al, you wouldn't believe the parties. Some of those chicks are so hot, especially when you get them off by themselves and away from their sorority sisters."

"No kidding," I said taking a slurpy drag on my vanilla milkshake.

"But it's not all parties. Berkeley is a tough school, but we have files of old exams to help you out. "

"Old exams?"

"Yeah, old econ exams, old chemistry exams, math and what not. Many professors never change their exams from year to year, or if they do, not by much. Those files have saved a lot of frat brothers."

"No kidding," I said, amazed.

A few evenings later, Gerard drove up with Denise, a dark brunette in short-shorts who he introduced as a friend from one of the sororities with which Alpha Kappa Lambda was affiliated. Denise didn't say much. She simply smiled as she sat on the couch in her short-shorts, her smooth legs curled up, gazing at Gerard as he continued his pitch:

"It makes sense to join a fraternity at a school like Berkeley, Al. The place is so huge, you can easily get lost. Twenty-six thousand students or thereabouts. So no matter how smart you are, it pays to have some friends who can show you the way."

As he smoothly explained this, he flipped out some pictures of past parties with good-looking women.

I was intrigued.

Gerard went on to say that over the summer, there would be a series of informal rush parties to give prospective fraternity brothers a preview of what awaited them should they decide to join.

"And you know the cost is about the same as living in a dorm, and I guarantee you the food is much better, as well as the scenery," he concluded.

My tongue was hanging out.

Gerard gave me a list of rushing events for the summer. Swim parties at homes in Orinda, a beach party at Tomales Bay in Marin County and a '49er's football game in August. I was impressed. I was sold. I decided go through fraternity rush and join a fraternity, maybe Alpha Kappa Lambda.

3. FRAT BOY

I spent my first week in Berkeley staying at the local YMCA. The place was a dump with the bathrooms down the hall and it was full of freshmen who were rushing fraternities. Most of us slept late because of the nonstop parties. We rose around noon, stood in line for a shower and then went off for another round of pool parties, dinner parties and cocktail parties. Sometimes we went to San Francisco for a rush outing. After four days of this, my head was spinning. Classes would begin soon, so the pressure was on to pledge a fraternity before the end of the week.

I had gone to several rush events with Alpha Kappa Lambda (AKL) and a few other fraternities. Delta Kappa Epsilon (DKE) had shown me a great time, and they had a beautiful house on the south side of campus. In addition, they seemed rather sophisticated. They talked of their ambition to go into law and medicine and many had spent summers in Europe. The guys in AKL, by contrast, were friendly, but some struck me as clueless. A few lived at home in Oakland or El Cerrito and only showed up for meals at the fraternity house. The fact that Gerard and Ken (my old tennis teammate) were house members and from Martinez made AKL seems an extension of high school. Still, there were a few cool members such as Bill Singleton, Jim Dougharty, and Rich Petrillo, all upperclassmen who were active on campus and knew their way around. I didn't know what to do, but I had to make up my mind fast or else live at home in Martinez and commute to Berkeley, since I had forgone the opportunity to live in a dorm.

While I was debating all this, I went to one more rush party at the FIJI house (Phi Gamma Delta). The first floor of the Italianate style brick house had been transformed into a South Pacific island with fake palm trees, colored lights, a roast pig and a lethal punch that bubbled up like lava from an erupting volcano. The guys were in loincloths, the girls in sarongs. It turned out to be a drunk-fest. I had never seen so many people passed out, lying about in the living room, in the basement, up in the sleeping rooms and out on the lawn. I had crashed on a couch with a dim memory of making out with some tipsy sorority girl. All the while, I was thinking, no way could I pledge a house like this. It would be a sure invitation to academic disaster. In fact, one drunken Fiji proudly told me their house was always on academic probation and near the bottom of the dean's list.

"Somehow, most of the brothers make it through," explained my host. "Like, man, you got to have a good time at college. That's what my ol' man always tells me. 'Don't worry about grades, just get through', he says. 'Business loves guys who are sociable. They don't give a damn about grades'. "

The next day, I had offers to join AKL and DKE. I debated the pros and the cons. With AKL, at least I would have some old friends and rides home to Martinez on the weekends. In addition, the AKLs were friendly and down to earth. The DKEs mostly came from Orinda and Lafayette and obviously had money. I didn't know if I could keep up with them, their sports cars and their trips to San Francisco to party and club. Yet, I knew membership in their house could mean connections that might pay off later in life. Still, I was confounded. Finally, I flipped a coin and it came up AKL. The next day I moved in.

***

Alpha Kappa Lambda was the archetypical frat house, with a spacious entrance hall, an extensive living room, a central flagstone fireplace, a dining room hung with house banners, a beer cellar downstairs, and upstairs, sleeping rooms and sleeping porches. It was a friendly, comforting place full of mementos documenting its fifty-year history.

Life in the fraternity soon settled down to a routine. I was assigned to a stuffy little room on the second floor that I slept in for a few nights, and then I moved to the sleeping porch, which had more room and plenty of fresh air. My roommate was upper-classman Jim Dougharty, a political science major who never studied yet wrote long, involved papers on the more arcane aspects of the U.S. political process such as the role of lobbyists in government. Jim went out drinking nearly every night and slept through the day, missing most of his classes, yet he main-tained a B+ average. As he used to say, "It's all in the art of bullshitting, Al. Read a book or two, maybe the *New York Times,* write some compel-ling bullshit and you'll do well in this major, if not in life."

Monday night was house night, an hour-long meeting to discuss house business. Pledges did not attend. We were supposed to be study-ing. On Tuesday night, special committees such as the rush committee or the social committee met to plot their next event. Wednesday night was often movie night for those who needed a break from the week's rigors. Thursday night was drinking night. Around nine o'clock the call would go out for a beer break. Ten or twelve brothers would pile into cars and roar off down Hearst Avenue to La Vals, or some other beer joint with peanuts on the floor, an off-key folksinger. Invariably, there was an ID checker didn't look too closely at the fake ID's. We would consume a few pitchers of beer together with several pizzas and then return to the house around midnight. After all, there were classes the next day. Attendance at Friday classes was a spotty affair for many of the brothers. However, for pledges, it was mandatory. We dutifully made our down to campus for classes that we sat though nearly comatose.

Friday night was usually an exchange with a sorority or a woman's dormitory. These were low-key mixers, designed to scope out likely prospects for future dates. The process was usually Darwinian with the most attractive guys hooking up with the most attractive co-eds and the others pairing up as best they could.

In the fall, Saturday was game day. A day to put on our white shirts and trudge over to Memorial Stadium to watch the Cal football team do battle with teams from the Pacific Coast Conference. Fall of 1958 was an outstanding season, with quarterback Joe Kapp leading Cal to the Rose Bowl. Cal went to the Rose Bowl with a 6-1 record, yet lost to Iowa 38-to-12.

Even more fun than watching the game was sitting in the rooting section and holding up large colored-coded stunt cards that, when seen from across the stadium, formed words or designs insulting to the op-posing team. At the end of each game, we flung these cards high into the air and watched them sail across the football field. Occasionally someone was hit on the head or even lost an eye from these missiles.

The other football highlight was watching the high-kicking cheer-leaders go through their pom-pom routines in their short little skirts. Looks and skill were everything. These cheerleaders often inspired drunken male striptease, sometimes right down to bare butt. Throughout this mayhem, Oski, the Cal bear mascot would race around the field dancing with the cheerleaders and leading the Cal Fight song: *Fight on you golden bears...*

Half time featured the high-stepping Cal Band, in their navy blue and gold uniforms, marching smartly across the field, playing in complex, choreographed formations. The Cal Band always blew away the competition. They routinely won collegiate band contests and traveled through the U.S. and Europe. Gerard was a proud member of this group, playing his trombone for hours until his lips bled.

After the game, we retreated to the patio deck in front of our fraternity house and continued the party with alums, girlfriends and whoever else showed up. Beer flowed from the kegs and rock'n' roll blared from the loud speakers.

Saturday night was a continuation of the party with a spaghetti dinner, wine and often a bread fight with chunks of sourdough flying about. Out of season, Saturday night was perhaps a cocktail party at somebody's private home up in the Berkeley hills or a trip to the nightclubs in the City. Sunday was a day of rest, a day of study, a day to do laundry or perhaps take the laundry home and have Mom do it. The frat boy beat went on.

***

With the fraternity as the hub of my residential and social life, I set off daily to do battle with the academics of the university. This involved hiking down through the north end of campus to Dwinell Plaza and joining in the crush of some twenty-six thousand students as they surged through the main campus entrance, Sather Gate.

Between classes, I would sit on a nearby bench on the plaza and watch in amazement as hundreds of attractive co-eds fluttered on by in their cashmere sweaters and poodle skirts. All shapes, all sizes. Blondes, brunettes, an occasional redhead, all forging ahead, books in their arms, intent on getting a college education and maybe meeting Mr. Right. Then there were the men, mostly clean-cut with close-cropped hair, wearing short-sleeve dress shirts, some with ties and neatly pressed khakis or slacks. Now and then, a bearded, longhaired student in dirty jeans wandered by with a book bag slung over his back.

Only the Asians broke up this sea of white faces. About a third of the Cal student body was Asian. Most were Japanese-Americans who lived at home in the East Bay and commuted to school. Nearly all were majoring in the sciences or engineering. They stuck to themselves and rarely interacted with their Caucasian peers. The only blacks that I saw on campus were usually African students, the sons and daughters of the ruling elites. Occasionally, I ran into an American black from back East who had gone to a private prep school and whose parents were either doctors or lawyers.

My classes ranged from small sections of twenty-five students to five hundred in large lecture halls with professors mumbling at a distant podium. Every criticism that I had heard of Berkeley—that it was huge, impersonal and tough—proved to be true. The unstated goal was to flunk out at least a third of the freshmen class. Nonetheless, I felt a sense of liberation, a sense of being entirely on my own with no one looking over my shoulder. I could attend class or not. I could study or not. Nobody cared. Only the midterms and finals counted. Show up for those, do well and your grade was assured. I was no longer in high school.

The first semester I took freshman chemistry, pre-calculus math, speech and ROTC. It was a light load, only thirteen units. Fifteen units per semester were considered average. However, I had been warned against a full load.

"I've seen more brothers go down the tubes because of a heavy class commitment," said Dougharty. "They think they can do it all. Be in a house, party and maintain a C average. It doesn't work that way."

I took his advice and was glad I did. Even the thirteen units were a hassle, especially the five-unit freshman chemistry course, Chem. 1A. High school chemistry had been a breeze, but this course made no sense to me. The professor's lectures didn't relate to the textbook; rather, they usually focused on some obscure pet project of his. The chemistry lab related neither to the book nor to the lectures. It had its own weird internal logic that I usually failed to grasp at 8 AM on a Saturday morning. As a result, I was flirting with a D throughout the course, and I was afraid of flunking the final. Then I heard about Ballard Brothers, a tutoring outfit that prepped students for the Chem. 1A final. It offered a two-week course, meeting several nights a week on Shattuck Avenue. The instructors taught us useful formulas, showed us how to derive them and gave us several practice finals. Therefore, I was somewhat prepared for the final and received a B- for my efforts, which, averaged with my other grades and lab work, gave me a C for the course.

"Nice work, Mr. Brown. You pulled it out," remarked the teaching assistant as he handed back the bluebook finals.

"Thanks," I replied. "It was tough."

"Yeah, I know. But it only gets worse from here on, Mr. Brown. Wait until you have to take physical chemistry and for that matter, engineering physics."

"I hear you," I said.

I fared better in math. I was taking a pre-calculus course, and for the first time, I felt I understood advanced algebra. As a result, my transition to calculus was smooth. However, my self-confidence didn't translate into a B. For some reason, maybe over-confidence, I received only a C on the final.

As far as the language arts were concerned, I had initially wanted to take freshman English, but again, I was counseled by the brothers to avoid it. The grading was chickenshit. The teaching assistants apparently took great glee in flunking those they deemed unworthy of pursing an English major.

Instead, the brothers suggested I take Speech, which satisfied the same requirement and was much easier. However, the only section I could enroll in was one designed for pre-law students taught by a Dr. L., a pudgy, curly-haired guy who spoke with a lisp. We studied a few landmark Supreme Court cases including *Brown v. The Kansas Board of Education* and argued the pros and cons. I struggled to write two papers for the course in some form of legalese for which I received two C's. In the end, I got a C in the course.

Reserve Officer's Training Corps (ROTC) was compulsory, and it was my downfall. It was only two lousy units, yet it was so boring and ridiculous that I blew it off and received a D for my lack of effort. More on this later.

Thus, at the end of my first semester, I had three C's and one D, giving me less than the required minimum C average. Therefore, I was duly placed on academic probation. At first, I panicked. I had visions of returning to Martinez in disgrace and attending Diablo Valley Junior College. Then, I calmed down and resolved to earn some B's in the next semester to bring my grade point average up.

I also knew I had to get out of the chemical engineering curriculum. No way was I going to take another chemistry course. However, I was unsure in which direction to go, so I visited the counseling center, housed in a World War II temporary building that had long since become permanent. The counselor gave me a battery of aptitude and interest tests and then discussed the results.

Counselor: "Well let's see here, Mr. Brown. You scored reasonably high in the aptitude portion, not a genius, but good enough to major in anything except the hard sciences or math."

Me: "Funny, in high school I was told that I was good in math."

Counselor: "That may be, but this is Berkeley, a much bigger pond. Math and science geniuses come here from around the world. If you wanted to pursue chemical engineering, perhaps you should have gone to a state college like Cal Poly."

Me: "Yes, I have heard that before, except now I want to stay here at Berkeley, but major in something else."

Counselor: "Yes, well let's take a look at your interest profile. It's rather informative."

Me: "Really?"

Counselor: "Yes, you come out high on the artistic, creative side. You score in the same brackets as musicians, writers and architects. In addition, you have many interests similar to those of ministers. This doesn't mean you would excel at any of these, simply that you have the same interests. The one that intrigues me the most is the architect category. Architects are a hybrid of engineers and artists. You certainly have the quantitative skills necessary and perhaps, the artistic ones. Have you given any thought to studying architecture?"

Me: "It has crossed my mind, but I don't think I'm creative enough."

Actually, I thought, no way. Architecture was a five-year degree and it was a ball-breaker. I knew two fraternity brothers in architecture who stayed up night after night, trying to complete their projects. Both were walking zombies. I wasn't up to that.

The counselor pointed out that since I had many of the hard science and math prerequisites out of the way, I could launch right into architecture and still graduate on time.

"I'll think about it," I said as I got up and shook his hand. "Thanks for all your help." In fact, I never gave architecture another thought.

Having disposed of chemical engineering, I continued in the College of Liberal Arts and Science. The next semester I took speech, economics, French and ROTC.

Of course, I had to hear from my father, "What are you going to do with all these liberal arts courses, son? Teach?"

"I don't know. I find them interesting," I answered.

"That's nice, Allan. Enjoy yourself. Just plan on graduating in four years and getting a job."

I found more support from my mother. "Don't be so narrow, Ray. I think it's good for Allan to broaden his mind with these courses. Who knows where they might lead?"

I wasn't sure where they might lead either. What I did know was that I was a busy boy with my liberal arts classes, the fraternity and now crew.

4. CREW

"On average, it's only three hours out of your life a day," declared Jim Lemmon, the freshman crew coach. "You probably waste more than three hours a day hanging out at campus or back at your dorm or fraternity."

Lemmon, a tall, freckled-face Irishman, was standing by a sign-up table for crew at Harmon Gym. The UC coaches used fall registration as an opportunity to recruit for their particular sport. Lemmon was looking for tall, strong kids to man his freshmen boats. He didn't expect rowing experience, although a few who signed up had rowed in prep school crew. As we filed by, Lemmon looked us over one by one. If you topped six feet and otherwise met his specifications, he asked if you were going out for any sport such as football, basketball or baseball. Usually, the answer was no, and then Lemmon would launch into his pitch: "We know your studies come first. We want good students. We try to keep the time commitment to a minimum. Crew is that kind of sport. You can have a hell of a workout in an hour or an hour-and-a-half. It's intensive, yet very short compared to the hours of practice required for football or basketball."

" Sounds interesting," I said after the pitch. I had heard about crew from the fraternity brothers, who thought it was a cool sport and who wanted jock representation from the house. I didn't know much about crew, but from what I had seen in newsreels and TV, I was struck by the elegance of the sport with the spider-like oars dipping into the water and the long narrow shells gliding over a lake or a bay, all in a perfect, harmonious motion.

"This is only an interest form," said Lemmon handing me a piece of paper. "We'll take a bunch of you fellows down to the boathouse and show you around. If you like what you see, we'll get the final forms out and then you can sign your life away," he chuckled.

The next afternoon, I, along with other freshmen recruits and climbed aboard a rickety old school bus outside Harmon Gym for an hour-long drive down to the Cal Boathouse on the Oakland Estuary. The boathouse was a weather-beaten two-story building sandwiched in among a row of warehouses. The entrance hall was lined with photographs, placards and trophies from past crewing glories. The Cal crew had rowed in several Olympics and won three gold medals. I paused before the picture of the 1939 junior varsity crew. This crew had won no medals or championships; however, an arrow pointed to one of its members, a skinny, gaunt-faced young man with a shock of black hair. A little note to the side said this was Gregory Peck, soon to be a movie star. Yes, Gregory Peck had gone to Cal and rowed on crew. Celebrities aside, part of Lemmon's pitch to us had been that we would be in position to try out for the 1960 Summer Olympics in Rome. We could add another chapter in Cal's Olympic rowing glory.

Next, we toured the dressing room, a rather dingy affair with beat-up lockers, a cement floor and showers off in an alcove that looked as if they belonged in a concentration camp. Out back was the boatshed that housed the wooden shells and the oars, along with other rowing paraphernalia. Behind, the boatshed ran a long ramp down to the estuary itself. It should be noted that the Oakland Estuary wasn't some bucolic stretch of water off in nature. No, it was an industrial shipping lane with giant freighters constantly plying the waters day and night, coming in and out of San Francisco Bay. However, Cal crew rowed here because the estuary offered the only straight three-mile stretch of calm water in the East Bay, a distance considered sufficient for most crews to practice and race on.

Lemmon had the junior varsity crew demonstrate putting one of the sixty-foot shells into the water and arranging their oars in the outriggers. Once that was completed, the eight-man crew slipped into the shell and rowed off across the estuary.

"Aren't those ships a hazard?" asked one worried looking freshman as he spotted a freighter passing by only yards from the crew which was now in the middle of the estuary.

"Nah, son," said Lemmon glancing around, "You learn how to dodge them. Also, I'm out there too in a launch with a loud bullhorn to warn them off."

"Oh," said the freshman, unconvinced.

By the time the tour was over, I decided to join up. My companions on the bus appeared to be good guys and enthusiastic about the sport. Those going out for freshman crew could be divided into two groups: the big West Coast lugs such as me, six feet and taller, who had never rowed in their life, and the smaller East Coast men who had rowed in prep schools. Crew was their big sport. Only one of the preppies was over six feet. This was Tony, a tall skinny lad who had a long neck and wore thick glasses giving him the appearance of an intelligent goose. As it turned out, Tony was the only preppie to make it into the first freshman boat. This was a bitter pill for the other preppies to swallow and most dropped out later in the season.

Crew was a sport for big men except for the coxswain, little guy who sat up in the front of the boat and called out the beat. With his megaphone, he would bellow, "Stroke, stroke, stroke." He would also function as a cheerleader. "Come on you guys. Put your legs into it. Keep up the rhythm." They were usually funny little twerps who got a charge out of bossing big men around. However, a good one was often the difference between winning and losing. The head coach of Cal Crew, Ky Ebright, was a former coxswain. He had been at Cal some thirty-odd years and had won three Olympics and numerous other championships. A tough little bugger in a slouch hat and baggy dungarees, Ebright would stand like a little Napoleon in his motor launch with his bullhorn at the ready and work the varsity crews until they nearly fainted from exhaustion. Occasionally, someone did pass out and fall into the estuary. Ky would nonchalantly fish him out.

Crew had two seasons: the practice season in the fall and the regular season in the spring. The eight-week fall season was the worst because there was no real competitive goal except a few practice races. Lemmon said it was important to be out rowing in the fall even though in November it was dark on the estuary by 5 PM. Fall was time to develop skills and conditioning. Also, it was a time to fool around with combinations of rowers in different boats. Those who rowed in the varsity and junior varsity boats were a varied lot: some tall, some short but stocky, others skinny and scrawny but apparently tough. Our freshman boat, however, was about as perfect as a crew could be. All of us were around 6'2" or 6'3", well-built, weighing about 180 to 200 pounds. From day one, we worked well together, and as our skill increased, we thought we had the best rhythm of all the boats. Later in the season, we routinely beat the junior varsity boat and sometimes the varsity boat. Lemmon often exclaimed, "Best frosh boat I've ever had."

Workouts were grueling. We rowed miles up and down that stinky estuary, always trying to follow the beat, the rhythm, striving for the surge. This was accomplished by sitting on a sliding seat in the shell, which enabled the rower to meld leg and arm power into one powerful stroke. If all eight rowers did this in unison, the shell would surge ahead.

Saturday workouts were the longest and the toughest. If the bay was calm, we sometimes rowed over to Yerba Buena Island, about five miles away in the middle of San Francisco Bay. This added a sense of adventure. Here we were in the open bay with monster tankers and cargo ships cruising by, sometimes blowing their horn at us, their wakes threatening to swamp us. We often rowed within fifty yards of Yerba Buena and then sat, resting on our oars and gazing up at the white military mansions on the hill, interspersed among the eucalyptus trees.

However, these moments of calm reflection out on the bay were rare. By the time we had rowed back to the Cal Boathouse, we were limp, exhausted young men who could barely stagger up the ramp carrying the shell and our oars. After one of these grueling workouts, the bus driver usually stopped at an ice-cream shop in Oakland where we all gorged on milkshakes, sodas and sundaes in the hope that the sugar high would revive us. However, I usually slept all afternoon back at the fraternity house, trying to recover from the workout.

Despite all the hard work, crew did have its compensations. I was designated as a house jock since there were only two of us going out for a varsity sport. As such and because of the long practices, I was excused from many pledge duties. I didn't have to do the menial chores of house cleaning during the week or the big clean up on Saturday morning. I did not have to attend pledge meetings, and I had special meals prepared for me when I came back from practices. For a pledge, I was king shit. Of course, this caused some resentment among the other pledges. I often overheard comments like, "That Brown thinks he's hot stuff," and, "He'll get his when crew season is over."

The other benefit was developing a great physique. I had gained about five pounds of muscle mass. My arm and back muscles rippled. I had a six-pack abdomen and bulging calves and thighs. The fraternity brothers used me as a prop at beach and pool parties to attract potential pledges: "See Brother Brown. See how he's ripped. Crew did that for him. He gets a lot of girls. You could be like him if you join our house and go out for a sport. We support jocks."

***

The highlight of the 1959 spring season was a trip to Seattle to row against the West Coast powerhouse, the University of Washington. The crews of UW routinely went undefeated all season. Occasionally though, Cal beat them.

"The Washington frosh crew is tough," lectured Lemmon on the way to the airport. "They're big and strong and, unlike some of you fellows, they know how to translate that power into speed on the water. They spend more time on the water. After all, they have Lake Washington right at their front door. We don't have that, but I think you men have a shot if you put your backs into it."

We all nodded and silently vowed not to let Lemmon down. After all, we were off on a big adventure: a flight to Seattle, a stay in a hotel, the race itself and maybe parties afterwards. As instructed, we were all dressed up in coat and tie, our hair freshly cut, our faces freshly shaved, our underwear clean and crisp, our small suitcases at our side with three changes of clothes. We were to be the face of Cal up in the Northland, and we were expected to act like gentlemen.

Upon landing at the Seattle airport, we retrieved our baggage and boarded a charter bus that took us to a hotel on the edge of the University of Washington campus. With peeling wallpaper and a beer stained carpet, the hotel was a well-worn place for students to stay before they joined a fraternity or found some dorm housing. Luckily, for us, we didn't have to eat there. As soon as we arrived, we were bused to the UW training table at one of the dorms for a big steak dinner. All the UW crew was there along with jocks in other sports. The UW crew had its own table and a few of the guys motioned for us to join them. They were a friendly bunch. All were six feet and over. Handpicked. Selected.

After dinner, back at the hotel, we were ushered into a meeting room where Ky had set up a movie projector to show us a newsreel of last year's Henley Regatta at Oxford, England, in which the Washington crew competed. UW coach Al Ulbrickson and his team were undefeated all season and then beat everybody except the Russians at the Regatta. The following week, UW crew went to Moscow for a rematch and beat the Russians on their home ground, much to the shock of the rowing world.

When the film was over, Ky remained silent and curiously detached. The rumor was that he was going to retire at the end of the 1959 season and that he wasn't happy about it. At the time, Cal had a compulsory retirement age of sixty-five. Lemmon was being groomed to succeed him. It was he who delivered the pep talk: "So you see fellows, what you are up against. UW is a real powerhouse, but they can be had. Cal has beaten them on several occasions both here on the West Coast and back east. Sometimes success can breed overconfidence. If you lads stay hungry and are willing to row your guts out, you can beat them.

That's it for tonight. Get some rest because tomorrow we have two practices. The bus leaves at 6 AM. If you want breakfast, eat light."

***

At 6:30 AM the next day, we pulled up in front of the Conibear Boathouse right on Union Bay, the rowing venue for UW. We were struck by the gorgeous setting: the tranquil bay surrounded by a pine forest—very different from the industrialized Oakland Estuary on which we rowed. The Conibear Boathouse itself was a huge, barn-like building that housed hundreds of shells, oars and all the latest rowing accessories. Remarkably, the building also contained a dormitory for the crew a few steps from the water. No downtime coming and going. I could instantly see why UW was such a powerhouse in rowing. It was a dream set up.

We changed in their locker room and minutes later were out on the water in our own shells going through our paces. At first, it was all rather leisurely. The water was calm as glass, sparkling in the morning sun with the promise of a bright and warm day. The air was filled with the scent of pine. Birds chirped, insects buzzed and fish jumped in the water. A little bit of paradise. The spell was soon broken when Lemmon put us through the racecourse that we were to take the next day. Lemmon treated the course as if it were a minor wind sprint. For an hour and a half, we raced up and down the two-and-a-half-mile course with barely a pause between sprints. I thought the frosh boat felt pretty good. We had a great rhythm and speed, usually beating the junior varsity boat and close on the heels of the varsity. Finally, as the morning wore on, Lemmon called a halt to the practice from his launch, joking that he didn't want to wear us out too much. We rowed back to the boathouse, changed and were then free until 3 PM to roam the campus.

***

The UW campus with its neo-gothic architecture was huge, some seven hundred acres, almost as large as Cal. The university location was spectacular, situated as it was, right on Lake Washington. Despite its size, the campus felt cozy because of its garden-like setting—spacious lawns interspersed by groves of cedars, redwoods and other assorted trees. The students were friendly, sunny and laid back. No stress here, no academic panic attacks, no fear of flunking out. UW accepted just about anybody who applied, yet it was noted for providing a decent undergraduate education and for being an outstanding research university.

The weather was a dream, although I knew it was often cloudy and rainy in Seattle. I ate lunch on the student union patio taking in the scene. I noticed the women here appeared free and easy unlike the up-tightness of many Berkeley co-eds. I vaguely wondered if I should trans-fer here to go to school. It would be an easier time academically, and I would have a chance to row on a championship crew. As I mused on that possibility, the hours slipped by and before I knew it, it was time to make my way back to the boathouse for the afternoon practice session.

Unlike the morning session, the afternoon one was a breeze. Our boat was rowing better than ever as we clicked off the miles in a leisurely row around Union Bay. It was almost a pleasure cruise. We felt ready to trounce that UW frosh boat. Even Ky was smiling, no doubt savoring the prospect of beating his archrival once again.

***

Saturday morning dawned windy and wet. Typical Seattle weather was back. At 10 AM sharp, our crew was standing around, shivering on the dock, waiting for the freshman race. Looking at the white caps break-ing on Union Bay, Lemmon tried to make light of the situation, "A little choppy fellows, but you can handle that. Remember, the UW frosh team has to put up with the same thing. The rough conditions are a great equalizer."

With our oars at our side, we shifted uneasily. We knew the rough water was a serious handicap for us. We seldom rowed in such condi-tions; maybe once or twice out on San Francisco Bay when the weather turned bad unexpectedly. Dealing with the wake of big cargo ships was easy compared to this. We would have to power through these white caps and lose valuable forward motion. God only knew how it would disrupt our rhythm, a rhythm we had down pat yesterday.

So full of anxiety, we got into our shell and paddled out to the start-ing line, lurching and bucking the waves. I glanced over to the Washing-ton frosh boat that was following us. They were thrown around too, but it didn't appear to bother them. They took it in stride. Finally, we were all lined up at the starting position. Lemmon was in his launch on our side, the UW coach in his launch on their side. In the third launch was the starter with his starting gun. After a few tense moments steady-ing the boats, the starter pulled the trigger. The gun cracked and we were off.

Despite the waves, our boat surged forward. We managed to get a good grip on the choppy water. The rhythm seemed right.

Stroke…slide…pause…catch…stroke…slide…pause…catch.

"Come on you guys! Put your backs into it!" screamed the cox-swain, more annoying than inspirational. Nevertheless, about a half mile into the race, we seemed to be moving along. Then glancing over to the UW frosh crew, I saw they were neck and neck with us. We increased our rate to forty strokes per minute and were starting to pull ahead when a rogue wave hit us. A three-foot motherfucker from out of nowhere. It was as if a phantom cargo ship had cruised on by and engulfed us in its wake. Later, somebody on the UW crew said it was just one of the goofy quirks of Union Bay. Something about the water on a windy day being funneled in from the main body of Lake Washington. Regardless, the rogue wave threw us off our rhythm and we scrambled around for a few strokes, but it didn't seem to affect the UW crew. They rode it out barely losing their beat. By the time we had reorganized, the UW frosh crew was a length-and-a-half ahead of us and moving out. We tried to catch up...oh how we tried. Yet, we couldn't do it. We started to scramble, lost our rhythm again and fell even farther behind. In the end, UW beat us by a good three lengths. I felt like throwing my oar into the water.

Later Lemmon tried to console us, saying, "You lads gave it your all, but you got a bad break with the rough water, especially that one wave. Had this been held on the estuary, I have no doubt that you would have been victorious."

The Cal junior varsity and varsity crews met a similar fate. The JV race was a rout. An oarlock on one of the outriggers came loose on the JV shell and the rower nearly lost his oar. The boat was thrown off balance and that coupled with the rough water caused the JV's to lose by a good stretch. The Cal varsity boat did better, but the rough water hampered them as well, and they lost by over two boat lengths. Overall, our meet with UW was a bust. Afterwards, the UW crew was gracious, lamenting our bad luck too.

"We ought to go for a rematch on a calmer day," said one. "This was unfair to you fellows. We're used to this shit."

Another UW crewmember while sympathizing with us, noted that, "It's the breaks of the sport. You can't control it. We too get screwed from time to time, such as when we row at Syracuse in that muggy heat in upstate New York. We wilt like a bunch of pansies. It's so hard to breath in that humidity. I don't know how those eastern crews do it."

***

Despite our loss to Washington, the 1959 Frosh crew season ended on a high note. We came in second in the Pacific Coast League. Of course, UW came in first. We were all looking forward to the 1959-60 season and a shot at the 1960 Summer Olympics in Rome.

"Believe it. It's possible, men! Cal has done it before. We won gold in 1928, in 1930, and in 1948. We expect to be in the running in 1960."

So sayeth Jim Lemmon, full of confidence and a little bit of arrogance.

5. ROTC

You're in the Army now.
You're not behind a plow
You'll never get rich,
You son of a bitch
You're in the Army now.

Old Army Marching Song

Army ROTC was my downfall at Berkeley that first semester. In 1958, male students at land grant colleges and universities such as the University of California were required to participate in mandatory ROTC (Reserve Officers Training Corps). The idea was to have a corps of college-educated officers in the three branches of the military: Army, Air Force and Navy. Behind all this was the threat of the draft. Those who did not attend college were usually conscripted a year or two after high school. Those who did go to college received deferments if they were in good academic standing. However, if one screwed up and dropped out of school, a friendly draft notice might arrive in his mailbox a few months later. The stated rationale for the Selective Service Act was that young men eighteen and older owed a debt of service to their country. Essentially, Uncle Sam wanted a constant supply of fresh recruits in case the Cold War turned hot.

I had a chance of entering the military at the highest level. In my senior year, my high school principal, Grenville Jones encouraged me to apply to one of the service academies. I can remember his exact words: "Allan, you are an excellent student and a good athlete. You did well on your College Boards. You are precisely what the military is looking for in its officer ranks. I'm sure it will be no problem to get a recommendation from Congressman Baldwin. Think about it. A free education and a chance to serve your country."

I did think about it and mentioned it to my father, who said the decision was up to me. Yet he cautioned me about what would lay ahead.

"A golden opportunity, son, but you have to want it badly. Those service academies are tough and heavy on discipline."

"Discipline?"

"Yes, a lot of it," he said and then added, "Remember only you can decide what you want to do. We'll be proud of you no matter what you choose."

In the end, the whole idea struck me as absurd. As someone who had an aversion to authority, I couldn't imagine myself as a military officer. I was going to stick to my plan of attending Berkeley, even though I knew that I would have to contend with ROTC and later the draft. I figured I could find some way of getting out of both.

***

As it turned out, there was no way of avoiding ROTC at Cal unless I became a conscientious objector, which I wasn't prepared to do. I wasn't against fighting, just against authority. So the question was which branch of ROTC should I join to get through with the least possible sweat.

During registration at Harmon Gym, I spoke to the Air Force recruiter, who said in effect:

"Yes, it's a four-year commitment, but we have an exciting curriculum. The summer camps are spent at Air Force bases around the country and overseas. Many of our students end up flying. Of course, you are a second lieutenant when you graduate but you do have a four-year service obligation."

That sounded attractive, but I wasn't sure about a four-year service obligation in the Air Force after college.

On to the Navy Recruiter who essentially said:

"We are the Cadillac of the services. We believe in training officers and gentlemen. Of course, our food is the best. Our officers live well on board ships with their own cabin and a personal attendant. There are many options in the Navy. You can fly. You can join the Marines for assault combat. Or, you can sail around on the latest warships and spend days in many interesting ports-of-call. The old slogan, 'Join the Navy and see the world' is literally true. It is a four-year commitment during college and three years afterwards. We want only those who are serious."

Three years of life at sea? I didn't think so. I remembered the World War II stories my uncle used to tell about being in the Navy — months of boredom and monotony at sea punctuated by danger and terror. He barely escaped with his life in the Battle of Leyete in the Philippines.

Finally, the Army with this pitch by a barrel-chested sergeant:

"Only a two-year requirement, kid. Of course, if you get inspired you could continue for another two years and become an officer upon graduation. Even after graduation, you don't have to go on extended active duty. You can do six months and then jump into the reserves. The bottom line is two years and minimal class and drill time. Remember though, the two years doesn't get you out of your service obligation. You are still subject to the draft, but if you are drafted, you will go in as a buck private and not a lowly E-1. How about it?"

"I guess," I said unenthusiastically, figuring the Army was the best of a bad lot.

"Sign right here," he said, handing me a pen.

So, I signed up for Army ROTC and resigned myself to being a dogface at Berkeley.

***

The Army ROTC lectures were not too bad, only two hours a week. Most of my classes were taught by a Major Scott, a ramrod straight West Point graduate. Major Scott knew his stuff, covering the predictable topics: history of the Army, military theory and major battles. He was especially fond of the Civil War battles and frequently pointed out that the Confederate Generals such as Robert E. Lee and Stonewall Jackson were by far the most brilliant of the war. "However, in the end it was the mass of northern industrial might — men and material that beat the South, not the strategic brilliance of the Union generals," he invariably concluded.

The major also lectured on current events and the role of the Army in today's world. At various times, he pulled down maps of Europe, Asia and North America and, with a pointer, commented on the hot spots around the world that the Army might be called upon to engage in.

> **Soviet troops in Eastern Europe:** "A current and long-standing threat. You never know what those Russians will do. They gobbled up Eastern Europe and may try to do the same with Western Europe. Two years ago, they rolled into Budapest and put down the Hungarian Revolution. Good fighters though. Tough. The Soviets lost the most men fighting the Nazis in World War II. Nevertheless, we are prepared to meet them in the field. We

have a hundred-thousand man force in West Germany to blunt any initial offensive they undertake. In addition, our military hardware is the best in the world. They don't stand a chance."

North Korea: "The fighting may have stopped with the armistice in 1953, but this is still a war zone with fifty thousand American troops in the Demilitarized Zone (DMZ). These North Koreans could re-invade South Korea at any minute. We have to remain vigilant. This is the first war that Americans ever fought in without an outright victory. It's hard to live with that. However, the Army does not question our civilian Commander-in-Chief."

Cuba: "A small blip on our national security radar screen. However, it could blow up at any minute. Last August, a small army of rebels came down from the Sierra Maestra Mountains and overthrew the Batista government. The rebel leader, Fidel Castro, has assumed power. Washington thinks he's a communist who has the backing of the Soviet Union. If Castro and his boys get too far out of hand, you can bet the U.S. Army might become involved. The thought of a communist country only fifty miles from our shores is intolerable."

Vietnam: "This Southeast Asian country is dicey. The North Vietnamese communists have been waging civil war for years trying to take over the South. They defeated the French in 1954 at Dien Bien Phu. We have been trying to help the South Vietnamese government, but they have no idea how to fight a war. This could be an important place to stop the spread of communism. Stay tuned."

At one lecture, the barrel-chested sergeant discussed and showed off the latest rifle in use by the Army: the semi-automatic M-14 rifle. Of course, we never got our hands on it. We drilled with old M-1 rifles with no live ammunition. The sergeant, a walking encyclopedia on weaponry, also gave us a slideshow on the latest tanks in the field, the latest machine guns, rocket launchers, flamethrowers, hand grenades, etc. All stuff, he said, with which we would become intimately familiar if we continued in ROTC or had the misfortune to be drafted into the army as dogfaces. A fate Major Scott encouraged us to avoid.

"I'm telling you men," the major often repeated, "you're all a bright bunch or you wouldn't be here at Berkeley. Don't let yourself be drafted.

Hang in ROTC and go in as an officer. Life is much better. It will set you up for life."

***

The weekly drill was the heart of the Army ROTC. It was also the most despised part of the program. Once a week, I had to put on my Army ROTC uniform for the afternoon and walk through campus to Harmon Gym looking like a military geek. A few gung-ho types put on their uniforms in the morning and sat in class in full regalia, often enduring the snickers of other students. Patriotic fever at Berkeley was at a minimum during the late 1950s. In fact, there were occasional protests to kick ROTC off campus staged by SLATE, the most radical of the student organizations.

The drill was held for two hours on the football practice field of Harmon Gym. It was boring, standing at attention with our M-1 rifles by our sides, in long ranks, arranged by platoons, bossed around by a wannabe ROTC lieutenant. "Right face...Left face...About face...Port Arms...Forward march." As it was explained to us, marching was the essence of the Army. It instilled organization and discipline and had the practical function of moving large numbers of men from point A to point B.

"What about the trucks?" I asked once. "I always see army troops riding around in trucks."

"Transport isn't always available or feasible in battlefield conditions," explained the sergeant.

Behind me, I heard one of the more radical cadets mumble, "Fuckin' robots, just ciphers, only numbers to the Army."

We also had to stand for inspection. We were expected to have short haircuts, which most of us had anyway. Our full-dress uniform had to be clean and neatly pressed, our black Army oxfords shined to a high gloss, our brass buttons, emblems and belt buckles gleaming. Our M-1 rifles had to be clean and freshly oiled. As the inspecting officer presented himself, the individual cadet would crack open the rifle bolt and pass it smartly to the officer for inspection. Of course, at this point, no one had fired a live M-1 round despite the constant refrain that the rifle was our only friend. Or as the Army ditty goes:

> *This is your rifle*
> *This is your gun (pointing to the crotch)*
> *This is for fighting.*
> *This is for fun*

Many of us did all we could to get out of drill. Some faked doctors' notes about illnesses; others simply didn't show up, which was my undoing. Twice, I overslept from much-needed naps. Another time I had to study for a midterm the following day. If a cadet missed three unexcused drills in a semester, he was flirting with failure. I also scored D on an ROTC midterm that I had underestimated. As a result, I was heading for a D in Military Science for the fall semester. At the time, I wasn't too concerned. I was under the illusion that Cal didn't average your ROTC grade into the other grades.

My other weak point in Army ROTC was military comportment. I slouched along, often out of step. I had a problem distinguishing left from right. In addition, a group of us actively sabotaged a mass formation by turning in the wrong direction and throwing everyone else off while under review of the ROTC commandant. The officers knew it was sabotage, but could never pinpoint exactly who was responsible. Furthermore, when it was my turn to conduct squad drills, I often screwed up the commands and the squad milled about in confusion.

"What are you doing, Brown!?" screamed the wannabe lieutenant from the sidelines, his arms rigid, his fists clenched.

"Just trying to do my best, sir."

"Get back in rank, Brown. You're pathetic."

It all added up in the eyes of the Army ROTC honchos. I received a D for the drill component of my first semester of ROTC. Overall, my grade averaged out to a D for the semester, a grade, which did indeed drag down my overall grade point average.

***

One of the more ambitious student ROTC officers was Redman, a fraternity brother two years ahead of me. He always conducted himself with perfect military bearing. Even out of uniform, he looked as if he was in uniform, always erect, immaculate and well organized. Redmond was on his way to becoming the student commandant of Cal's Army ROTC.

"Are you going to blow off drill again, Brown?" He often asked over breakfast.

"Red, why do you concern yourself with an insignificant dogface like me when you have the whole company to worry about?" I would respond.

"I worry about each and every one of my men, Brown. Play ball and I can do things for you. Right now I'm embarrassed to have such a fuck-up in my company, my own fraternity brother."

"Red, you should have gone to West Point since you're so gung-ho," I said.

"Don't think I didn't try. Some other prick beat me out. Academy slots are limited in our congressional district. A lot of competition out there."

"Well at least promise me a C this semester in ROTC," I begged. "Those assholes gave me a D last semester."

"I'll see what I can do, Brown. Meanwhile, shape up."

The following year, Redman, as a senior, took command of the whole ROTC regiment. During mass drills, he stood on a high podium overlooking the drill field, and with a microphone, barked out commands for hundreds of ROTC mucks like me. Amazingly, everybody did his best to look sharp as we went through out paces.

I was certain that Redman would make the Army a career. He was brilliant. When he did go on active duty, he served two years in Army Intelligence. He dressed like a British banker, rarely wore a uniform and spent most of his time looking for security breaches in Bay Area military facilities. After his hitch was up, Redman went to law school and became a lawyer. Years later at a fraternity reunion, he told me he had specialized in divorce and personal injury. I thought that was a waste of talent and asked him why he hadn't made a career in the Army.

"What? And spend my life with those morons?" he responded. "Two years of Army life was enough to convince me that I belonged elsewhere. Good thing I got out when I did."

6. PARTY TIME

Shag...
Shag…
Shag some more.
Shag until the fun is over
Giddy I ay, giddy I ay
Shagging with O'Reilly's Daughter

Old Drinking Song

The songs were raunchy, the banjos hot and the beer cold. Everybody gathered around the house *song-meister* Rich and sang away, beer mug in hand. The songs were great icebreakers at these exchanges, and soon the brothers struck up conversations with the co-eds, eventually asking them to dance. One of the bolder brothers might go for the cool blonde sipping her beer, ignoring everyone. Another might approach a plain Jane huddled in a corner with a few of her sorority sisters. We more or less conducted ourselves like gentlemen at these exchanges, dancing and singing with various women, trying to find out if any were worth calling up sometime later.

Exchanges were popular in the fall when everybody was looking for dates. Of course, the quality of women depended on the sorority in question. Some houses were known for being "dog" houses with few attractive women; other houses were known for their campus queens—good-looking, cheerleader types who dated the hottest guys. We avoided having exchanges with the "dog" houses and since the beauty queen houses were out of our league, we usually wound up exchanging with sororities filled with pleasant women similar to our own middle-class background who came from the suburbs or small towns around the Bay Area.

Even so, I rarely met anyone at a sorority exchange who aroused my interest enough to take out later. For the most part, these were women whose main goal in college was to get an MRS. degree from MR. RIGHT. That usually meant a hunt for some bright male student bound for a career in business, law or medicine. These girls had been trained at their mother's knee.

The cocktail party was a more refined form of socializing. It was usually held at some alum's house in the nearby Oakland hills. This was a dress-up party. Suits for men and little black dresses for women. No beer here. Hard liquor only. The height of sophistication was sipping Johnny Walker Red on the rocks and chitchatting about school, movies or sports.

It was all very proper for the first few hours, but later the party usually degenerated into a drunk-fest since most of us were not used to large quantities of hard liquor. Some passed out, others got sick in the bathroom. A few committed the ultimate *faux pas* and barfed on their date.

When it was time to return to Berkeley, many of the drivers were half-drunk and thought they were in a road race. I remember one wild ride along the Warren Freeway in the Oakland hills. Brother Mike had a Ford Galaxy with a souped-up 400-horsepower police engine in it. We hit 140 miles an hour, oblivious to everything.

By far the most popular event was the toga party that was given once a year. Weeks of planning went into its preparation. The entire house was decorated on a Roman theme with pillars, fountains, bowers and plenty of cushions. There was always a tunnel lined with mattresses leading to the main party room. The libation was a killer punch filled with rum and vodka, disguised by gallons of fruit juice. Food was most often a roast pig cooked outside on a spit. Partygoers had to dress up as Romans in togas. The whole idea was to simulate an orgy of drinking, feasting and making out.

While the drinking and feasting were done in the main room, the making out was carried on in the side alcoves. Most people had dates; a few did not. The adventurous women who showed up without dates were quickly picked off by dateless brothers. Also, a fair amount of "bird-dogging" or date swapping took place. Towards the end of such a party, total strangers were grappling in the various nooks and crannies. Often, the next morning, nobody could remember exactly who was with whom. Sorority houses usually gave blanket amnesty to its women who were carried away at a Toga party. The co-ed wasn't responsible for her actions. She only had to make sure her period came on time.

The toga party was also an occasion for the start of a life-long commitment. Many an unwary fraternity boy brought his steady date to such a party where he got a little taste of the flesh and pledged undying love. The steady often went back to her sorority with a fraternity pin and the promise of an engagement.

Wedding parties were also popular among the brothers. When one of the fraternity brothers walked down the aisle, it was playtime for the other uncommitted brothers because the sorority sisters were out trolling—hot and willing, so caught up in magic of the moment.

Harvey, a soon-to-graduate-architect, held his wedding reception at the Brazil house in Tilden Park. It was a lavish affair with a strong alcoholic punch spurting forth from a fountain centerpiece. Champagne was also on hand for the more traditional. Caterers stood by carving off slices of savory prime rib. Seafood was abundant as well as other tasty hors d'oeuvres. Mounds of strawberries, melons along with ice cream and wedding cake beckoned as desert. Tipsy bridesmaids and sorority sisters giggled, flirted and flitted about like flocks of birds. The brothers moved in for the kill. Snatches of overheard conversation:

"Why yes, they make a charming couple."

"Why no, I am not seeing anyone presently."

"I do plan to spend the summer in Europe, so I'm at loose ends right now."

"Would you care for some more punch, my dear?"

"Let's stick to the bubbly."

"It's so noisy here. Why don't we go upstairs where we can talk?"

***

If all else failed in the brothers' constant pursuit of getting laid without incurring obligation, there was Moonlight Ranch, a whorehouse near Reno, Nevada. After a night of heavy beer drinking and "Red Cross" movies, some of the brothers were invariably horny. So periodically, in the dead of night, they would make the run to Moonlight Ranch, about a five-hour drive from Berkeley.

Brother Joe lost his virginity that way. Joe was a cherry lad who went to Catholic mass every Sunday. Up to that point, he had had no physical relationship with woman. The brothers were celebrating Joe's twentieth birthday late one night when the more experienced among them felt a good deed was in order. It was time to introduce Joe to the joys of the flesh. Hence, the run to Moonlight Ranch on that particular evening. As Joe related it, he was half-nauseated, cold and shivering when he entered the ranch after the long drive. The Madam took pity on him and gave him a particularly warm and voluptuous young blonde who took it slow and easy with him. Finally warmed up, Joe reportedly performed like a stallion, several times within two hours until the gentle blonde finally threw him out, pleading sleep deprivation. Back in Berkeley, Joe confided in me that while he enjoyed the encounter, he felt a deep sense of guilt and shame. Of course, he promptly confessed all to the local Newman Club priest.

***

The Moonlight Ranch was not for me. There were too many willing women around if you knew where to look. While, the sisters at the fraternity parties and the weddings were enjoyable, my preference ran to those young ladies who had no organizational affiliation, the Independents. Gwen was one such co-ed. I met her at a Cal sponsored dorm dance. Tall, blonde and willowy with a pair of dark glasses perched on her head; she looked interesting in her black turtleneck sweater and black skirt. Totally unlike the sorority girls that I had known. I asked her to dance. She moved gracefully and fluidly, following me with ease.

"I haven't seen you around here," she remarked.

"I don't live here. I'm in a house. I dropped in to see what was going on."

"Slumming with us dormies, huh?"

"Not at all. It's a relief to see some variety."

"What house?"

"Alpha Kappa Lambda."

"Never heard of it, but then again, I'm not into fraternities or sororities. I believe you're the first fraternity boy I've talked to at Berkeley, let alone danced with."

"Gee, I'm flattered."

Gwen soon let it be known that she was politically active in SLATE, a controversial student group involved in off-campus issues such as protesting against the House Un-American Activities Committee.

"Are you active?" she asked.

"Not at all," I responded. "I'm too busy with my classes and crew."

"Crew? That's an elegant sport and that explains your arms," she said giving one a squeeze.

"Well thanks."

"Oh, I probably shouldn't have done that," she said, giggling. "My mother has warned me about being too forward."

"Don't worry. I like straightforward women."

Gwen talked on. Her parents lived in Oakland. Her father was a union organizer for the painters' union. Her mother was a writer who worked from home and raised her little sister.

I suggested that we leave the dance and walk down Telegraph Avenue for an espresso. Gwen agreed and we strolled down to the Mediterraneum Café, the local beat hangout that featured exotic coffee drinks from around the world. The place was crowded as usual on a Friday night with beards and sandals. Cool jazz played in the background.

"For a fraternity boy, you seem right at home in this crowd," she remarked.

"I've been here before. I may not have a beard, but I did read *On the Road* by Kerouac. I once met Allan Ginsberg at a party in North Beach."

"How did that happen? He doesn't seem like your type," she said taking a sip of her espresso.

"Oh it was simple enough," I explained. "We were on a rush outing on Broadway in San Francisco. Somebody came up and handed us a flyer about a fundraising party to raise bail for some beatnik. We were feeling our oats, so we went primarily to make fun of them. When we arrived at the apartment, the beats greeted us like long lost friends. We paid two bucks each, sat down on the floor and joined them drinking cheap jug wine. One bearded Jewish looking guy came up and started asking us all sorts of questions about fraternity life. He said his name was Ginsberg and he liked talking to fraternity boys. He was very modest and pleasant. I hadn't read *Howl* so I didn't know who he was. Later, I learned he was queer and that was probably why he was interested in fraternity boys. At the time, he seemed harmless enough and after talking to us for a while, he drifted off. I also talked to some black dude who told me he was a jazz player. I don't remember his name. There was also an assortment of beat chicks around. They looked a little scruffy and smoked too much for me."

Gwen nodded. "Well I hope I look clean enough for you."

"You sure do," I said as I checked out her shiny blonde locks. "Say, why don't we go see a movie sometime together?"

And we did. The next weekend, we saw *Wild Strawberries*, a new Ingmar Bergman film and later had the obligatory discussion on what it all meant: life, death and the cycle of existence. Finally, we headed for the hills for some stargazing.

***

Grizzly Peak Boulevard winds along the crest of the Oakland hills. At every turn, it offers a stunning view of the Bay Area at night. It also features roadside turnouts hidden in groves of eucalyptus trees where one can park and take in the spectacle. However, we weren't paying much attention to the view that night.

"I can't believe I'm making out with a fraternity boy," said Gwen.

"Life is strange," I said, slipping my hand under her sweater and snapping open her bra.

"Hey, what are you doing?"

"What do you think I'm doing?"

"Not so fast, I may be a freethinker, but I'm not that free, at least not yet."

And so it went.

Several dates later, Gwen, finally tiring of conversation about world problems and injustices, gave in. She told me she was a virgin.

"A worldly girl like you," I teased.

"You shit! If you didn't have such great arms, I never would have given you second glance," she said hitting my arm. "Even if you are bright and curious, you're still a fraternity boy."

"That's true, but I'm thinking about going to Europe next year. Maybe, it'll broaden my horizons."

"That sounds like a good idea because I won't be here either. I'm definitely transferring to St. Johns College in Maryland, where they read the Great Books and don't have all those stupid science requirements like Berkeley does. I certainly don't want to become entangled with somebody like you again. It's too distracting."

I reached over and we went through another round, parked in the Berkeley hills on a star bright night.

7. ACADEMICS

Despite all the fun and games of fraternity life, I still had to contend with the academics of Cal. Since I had dropped chemical engineering after my terrifying first semester, I now faced an array of liberal arts requirements including a foreign language. Luckily, chemistry and calculus had taken care of my science and math requirements. So, spring semester of 1959, I dutifully took history, economics, speech, French, ROTC and crew as a P.E. course. A full load. Initially, I wasn't sure what to major in. I thought possibly business administration or maybe pre-law. I also had an inclination to simply go with the liberal arts flow and see what captured my fancy. As my mother had told me, I would have this freedom only once in my life. I should take time to smell the academic roses.

***

My favorite course was Western Civilization. Along with several hundred other students, I sat in Dwinelle Hall and listened to words of historical wisdom from Professor J. Even though his course was a survey of Western history, Professor J. lectured often on East European history, rattling off the names of countries and empires that I had never heard of before.

"Fundamentally, the history of modern Western Europe was shaped by the Eastern empires: Byzantium and Islam," he lectured. "During the early Middle Ages, Western Europe was an intellectual backwater compared to the East. It was the transmission of Eastern knowledge to the West that was key to the development of Western Europe."

That was what I liked about history: the big picture, the big sweep. Mongol hordes and Islamic warriors charging across Europe. The notion of zero, algebra and even the alphabet coming out of the East. Of course, I had to wrestle with and memorize the names and date, but I never let the details get in the way of the big idea. As a result, I thought I could do well in history although the fraternity brothers had warned me it was a tough major.

"Why not major in political science? It's a breeze compared to history," said Jim Dougherty, who, as noted, could churn out a plausible political science paper in only a few hours while drunk.

"Nope, not for me," I said. "I sat in one political science course for a week and it was too nebulous for my taste. History gets right to the point."

***

By contrast, the lectures for my Introductory Economics class were a bore. The professor read from his lecture notes in a dull monotone that put half the class to sleep. Many students skipped the lectures since they varied little from year to year. Instead, they bought the lecture notes from one of the many note-taking services in Berkeley or, like me, rifled through their fraternity or sorority files and found last year's notes.

The most interesting aspect of Introductory Economics was my teaching assistant, Jeff. A little, red-haired guy in a moldy green corduroy coat and sporting a goatee, Jeff was a self-admitted communist. He believed in state run economies and the primacy of the workers.

"You know that Roosevelt was a socialist at heart, don't you?" he said once, half in jest.

"No way," came the class response. "Roosevelt was a rich guy from an old New York family."

"That may be, but when he was elected president in 1932, he signed on to the progressive agenda. What do you think the New Deal was? Roosevelt basically co-opted programs being pushed by the American Communist Party and the Socialists. Ideas such as social security, the WPA, unemployment insurance and the Labor Relations Board. That's why the wealthy elite hated him. 'A traitor to his class', they used to call him.' "

In spite of his left-leaning rhetoric, Jeff knew his capitalist text. He thought our textbook by Samuelson (*Economics: An Introductory Analysis*) provided a clear explanation of how capitalist system worked and how it had been modified by Keynesian theory.

"It was Keynesian policy that saved America's ass in the 30s," Jeff claimed. "Once and for all, it was established that government had a role in stimulating the economy and also the responsibility for taking care of the poor and disenfranchised."

With Jeff, the twice-a-week Economics sections were interesting and sparked lively debate. Half of the students in the class were planning to major in business, so they often took issue with Jeff and pointed out that despite its faults, capitalism created jobs and prosperity. Jeff conceded the point, but also stressed the occasional need to rein in the capitalist stallion.

Then one day late in the spring semester, Jeff came into class looking half-dead and bedraggled. His clothes were more rumpled that usual. He was bleary-eyed and unshaven. "I've been up for three days drinking cheap wine," he confessed. "The reason I went on this binge was to get over my shock at being thrown out of the Communist Party. Those San Francisco apparatchiks decided I was too unorthodox, too undisciplined even for them. Well fuck it."

Jeff left UC after that semester. I don't know if it was related to his communism or not. Teaching assistants were always coming and going for a variety of reasons. Some couldn't cut it academically for a doctorate and had to transfer to other schools. Most often, they were awarded a Master's degree from Berkeley as a consolation prize. A few said the hell with it, dropped out of school and hung out at the Med on Telegraph Avenue. Some became active in various off-campus radical groups.

***

I continued with Dr. L. in second semester Speech. This time the course focused on spoken persuasion. We studied the speeches of Hitler, Roosevelt, Churchill and Lenin.

Dr. L. would stand in front of the class in his tight pants and in his high, lispy voice and lecture on Hitler's persuasive oratory, which he illustrated by playing film clips of various speeches:

> *When the question is still put to us why National Socialism fights with such fanaticism against the Jewish element in Germany, why it pressed and still presses for its removal. Then the answer can only be: Because National Socialism desires to establish a true community of the people.... Because we are National Socialists we can never suffer an alien race which has nothing to do with us to claim the leadership of our*

working people. (Hitler's Closing speech at the Nuremberg Party Conference, Sept. 12, 1938)

"So you see, this is Hitler using a pseudo-rational approach, patiently and logically explaining why the Jews had to go," lectured Dr. L. When Hitler says a 'true community of the people', he is referring, of course, to the Aryan people. Hitler also takes a swipe at labor unions, which he claims are controlled by Jews as well, thus further demonizing a people."

Dr. L. continued by noting Hitler's use of stereotypes, emotional appeals, and his constant restatement of the "big lie", which declared that Jews were a subhuman race.

Everyone in the class was required to give a presentation on one of the orators we were studying. I chose Winston Churchill and examined several speeches he gave rallying the English people during the early, dark days of World War II. In particular, I focused on the so-called *Blood Sweat and Tears* speech he gave before the House of Commons in May of 1940:

> *We have before us an ordeal of the most grievous kind. We have before us many, many long months of struggle and of suffering. You ask, what is our policy? I can say: It is to wage war, by sea, land and air, with all our might and with all the strength that God can give us; to wage war against a monstrous tyranny, never surpassed in the dark, lamentable catalogue of human crime...*

I pointed out how Churchill used many of the same persuasive techniques that Hitler did, such as emotional, patriotic appeals and references to the past glories of Britain's power and prestige in the world. Of course, he buttressed his message with the eloquence of his language. I managed to get a B in Speech that semester, which I desperately needed to make up for the D in ROTC that I had received my first semester. However, I was still in trouble in French.

***

My French I class was held in one of the many temporary class buildings left over from World War II, a nasty olive-drab structure with a sagging floor and lighting. Its only virtue was that it was on the northeast portion of campus and near my fraternity house. Even so, I was often late for my 8 AM class because I constantly overslept. When I arrived ten minutes late or so, the conversation with my French teacher, Reginald, usually went like this:

"Glad you could join us, Mr. Brown," Reginald would say in his most arch Oxford accent. "Do you have your homework?"

"Sure...sort of." I would hand him a few wrinkled pages.

"Thank you, now please sit down and conjugate the past tense of the verb, *être.*"

"Ah..." was my initial reaction and I could only manage to get four out of the six conjugations correct.

"Thank you, Mr. Brown," Reginald would say turning to another student. "Karen, please finish what Mr. Brown started."

French I and I was headed for a D. I probably should have continued with Spanish. After all, I had taken two years of it in high school. For some reason, I had thought it would be simpler and easier to begin a new language, so I chose French. Now, for better or for worse, I was stuck with French.

Despite his Oxford sarcasm, Reginald was a cool teaching assistant. Thin, with long blond swept-back hair, thick lips and an Afghan dog that looked like him always by his side. He even brought it to class. Reginald had told us he had taken a second at Oxford. He explained that a second at Oxford was good but not great. He said he took this teaching job because he wanted to see America, especially the Bay Area and San Francisco. One day, a month before the final, I went to see him in his office.

"So Mr. Brown, why are you taking French?" Pause. "No don't answer," he said leaning back in his rickety swivel chair. "Of course it is to fulfill a language requirement."

"Of course," I said.

"Well, as you know, you are not doing too well. However, I do want you to succeed. After all, you are a nice lad, but obviously, your talents do not lie in French. You are not planning to major in French are you?"

"Oh no, I have two more semesters after this. French II and French III-Reading and then I'm done," I answered.

"Right. Just as I thought. Watch out for French II. It's a bitch. Study hard. French III-Reading is a breeze. You can't get into too much trouble there. You will read the easy stuff such as *L'Étranger* by Camus and *Les Jeux sont Faits* by Sartre. "

"Well, that's a relief. But I'm in trouble now," I said.

"Here, I'll tell you what I'll do. I have a bunch of old final exams. I'm supposed to concoct a new final out of these for your class test. I'll give you copies of these old exams as a study guide. You can find them in the library too, but this will save you a lot of trouble. Just do the questions and you'll be all right."

"Thanks."

"Don't mention it." Reginald smiled, glancing at my bare arms, "Mr. Brown, do you do sports?"

"Just crew."

"Nice sport, very graceful. If all the lads are as big and strong as you, you probably have a championship boat."

"Well, not quite. Come on down to the boathouse sometime and take a look around," I said, sensing an opportunity to score points. "We're having a race at the Oakland Estuary this Saturday."

"Maybe I will." He shook my hand gently, holding it a little too long.

Yes, I knew Reginald was queer. It was written all over him. Still, I liked him. He was interesting to talk to, especially about France. Yet, even with his help on the old exams, I could only muster a C- in the course.

A few days later, after the exam, I ran into Reginald at the student union going through some travel brochures for France. He mentioned that he was going to spend the summer there. Over coffee, we discussed studying abroad.

"Mr. Brown, if you are serious about learning French, consider going there to study for at least a semester. I know of a great program in the South of France, Aix-En-Provence."

"Ah, where is that?"

"Near Marseille."

"Why not Paris?" I asked.

"Paris is O.K., but for a California boy, I think Aix might be better. Good weather, beautiful scenery, plus the history—Greek, Roman, Medieval, Provencal. If you go, do it right. Total immersion. Don't hang out with English speakers. Bury yourself in the culture. Find a girlfriend or whatever. Pillow talk is the best way."

I told Reginald his idea was intriguing and that I would think about it.

***

When I received my final grades in the mail in June, I was notified that I was officially off probation. It was my three-unit B in Speech along with a one-unit A in crew that did it. I received C's in the rest of my spring courses. I was hanging on by a thread at Berkeley, but it was a strong thread. I was surviving.

8. DON

While I was doing battle with my classes at Berkeley in the spring of 1959, my brother Don was debating whether to apply to the U.S. Air Force Academy. Don was a year behind me in school. Everybody expected him to go to Cal. However, after much debate, he responded to the siren call of the military academies. Don had been listening to his friend Carr who was gung-ho about going to West Point. Carr was a true believer in the military. His father Carr Sr. worked as a civilian for the Army on mysterious weapons projects at the Army Weapons Depot near Vallejo. All the talk around their dinner table focused on how great the Army was.

One day in September of Don's senior year, Carr told him that he was going for a physical over at Travis Air Force Base as an initial step to getting into West Point. He would get out of a day of school to do it.

"A day off?"

"Yeah. It'll be great," said Carr. "We'll see the base and screw around after. My dad said I can use his car."

"Sounds good to me," said Don. "Count me in."

Therefore, as a lark, Don and another friend, Andy, went along with Carr. When they arrived at the examination center at Travis Air Force Base, a Sergeant announced that those who were applying to the Air Force Academy could go first. Don thought 'what the hell, I'll go first.' So he did and he passed the physical. Andy, who was interested in going to the Coast Guard Academy, passed too, but Carr flunked his physical because of poor eyesight.

After that, Don forgot about the Air Force Academy until he was approached by his high school principal, Mr. Jones, who asked him to step into his office. As he did with me, Jones extolled the virtues of the academies.

"Don, the military academies are looking for bright, athletic boys like you. What are your college plans?"

"Ah," responded Don. "I thought I would do engineering at Berkeley."

"Well, yes. Berkeley is a great school for engineering. However, if you want to follow up on the Air Force Academy, I could recommend you to Congressman Baldwin for a possible appointment. It's a great opportunity, a fine engineering education, the fulfillment of your military duty at officer rank and best of all, it's free. Something I'm sure your parents might appreciate. Think about it."

Unlike me, Don did give it serious consideration. He thought it might be great to fly jets. When he mentioned the Air Force Academy to our parents, my mother was cool to the idea, but my father was enthusiastic. After all, he was now facing the prospect of putting two boys through college and that would be a financial burden for him. A free government education for Don was enticing.

Don talked it over with Andy. Andy said he was definitely going to apply to the Coast Guard Academy in Connecticut. He was a feisty, red-haired kid, always getting into scrapes and talking his way out of them. He was also something of a genius. He built Heathkit ham radios from scratch and constructed motorized model planes that flew. His goal was to go to college and become an engineer. The only problem was his family was broke. His mother was a schoolteacher and his father an occasional car salesman who drank too much. Thus, getting a free education was a tantalizing prospect to Andy. He chose the Coast Guard Academy because as he put it, "The Coast Guard has the most rigorous courses and a Coast Guardsman hardly gets shot at. All they do is protect the coastal waters of the U.S. That sounds about perfect to me."

The application process was long and tedious requiring letters of recommendation from Mr. Jones and various other teachers, as well as one from U.S. Congressman John Baldwin. In the spring, Don received his response. The Air Force notified him that he was a second or third alternate for a slot at the academy. Don thought that was a long shot, so he resigned himself to entering Berkeley in the College of Engineering in the fall. Then, a few days before his high school graduation, he received another letter from the Air Force Academy informing him that a slot had opened up at the academy and it was his if he wanted it. Don was in a quandary. Should he go or not go?

"Think about it carefully," I warned. "My ROTC experience has taught me that the military is basically run by little pricks who want to boss bigger guys around. You, at 6'5", will be a target."

"What am I supposed to do, cut my legs off?" he responded. "I want to fly jets. My eyes are perfect. They want cadets with perfect eyesight. You would never make it 'cause you wear glasses."

"Your eyes may be perfect, but you're too tall," I said. "You'll never fit into those tiny jet fighter cockpits."

"Hah, if my height was a problem, they would have said something. They took me in, didn't they? I can scrunch up," argued Don.

"Whatever you say, Don."

Then in a more thoughtful vein, Don added, "You know, Allan. I'll never have another chance at something like this. This is a once in a lifetime opportunity. Even if I'm not sure that this is for me, I think I want to take a shot at it."

So in the summer of 1959, Don went off to Colorado Springs for summer training at the spanking new Air Force Academy. I had to admit that, based on the brochures, the place looked great—sleek, space-age architecture, all set before the dramatic backdrop of the Rocky Mountains. It had taken five years to build this thing. Prior classes had trained at Lowery Air Force Base near Denver. Don's class would be the first to spend four full years at the new academy.

I was jealous. Don would be flying jets. They promised all cadets the opportunity to fly training jets regardless of whether they became pilots. Here was adventure, discipline and military glamour. Even though I thought ROTC was a joke, I had a nagging feeling that maybe I had passed up an opportunity by not applying to West Point or Annapolis.

A few weeks later, Don's letters started to arrive. He was in shock:

July 15, 1959

Hello all,
This place is tough. Basic cadet training or "beast" as they like to call it, is like a high-speed Boy Scout camp with the upperclassmen bossing and shoving us "doolies" around. The minute we arrived, they started yelling at us, and we had to go down for one hundred pushups. Not many could do that. So we got yelled at some more for being such wimps. We have to stand for hours at attention in the broiling sun for stupid-ass inspections. I don't mind the physical exercise stuff, the running around, obstacle courses, the hikes, the combat training. It's the chickenshit stuff that I hate like unannounced white glove inspec-

tions. They give you demerits for a piece of lint on your dress uniform. And, as you said, Allan, I'm a target because of my height. And I have trouble distinguishing right from left, like you. I guess that's the penalty for being left-handed. This plays havoc when we march in formation. I'm always turning the wrong way. Also, I can't seem to get enough to eat. I have lost ten pounds since I got here and, as you know, I was pretty skinny when I left a month ago. Thank God, I only have another four weeks to go with this summer camp gig. I'm looking forward to regular classes starting. By the way, the Academy is beautiful to look at set up against the mountains but so far it's just been a beautiful hell.
Love, Don

Sept. 1, 1959

Dear folks:
Classes have started and they don't seem too hard. Though, a lot of my fellow doolies complain that they move too fast. Some of them don't seem too smart to me. Most really flounder when it comes to calculus. I think many of them were admitted because they are the sons of Air Force officers or because of some political connection. Anyway, those who come from military families breeze through the discipline and military stuff. They already know how to work the system, how to kiss the upperclassmen's asses. Also, if you are out for a team, especially football, then you have it made. You are excused from all the chickenshit. You get to eat at your own table and fill up to your hearts content, unlike us regular plebes. I still can't get enough to eat. I have to sit at attention while I eat and recite long verses of Air Force songs or slogans or Air Force regulations. I don't know how long I can last here. Free or not, this place is the pits.
Love, Don

Oct. 14, 1959

Dear family:
Things seem to be going better. I'm getting into the swing. I've managed to gain some weight back and am eating better. I guess my commanding officer noticed how skinny I was and told the upper class men to ease off on me. Anyway, classes are easier, although they don't give you much time to study. We just had a weekend pass to Denver. One of my fellow cadets has a car and we piled in and headed north. Denver is not much of a town, but this guy was from there and knew all the spots and where to find the girls. We were in uniform and that was a sure-

fire attraction to these local honeys. All the hotels and the restaurants treated us like royalty. We didn't pay for anything. Life was good.
Love, Don

Nov. 16, 1959

Hey Allan:
I flew in a jet-trainer jet last week. Guess what? Even with my long legs, I fit in. It was quite a blast, lots of barrel rolls, and although I did have a queasy stomach, I didn't throw up like a lot of guys. It was like a super high-speed roller coaster. The pilot said I held up really well for a first timer.
By the way, two guys knocked up their girlfriends and when they informed the higher-ups, they put it to them straight. "Either you resign and marry the girl, or you deny you are the father and continue at the academy." One guy resigned, another guy shut the door on his pregnant girlfriend and stayed in the academy. This place is cold. As they say, they are here to produce cold-blooded, cold war warriors and that's what they do very efficiently.
Love, Don

Dec. 15, 1959

Merry Christmas, all. I won't be coming home. Fourth Class doolies have to stay here at the Academy and undergo special training and projects. From what I hear, it's not too bad because most of the upperclassmen are away. Maybe I can catch up on my studies and eat better. I guess we will have a couple of days off. I plan to go skiing at Winter Park near Denver.
Love, Don

Jan 3, 1960

Hello All,
Hey, happy New Year. How time flies when you are having fun. That's a joke. Christmas break was cool. Like I predicted, no upperclassmen to harass us doolies. We even managed to go skiing for three days at Winter Park. The Air Force supplied us with all the ski equipment and the clothes. Also, we had free lift tickets. Boy, Rocky Mountain skiing is a blast. None of that Sierra cement. The snow is light and fluffy. 'Champaign powder' they call it. The only hassle was my roommate. The dumb shit went AWOL for several hours with his girlfriend over Christmas break. His parents showed up unexpectedly and the academy

was unable to locate him. It turns out he tried to cover his tracks by erasing my name from the sign-out sheet and replacing it with his name. Now they want to talk to me to see what I know about it. Well, I don't know anything about it, so I'm clean. I have to go now.
Take care.
Don

Jan 25, 1960

Dear family:
I'm bailing out of here. I can't live in such a chickenshit environment, free or not. As I mentioned in my last letter, my roommate went AWOL during Christmas for a few hours. He tried to cover his tracks by erasing my name from the sign-out sheet and filling in his name. The Commander wanted to know what I knew about it. I told them I knew nothing about it. I don't think they believed me and kept bringing up the Honor Code that required me to tell them everything I knew. I still said I knew nothing. They seem disgusted with me, but took no further action against me. Since that interrogation, life has gotten really bad. The upper class men are on me like a ton of bricks. It's back to the old dooly harassment game. I wind up doing extra guard duty for the slightest infraction. They don't let me eat much. I've lost ten pounds. I caught the flu and was in bed for three days with a fever. I was accused of malingering. Then I fell behind in my studies and got a couple of bad grades. Finally, I decided, who needs this crap. You're right, Allan. The military is full of little shits on power trips. Most are adept at covering their ass. The name of the game around here is violate every rule but don't get caught. Anyway, after several interviews and a lot of resistance, they are allowing me to resign. They reminded me that I still have to carry out my military obligation, very possibly being on active duty, but in the end, someone took pity on me and assigned me to an Air Force Reserve unit at Travis. Anyway, I fly into SFO next Friday. Can somebody meet me at the airport? I will give you a call.
Love, Don

***

When Don came home in February, he seemed like a different person. He was at least twenty-five pounds lighter and did nothing but eat. My mom had to buy double rations of everything. He ate day and night. When he wasn't eating, he was sleeping. As a cadet, he had to survive on five or six hours of sleep a night, now he was sleeping ten or twelve. The rest of the time, he lounged around, played with our little brother, nine-year-old Kenny or watched TV. He didn't want to talk much about the academy except to say he was glad to be out of it and wanted to go to Berkeley, but wasn't ready yet. Besides, it was already too late to sign up for the spring semester. This was fine with my father who was now faced with putting two kids through college. He suggested to Don that it would certainly help if he found a job for the seven months until the start of the fall semester.

After a few weeks of lying around, Don got into gear and started leaving job applications at the various oil refineries and chemical plants in the area, including Dow Chemical. He was hoping for a job as an ordinary factory worker, but the personnel department at Dow Chemical in Pittsburg took one look at his application and his test scores and decided to hire him as a research assistant. "Anyone with those high test scores and experience at the Air Force Academy needs to be properly utilized," said the personnel lady. Before he knew it, Don was wearing a white lab coat.

In addition, Don had use of a '52 Chevy coupe to commute to his job. This bummed me out because the car was originally mine. I had bought it at the beginning of the school year for $600. The purchase had depleted my summer savings, money that my father was counting on me using for college expenses. It was obvious from the start that I could not afford the car, so I tried to sell it a month later, but there no takers. It was a great little car, a tan coupe with white sidewall tires. Finally, my father bought it from me for $500, saying the family could use a second car in Martinez. It would be at my disposal on a weekend basis. However, when Don came home my father let him use the coupe full-time.

Don started putting his life back together. His job was interesting and paid well. He was an assistant to a couple of industrial chemists who were working with polypropylene to develop new products. He set up and monitored different types of experiments. Don also spent time in Berkeley partying with me and my fraternity brothers and chasing sorority girls with tales of the Air Force Academy. For a while, I thought he might even join AKL, but that never happened. Don easily passed the engineering entrance test given in May. Furthermore, he received several units of credit for his work at the Air Force Academy. As a result, he would be starting his first year at Berkeley a step ahead of the other freshmen in engineering.

Overall, Don was sitting pretty—all directed and defined, money in his pocket and use of a car. However, I was without wheels, nearly broke and wondering what to do with the rest of my academic life. Here it was

1960, the beginning of a new decade, and I was adrift. At one point, I was ready to chuck it all and become a ski bum at Squaw Valley where the Winter Olympics were scheduled to be held.

9. SKI BUM

The plan was this: Squaw Valley was hiring for the 1960 Winter Olympics. It would be mostly grunt work such as housekeeping, waiting on tables, kitchen work. If I was lucky, maybe outside, working on the lifts, taking tickets. I knew whatever the work, the benefits would be many—free room and board, free skiing and a front row seat to the Olympics. So when semester break came, I decided to put the plan to the test and check out ski life in the Sierras. If it worked out, I would say goodbye to Berkeley for a semester and ski for several months.

I had skied on and off since I was ten, starting with day trips to Dodge Ridge, a small ski resort in the Sierras on Highway 108 near Strawberry. I started out on beat up old wooden rental skis with archaic bindings, which would be outlawed today. Brother Don and I rode the rope tows, barely hanging on and then skied down chunky, un-groomed slopes, often falling as we went along. Later, in high school, we started skiing at larger resorts such as Sugar Bowl and Squaw Valley. By then, I was renting a better grade of equipment: skis with breakaway bindings and more advanced boots and poles. With my meager summer earnings, I had also bought a snazzy blue down parka and a pair of Bogner ski pants, along with gloves, goggles and ski hat. Last fall, I said goodbye forever to rental skis and bought a beautiful pair of Head skis. These represented the latest in ski technology. Sleek, black, light metal skis with Marker breakaway bindings. If you fell, the swivel toe-piece released your boot, greatly reducing the danger of a broken leg.

I had also taken a few lessons and could execute a variety of turns with a fair degree of competence. And while I had much to learn about the more advanced techniques of skiing, I felt at home on skis.

***

So it was, one sunny January day, I climbed aboard a local Union Pacific passenger train at Martinez with all my ski gear and took off for Norden and the Cal Ski Lodge near the Donner Summit. Although the engine was a modern diesel, the passenger cars looked and smelled as if they had been in constant use since World War II. The interiors were a dirty brown and green with trash littering the floor. Most of the passengers were a disheveled lot, half asleep in grimy raincoats, some occasionally sipping from small, brown paper bags. I figured many were heading to Reno for a few desperate days of gambling or perhaps a quickie divorce. I felt out of place in my bright blue ski sweater and knit cap, appearing as an eager Joe College without a clue in the world.

It took six hours to travel to Norden with the train stopping at every little town along the way: Fairfield, Vacaville, Dixon, Davis, Sacramento, Auburn and Soda Springs. Past Soda Springs, we began the climb to Norden at 6600 feet elevation. This was essentially the same route taken by the first transcontinental railroad that linked California to the rest of the continent. The Chinese workers had blasted the route out of the sheer granite cliffs while contending with thirty to forty-foot snowfalls during the Sierra winter. Both workers and rails were often buried in avalanches. In order to deal with the snow, the engineers built a series of wooden sheds over the tracks to protect the trains. At certain points, the sheds created a virtual underground city for the workers. Norden itself was still enclosed in a network of snow sheds tucked up against a granite hillside.

When I stepped off the train at Norden with my ski luggage, I was engulfed in the eerie half-light of a wooden catacomb. A dark figure waved a lantern at the end of the platform, signaling to the conductor that a lone passenger had safely descended. The train slowly moved on and out of the shed. I stood there with my duffle bag, boot bag, skis and poles, squinting into the gloom trying to find a way out.

"You lost, boy?" said a gruff voice in the distance.

"I guess. How do I get out of here?"

The figure came closer. He turned out to be a full-bearded flagman with a red nose and a dark, dirty uniform.

"Well, son, keep walking down to the end of the platform. You'll see an exit sign that will take you up to the highway."

"Thanks," I said, slinging my boot bag over one shoulder and my skis and poles over the other. With my one free hand, I grabbed my duffel bag.

He looked at me and shook his head. "All loaded up, eh? Here give me that bag. I'll help you out."

"Thanks," I said thinking maybe he wasn't such a scary guy after all. We walked through a dark passage and climbed a flight of stairs. Along the way, the flagman remarked, "Used to be a lot of college kids coming on the train to ski, but now most drive up. No use for the train. Don't blame them, though. They don't keep the trains up any more."

We emerged from the passageway at street level along Highway 40. It was dark now and, across the highway, I could see the lights of the Cal Ski Lodge beckoning. I thanked the flagman for his help. With a nod and a grunt, he disappeared back down the dark passageway, a mole man if I ever saw one. I lugged my ski equipment and duffle bag across the highway and up the wooden stairway to the lodge.

***

Cal Ski Lodge was a big, red, barn-looking affair with dormitory accommodations upstairs and a dining room and lounge downstairs. It was managed by fat Carl, of vaguely Germanic origin, who prided himself on running a tight operation.

"So, Mr. Brown," he intoned as he checked me in, "breakfast at 8 AM sharp, done at 8:30. If you sleep in, tough luck. Dinner is at 6 PM. However, I allow a full hour to savor whatever culinary delights I happen to prepare for the evening. The lodge door is locked and lights are out at 11 PM. Come back later than that and you will be out in the cold."

"O.K., whatever you say, Carl," I said, almost saluting.

I stashed my skis and poles on the ski rack in the entrance hall and carried my duffel bag and boot bag up a flight of stairs to the dorm. The bunks were stacked three high, narrow and stiff with grimy, green army blankets. I had brought along my own cotton liner to ward off the cooties. One glance at the bathroom told me it was generally unspeakable with whiskers in the sinks, toilet paper on the floor and dark stains in the toilet bowls. I knew that one didn't dare shower in the morning because the water was melted snow right off the summit. Hot water only at night. The dorms were split up according to sex. It didn't matter that you were married or going steady. Separate quarters for the sexes. As Carl once put it, "The motel is down the road."

So why I was I staying here? The first answer was that it was the cheapest lodge around. Only four dollars a night and that included breakfast and dinner. Secondly, it was fun if you followed the rules. There were always card and board games going on as well as plenty of books and magazines scattered about to amuse you. No television, only endless records of alpine and classical music. The walls were plastered with posters depicting such famous European ski resorts as Davos, St. Moritz, Innsbruck and Chamonix.

I warmed up in front of the fireplace for a few minutes and then sat down to dinner with about twenty other skiers. Carl had fixed pot roast and mashed potatoes that he claimed was sauerbraten. This along with a few scattered vegetables, washed down with pitchers of milk or ice tea, constituted dinner. Someone complained loudly that beer was the only beverage that should be served with such a meal. But Carl stuck by his rule. No alcohol allowed in the lodge.

"If you want beer, you should have stayed at the German Lodge, *Mein Herr*," said Carl.

This semester break the lodge was filled with foreign students from Germany, France, Austria and Switzerland. Most were doing graduate work in engineering at Cal. Still, all wore their technical expertise lightly, speaking excellent English, flirting with the American girls and in general acting sophisticated and continental. Skiing in Europe was the main topic of discussion. For hours on end, they would compare the Sierra ski resorts to those of the Alps.

"No trees, you see. Wide open slopes. Blinding white with beautiful mountain scenery. Of course we ski at a higher elevation than you do here, above the tree line," said Jacques, a suave Frenchman who claimed to be a graduate student but looked forty.

I countered, "I hear they don't groom their slopes and that most people ski only on narrow trails through those snow fields."

"That is true, but I think Americans take the challenge out of skiing by constantly grooming their slopes. In Europe, we don't make it so easy."

The consensus among the Europeans was that while the Sierras would do, nothing beat the Alps. However, it was admitted that the chairlifts were better here, allowing more skiing per hour.

"You have a great lift system at Sugar Bowl," said Rolf, a tall, thin Swiss student. "You can ascend rather rapidly. No long lines. In the Alps, it sometimes it takes an hour to get to the top of the mountain. Once on top we have to put up with T-Bars or even rope tows. That is annoying."

"Bah," said Jacques, "you Swiss are in too much of a hurry, like the Americans. You should relax and enjoy the scenery and the food. At French ski resorts, lunch is a leisurely affair."

"Yes," said Rolf, "sometimes a drunken affair."

"*Eh bien, mon ami,*" responded Jacques. "You are right. Sometimes we drink too much wine and the rest of the day is kaput."

As Jacques told it, the major challenge of the day came late afternoon when it was time to ski, half-drunk, down four thousand feet to the base of the mountain. "By the time you are back at the lodge, you are *très fatigué*. Perhaps a nap and then dinner at eight or nine. Then some dancing, more drinking. You are not in bed until two or three in the morning."

"So you see, Allan," interjected Rolf, "skiing in Europe can be very tiring for the French when you are trying to be so leisurely about everything."

This is not to say the party scene was lacking around the Cal Ski Lodge. Next door was the German Lodge, run by German-Americans. I had stayed there once with brother Don two years ago. They showed old ski movies and on the weekends, a polka band played. Best of all, they served beer. This was a favorite hang out. It was here you could get your second wind and dance the evening hours away. It was also a great place to meet women since the German Lodge was well known for its dances. The fun started early, around 8 PM, and went full blast until 11 PM. Many a night under a starry sky we stood hip deep in fresh fallen snow, drunk on beer, pissing long yellow streams into a field of silver.

About a hundred yards down the highway was the Sierra Club Lodge—a serious, low-key hostel. One came here for ski instruction and nature films. Already in the late 50s and early 60s, the Sierra Club was worried about the environment and offered lectures on the car culture of California with its pollution and suburban sprawl. The club pointed out advantages of driving those funny little European cars such as the Volkswagen Beetle. There were no real parties at the Sierra Club Lodge, just a sip of hot wine and earnest conversation. The Sierra Club had its own small ski hill out back of about 700 feet vertical. It was great for beginners but dull for more advanced skiers.

***

The following morning, after a breakfast of hotcakes and porridge, Rolf, Jacques and I drove over to Squaw Valley to see what was going on. Despite reports of poor snow conditions, we wanted to check out the new chairlifts and the new runs cut in preparation for the Olympics.

The day was clear and beautiful as we made our way over Donner Summit in Rolf's beat up Land Rover. We could see the distant snow-covered peaks and the lushly wooded Donner Lake down below.

Even Jacques was impressed. "This is *magnifique*. Such a view, but the road, it makes me dizzy."

Jacques was referring to the narrow switchback section of Highway 40 as it descended to the valley floor. Only a flimsy guardrail stood between us and a sheer drop of several hundred feet. Indeed, I was always anxious myself driving over the pass. Occasionally, we could spot the wreckage of a car or a truck in some gully, the result of careless driving.

We turned off at Truckee and drove down Highway 89 until we came to the Squaw Valley turn-off. As we entered the valley, we were confronted with an impressive cul-de-sac of mountains, glittering white in the morning light. Closer to the resort proper, we passed block after block of half-completed construction with cranes and workmen going about their business.

The new Olympic ice rink was only a skeleton of steel girders, although its massive slanted roof was taking shape. The dormitories for the athletes were almost complete, yet still raw around the edges with piles of construction debris. We parked and poked our heads in the main lodge, which had been rebuilt in a Neo-Alpine style with a high, vaulted ceiling, expansive picture windows, a huge central fireplace and a mahogany bar that went on forever. Overall, very impressive, but they had a long way to go before the opening only a month away. That combined with sketchy snow on the lower slopes made us wonder.

"It will be a miracle if this place is ready," said Jacques as he laced up his boots on the deck outside the lodge.

"You are such a pessimist, Jacques," said Rolf. "Of course it will be ready. Americans are like the Swiss. They complete their projects on time."

"Amen," I responded, hoping that Rolf was right.

Prior to its upgrade for the Olympics, Squaw Valley was a skiing challenge for most skiers. Groomed slopes were far and few between. If it had snowed the night before, you plowed through it on stiff wooden skis. Some skiers had mastered the weighting and un-weighting technique of parallel skiing, but most continued to rely on the old stem turn and the snowplow to make it down through the heavy, un-groomed snow. Serviceable but not graceful.

As I soon discovered, Rolf was an ace skier. He had the parallel technique down pat. He skied on a long pair of Kneissls, an Austrian made wooden ski. Despite the advent of metal skis, Kneissl was still considered the ski for the serious skier in 1960. Additionally, Rolf had no use for the breakaway bindings that instantly freed your boot from the ski if you fell.

"You see, Allan," he explained pointing to my Marker bindings. "Those bindings allow for little edge control. The boots are too loose on the skis."

I looked down at my Head skis with their gleaming stainless steel Marker bindings. I examined my leather Dolomite ski boots with metal buckles and felt their snug fit into my bindings. I shifted my weight on the skis, digging in one edge and then the other. It felt pretty good to me. It felt like edge control. I also felt fashionable in my black Bogner stretch pants, sky-blue North Face parka, black leather gloves, space-age ski goggles and a bright blue knit cap. The state-of-the-art skier on a mountaintop.

Coming back to the reality at hand on Squaw Peak, I told Rolf, "I'll take a little less edge control with my bindings and not break my leg, thank you."

"Suit yourself, but without complete edge control, the short-swing parallel turn is difficult. See, the boots must be securely fastened to the ski. This is best done by the thong. Watch." Rolf proceeded to thread two long leather thongs through metal hooks embedded on the top of his skis and then wrap the thongs several times around his boots, cinching them tight. Once this was done, it was virtually impossible to lose a ski even if the skier fell. Of course, Rolf did not fall. He glided gracefully over the cruddiest of snow or the largest mogul with a smooth up-and-down bending of the knees, in perfect short-swing turns, leaving me far behind.

Well, that was O.K. I didn't want to keep up with him. I had my own agenda, trying to reconcile my state-of-the-art skier image with the reality of actually skiing down Squaw Peak. For a while, I clunked around on top trying to ski through the six inches of new snow that had fallen that night. It was typical heavy, wet snow that we called *Sierra cement*. I made my way over to one of the main challenges Squaw had to offer: the *headwall*, a forty-foot, near vertical drop to a steep run below.

Skiers who screwed up on the headwall paid dearly, often sliding a hundred yards or so before coming to a stop down slope. Their skis sometimes continued the journey for another hundred yards because no security straps were required and this was years before the ski-brake that every skier must now have on his skis.

For an intermediate skier such as me, the headwall was almost a suicide run if you took it straight on. However, if you knew the slope, there was a way to traverse it at an angle and with one big turn, make it to the bottom. Technically, you had "skied" the headwall.

This is precisely what I did. I started down the headwall on a shallow traverse and then planting my pole, I swung around in a large arc, dropping some five feet or so. I was now positioned to traverse the rest of the headwall out to the bottom, which I did flawlessly.

I looked back up at the cliff-size headwall with smug satisfaction. I had made it down without breaking my neck. Of course, I had cheated somewhat, but it was good enough for me. All the same, I watched with envy as more advanced skiers pointed their skis straight out, jumped into thin air and came down mid-slope and then with a little check turn, ran it to the bottom.

After the headwall and skiing down the remaining slope, I felt confident enough to take on the other major challenge of Squaw Valley: KT-22. KT-22 was a steep, narrow run full of giant moguls. The technique for skiing moguls was a challenge for the average skier. So most merely skied over the bumps from one side of the trail to the other and then made a stem turn, or failing that, the skier would come to a stop and do a stationary kick-turn. Although awkward and a symbol of defeat, the lowly kick-turn allowed the skier to safely change direction 180-degrees in a tight situation without breaking his neck. The name KT-22 derived from the legend of the San Francisco socialite who had to do twenty-two kick-turns to make it down the run.

One run on KT-22 was enough for me. I had tried to avoid the kick-turn and take on the moguls head on, but it didn't work. I fell several times, sliding over those giant bumps and then becoming trapped in the ruts between them. Finally, I gave up and skied over to the edge of the run and side-slipped down the remainder of the slope.

I spent the rest of the day on the wide-open runs of lower Squaw Peak. The snow was thin, and I had to avoid some rock outcroppings, but the six inches of new snow was soon packed down and provided a comfortable cushion on which to ski. I had the most fun on a long straight stretch of open slope near the bottom where I could let my skis run full speed ahead, sometimes going over a gentle bump that sent me airborne for a few yards. Pure exhilaration. On this bright sunny day, this was the best that skiing had to offer.

***

Around four, I quit for the day and retired to the Squaw Valley Lodge for a bit of après-ski. I met up with Rolf, Jacques and a few other Cal students who had smuggled in a jug of cheap wine. In the mad crush of the lounge, no one noticed a group of college boys drinking their own wine. However, after an initial sip of this rotgut, I opted for a hot-buttered rum at the bar. Although only nineteen, soon to be twenty in April, nobody checked my I.D. It was wide open here. At 6'3", 200-pounds, I looked old enough to be twenty-one.

I watched as the bartender poured out a generous shot of Bacardi rum, dropped in a chunk of butter and sprinkled in some brown sugar and cinnamon. Then, he poured in hot water and presto, I had my hot buttered rum. This drink hit the spot after a hard day of skiing. I settled down in front of the fireplace and sipped my drink slowly, feeling the hot-burn of the rum sliding down my throat. After a few sips, I began to feel light-headed and mellow as Bobby Darin crooned his latest hit: *Somewhere beyond the sea, Somewhere, waiting for me…*

Various ski-bunnies were about, swaying to the tune as well, possibly waiting for someone to ask them to dance. These young women were decked out in the latest Bogner and Obermeyer ski fashions. With their perfectly coiffed hair and make up, most looked as if they had spent the day indoors grooming themselves, emerging only for the après-ski hour. Too plastic for me, but I did notice a tall, striking-looking girl leaning against the bar as if she belonged there. She had a ruddy, sun-redden face, long auburn hair done up in a Heidi braid. She wore a pure white cable knit sweater and lime-green stretch pants that fit her like a glove. She appeared to know the bartender and turned to him from time to time making cracks about something and laughing.

I finished my rum drink and decided I needed a beer. Easing in beside her, I ordered a brew.

"Which brand?" asked the bartender.

"Anything on tap," I answered.

"Try a *Dortmunder*," the girl interjected. "It's a German brew. It's popular around here."

"Really," I said smiling at her, then turning to the bartender, "O.K. I'll follow her recommendation."

After he delivered my Dortmunder, I took a sip and said, "You're right. This is good. How come you know so much about beer?"

"Fuck, I practically live on the stuff," she answered.

'*Fuck?* What kind of chick is this?' I thought.

Her name was Jerri and she made use of the whole vocabulary. Although she looked good from a distance, she really was a mountain hillbilly with her pug nose, freckles and one chipped front tooth. However, her hair was silken and her body sleek. Hmm, an interesting combination, I thought.

"A college boy, huh?" she remarked.

"Yes, I'm staying over at Cal Ski Lodge."

"Yeah, I know it. It's a dump, don't you think?"

"Well, it's cheap. What do you do here? Ski all day?"

"I wish I could, but I have to work. I do some part-time instruction, but mostly I wait tables at the restaurant. This is my day off. I'm trying to earn some money to go college myself. I want to go to the University of Nevada in Reno to eventually get a business degree."

"Not a bad idea," I nodded. "Very practical."

"Yeah, I'm not going to wait tables and instruct skiing all my life. I want my own business."

"Sounds good."

We chatted some more. She told me she lived with her mom at Kings Beach on the north shore of Lake Tahoe, a few miles away. I bought her a beer and then we sat down at a table with some of her friends, an assorted crew of college dropouts, ski bums and high-schoolers who never looked back. One kid, Jim, went to San Jose State but was taking the spring semester off so he could hang out at the Olympics.

"Yeah, like dig," he said. "I have a job busing dishes at the lodge restaurant. It's crappy work, but I eat and ski free. And when the Olympics start, I'll see it all. Imagine, watching that French guy, Jean Vuarnet. Goes like a rocket I hear."

I envied Jim. Ski free all day. Then work for a few hours at night. So what if it was busing dishes. I felt the siren call stronger than ever.

By now, it was getting late and people were hungry. Rolf, Jacques and the other Cal skiers were heading back, but I wanted to hang with these people and find out what the ski life was really like. I was sure I would find some place to sleep for the night, even it meant a couch. I told the Cal group I was staying behind.

"You sure?" said Rolf. "I know the Cal Ski Lodge isn't much, but at least you will have a bed."

"Not to worry, I'll find somewhere to crash," I responded.

"O.K., see you later." And with that, they took off.

After another beer, somebody mentioned there was a party going on at Joe's cabin. Some of the women were going to cook up a big pot of spaghetti and there would be unlimited Paisano red. That sounded good to me. Jerri was game for it too. We bundled up in our parkas and went out into the now dark and cold night, trudging after Jim, who knew where Joe's place was.

I was expecting some backwoods shed or a dorm-like hovel, but when we hiked up a side road for about a quarter of a mile, we came to a large A-Frame cabin with the lights blazing and a spacious deck that overlooked the valley. Joe came out to greet us. He was a tall, smooth looking dude with a mustache and longish hair, somewhat older than the rest of us.

The interior of the cabin was a radical departure from traditional Alpine décor. It was as if some hip 1960s designer had gone mad—a flagstone fireplace with a gas log setup that rendered a realistic looking wood fire flame; a long, curvy, burnt-orange modular couch that snaked its way across the "great" room; a thick, white shag throw rug on the hardwood floor with a vaguely bearish shape. Here and there, low-slung armchairs resembling overstuffed beanbags hugged the floor. A glass top table in the dining area encircled by strange looking modular fiber-glass chairs.

In the ultra-modern kitchen with gleaming white GE appliances, groovy tile countertops and dark oak cabinets, the gals began working on the spaghetti dinner

"Let's get cracking, ladies," said Joe. "I'm hungry. A man needs a hearty meal after a day of skiing."

"For sure, Joe," said one girl in pure white stretch pants that looked as if they had never seen a day on the slopes. "I'm fixing my grand-mother's old recipe."

Jerri set the dining room table while the guys repaired to the burnt-orange sofa in front of the fire, sipped on beer and listened to Joe hold forth:

"It's not a bad deal. My uncle made it big in the stock market in San Francisco so he built this little cabin for himself where he and his family could get away. Except for two or three weeks, it sits empty. That's where I come in. I live here in the winter and keep the place up, keep it clean, keep the pipes from freezing and in general make sure it's livable when they do come up. I can have people over as long as they pitch in and help, like I'm sure you guys and gals will do."

"So, what do you do here all the time?" I asked. "You can't ski all the time."

"You'd be surprised. This place keeps me busy. I read a lot and do some minor investing."

"Sweet deal," I said.

"Yeah, it works out although I do miss the City and go down there for a few days at a time."

Soon dinner was ready. The gal in the white stretch pants had in-deed cooked up a great pot of spaghetti. The noodles were done just right; the sauce was rich and tangy. This with a big green salad, toasted garlic bread and a lot of Pisano red wine to wash it down made for a de-licious meal.

Afterwards, we sat around the fireplace sipping Joe's Scotch. He put on a Sinatra LP and everything got dreamy. A couple danced, while others snuggled down and stared at the fire. Jerri was flushed and rather drunk but friendly. We danced for a while, and then I noticed one couple drifting off to one of the bedrooms. I led Jerri into a kid bedroom with a bunk bed. As we crumpled on to the lower bunk, I slipped my hand under her sweater and snapped open her bra. Soon, I had undone the side zipper of her stretch pants and was sliding my other hand down to her warm ass when she suddenly pulled away and stood up.

"Al, wait."

"Wait, wait for what?"

"Al, I just met you. I can't go all the way just like that."

"Why not?" I asked. "We seem to be attracted to each other."

"Yeah, sure. You only want to screw and then split. You'll go back to Berkeley and talk about the hick mountain chick you made it with."

"Oh no, Jerri. I want to see more of you. Maybe we could ski together tomorrow. You could give me some pointers."

"Yeah, yeah. Maybe. Right now, I really don't want to go on with this. I'm too drunk and sleepy. Let's crash…O.K?"

"Ah, sure, whatever you say," I said too bombed to protest.

Jerri climbed onto the top bunk, stretch pants half off, and passed out. I stayed on the bottom bunk and was soon fast asleep.

I got up the next morning feeling grungy and hung-over. Jerri was still asleep. I looked at her—a freckled-face mountain girl, her long auburn hair, now falling loosely on the pillow, her mouth half-open, lightly breathing, her broken front tooth, looking cute. I wondered. Maybe something was possible with this mountain girl.

I showered, sloshed some mouthwash around my mouth and climbed back into my ski clothes, funky now after two days of straight wear.

Two hours later, after a big breakfast of scrambled eggs, Canadian bacon and French toast and a quick clean up of the cabin, we were back on the slopes. Jerri and I took the chair up to Squaw Peak, got off right before the headwall and skied over to an intermediate slope.

She lashed her thongs to her Kastle skis and was ready to go. She motioned for me to ski ahead so she could watch my technique. I skied down the run making wide parallel turns and skidded to a stop. She followed with perfect short- swing turns and came gracefully to a stop.

"Well, I can see what your problem is, Al," she said holding her poles high. "You have to keep your center of gravity up. Hold your arms higher when you make a pole plant. Keep your hands out in front of you. Pretend you're holding onto a large steering wheel, driving a bus."

She demonstrated and I followed, standing up straighter, facing more directly down the fall line, keeping my hands up in front of me. It worked. I felt my skis swinging from side to side as I faced down hill. I was doing a series of short-swing turns, something that I hadn't mastered before. We took a couple more runs and then Jerri announced she had to go teach a class for beginner kids on the bunny hill.

"Well, maybe I'll see you after," I said.

"Yeah, maybe. You don't have to. I understand, Al. All I'm asking is, if I phone you up at Berkeley telling you that I'm coming down, you'll promise to take me out to dinner in San Francisco."

"It's a promise," I said.

She smiled a big radiant smile. "You know I've always wanted to go out all dressed up in San Francisco. You'll do that for me, won't you, Al?"

"Like I said, I promise."

We exchanged phone numbers and off she skied down the hill. Perfect, graceful, poetry on snow. I was left wondering, did I want to pursue her? She fit in so beautifully up here on the mountains. This was her element. But how would it be back in the Bay Area? What would we talk about? How would she fit in with the college crowd? Then I realized the problem wasn't Jerri. She was what she was—a cute mountain girl whose dream was to get a business degree. No, the problem was me. As much as I liked skiing, I realized I couldn't fit in with these ski bum types, waiting on tables, drinking cheap wine and partying with dropouts. There was no intellectual excitement here. No curiosity.

As enticing as the upcoming Olympics might be, I didn't want to bus dishes for minimum wage when I could be contemplating the great conundrums of Western Civilization. Moreover, if I dropped out for a semester, I would have to forego crew and give up a possible shot at the rowing in the Summer Olympics in Rome. Finally, I would be behind academically and would probably have to do an extra semester in order to graduate.

I skied for a few more hours and then decided to bag it for the day. I caught a ride back to the Cal Lodge, skied the next day at Sugar Bowl, which had better snow than Squaw. Then, I took the evening train back to Martinez, my ski outing over for the time being.

***

A few weeks later, on Washington's Birthday, I was sitting on Sam's Dock in Sausalito, eating cheeseburgers and drinking beer. The sun was warm, the breeze gentle, the water calm and the gulls flapping and screeching overhead. I had sailed over to Sausalito with the UC Sailing Club in four little sailboats. Now we were relaxing before sailing back.

Sam, the restaurant owner, had rolled out a large black and white TV on a stand so we could watch the highlight of the Olympics, the men's downhill. I had nearly forgotten about the Olympics since I had returned from the skiing.

We watched as the Frenchman, Jean Vuarnet, plunged down the headwall, in a perfect oval crouch known as *l'oeuf*, the egg. We watched as he raced along on his metal skis, making his turns in his wide-stance crouch, never changing the position of his upper body. We marveled as he plummeted down three thousand feet of vertical at speeds of over eighty miles an hour and flashed across the finish line with the winning time.

It was thrilling. It was live. Seeing it on television was almost as good as being there. In some ways, better. Because of the multiple cameras positioned up and down the racecourse, we could see the whole race rather than a portion of it like spectators on the scene.

However, as soon as the race was over, I returned to my cheeseburger and beer, now and then looking out over the bay filled with sailboats. The waters glinted in the afternoon sun with the still warm breezes. Spring was around the corner and those snowy white slopes up in the Sierras were a distant, fast-fading dream.

10. ADRIFT

So now that I had decided to forgo the life of a ski bum, I returned to the academic grind of Cal. The second semester of my sophomore year at Cal, I was taking French III-Reading, U.S. History, Modern European History, ROTC and Crew. With barely a C average, it was still a tough go. I had thought it would be easier after my freshman year, yet it seemed to get harder.

The myth was that if you had made it through Berkeley your freshman year, it was clear sailing. However, I knew several people who were invited to leave in their sophomore year because of a low grade point average. Berkeley was bucking to be as tough as the Ivy League. Many of the academic departments were run by former Yale and Princeton professors who had abandoned the East Coast with its cut-throat academic competition, harsh winters and cramped living quarters. (Housing in the Bay Area was still cheap compared to the more desirable places back East.) Even so, these very same professors continued to proclaim an Ivy League commitment to excellence and exclusivity. Their whispered agenda went something like this:

Yes, UC Berkeley is a state supported institution. Yes, we have to open the doors to mediocre high school seniors with barely a B average to keep the California politicians and parents happy. Once here, however, we can slam them, flunk them out and send them on the way to San Jose State or to their local community college. We want only the true pearls – the true intellects to care for and nourish.

I was not a *pearl*. I was not destined for intellectual care and nourishment.

I was flirting with probation again because of a D in French II last semester. As Reginald had predicted, French II had been a bitch of a course, far harder than French I. I studied hard for it, but it moved too fast for me. I was overwhelmed and lucky to get a D.

In addition, ROTC was once again giving me trouble. After behaving myself for two semesters and getting C's in ROTC, I slipped back into my old habits of skipping drill and displaying poor leadership skills when I did show up. I was once again rated F by an upper-division punk with big Army ambitions. Even Redman, my fraternity brother and overall student commander of ROTC, could not protect me. Averaging the F with my C for classroom work, the Army gave me another D and bid me good riddance.

My four semesters of mandatory ROTC at Berkeley were over. I had fulfilled my ROTC obligation.

Luck was with me, though. I managed to get a B in Modern European History, along with two B's in Crew. That gave me a lift above a C average and effectively put me beyond probationary status.

***

Still, those B's in crew annoyed me. When I was in the first boat in my freshman year, Coach Lemmon had given me A's. Now that I was in a junior varsity boat my sophomore year, I received only B's. When I mentioned that to him, he simply said, "Second boats rate only B's."

In fact, crew in general was getting annoying. This was the year of the 1960 Summer Olympics in Rome so we were rowing our butts off. The five-mile row out to Yuerba Buena Island had become routine. We sprinted up and down the Oakland Estuary as if it were a drag strip.

Somebody asked Lemmon, now the head coach, how he would choose his top boat for the upcoming Olympics. Would it automatically be the first boat varsity that went to the Olympics?

"Hold on there," he cautioned. "There's a lot of work to be done before we put together an Olympic boat. First, remember, that it takes the whole team, all thirty-two of you fellows to put the final eight men in the boat. Even if you don't go to the Olympics, you will have damn well contributed."

Contributed? Contribution was not enough. I wanted to be in the top boat.

Lemmon continued, "Throughout the season we will be shifting people around, as we do every year, to see who works the best and which combination gives us our fastest boats."

Despite what Lemmon had said about moving people around, we in the freshman boat fully expected to stay in the same boat because we were so good. And we did stay in the same boat for the first few weeks, regularly beating the JV boat and sometimes the varsity. However, as the weeks went by, Lemmon started shuffling the crews. Our old frosh team was split up among three junior varsity boats. All these boats sucked. We were different sizes, different temperaments and different styles.

Somewhat presumptuously, I asked Lemmon one day after practice why we couldn't keep the old freshman boat together as a JV boat since we were so good together.

"Can't do that right now, Allan. We have to mix it up. You never know. Sometimes you create a much faster boat. You fellows were good as freshmen, but you'll get even better in different boats."

Later in the season, I thought the varsity boat was mediocre, not at all Olympic material. Yet, Lemmon stuck with it. After the varsity boat lost again to the University of Washington, I asked Lemmon why he didn't try some of us sophomores in it.

Somewhat annoyed he responded, "These juniors and seniors have been rowing their hearts out for three and four years. They deserve their shot at the Olympics. I don't know how well we will do, but they have to have a shot. You fellows from the golden frosh boat will have your chance in a year or two."

"In a year or two? In a year or two there will be no Olympics," I countered.

"Yes, that's true, but there are other regattas, big ones too, such as the Henley Regatta in England. You lads will probably have a shot at that."

All the while I am thinking, 'What a loser. More worried about the upperclassmen and tradition than putting the best boat together.'

I was in funk. Although we were working hard with grueling workouts, trying to pace the first varsity boat, I had mixed feelings. During spring break in April, Lemmon had arranged for the crew to live together in a fraternity house vacated by its regular members. He pitched this as a time to bond, a time to coalesce as a crew. "It'll be great. We'll watch movies of the classic races, eat steak dinners and put in full three-hour practices."

Groan. I had had enough of his rah-rah. I decided to go home to Martinez and commute to the Cal Boathouse for the practices.

"So we're not good enough for you, huh, Brown?" said Lemmon a day or two after he realized I wasn't staying at the fraternity.

"Ah, Jim. I live only eighteen miles away. It doesn't make sense for me to stay at the fraternity when I have all the comforts of home, get my laundry done and visit with my parents and stuff."

"Yeah, I see, but this is a great bonding experience. I sometimes think you're too much of a loner, Allan. Crew is a team sport. You have to work together and think together. Living together helps accomplish that. God knows you have the physical size and skill, but I sometimes wonder about your spirit."

"My spirit is fine," I said. "I show up at the boathouse on the dot for practice and am ready to give my all. You won't see me goofing off during practice. I give one hundred and ten percent."

"Well," he scowled, "make sure that you do."

Lemmon's varsity boat never did make it to the 1960 Olympics in Rome. Navy beat them out for that spot in the Olympic trials at Syracuse New York. However, the Cal Varsity did win the Intercollegiate Rowing Association (IRA) regatta, also at Syracuse. So overall, it was a winning season for Lemmon. However, I was still convinced that if Lemmon had kept our old frosh boat together and worked us as hard as he had the varsity, we would have dominated that season and made it to the Summer Olympics.

***

When I didn't show up for fall practice the next season, Lemon sent me a note to come by his office in Sproul Hall. He was sitting behind his big desk fooling with his battery-powered megaphone when I walked in.

"Sit down, Allan. Long time no see."

"Yeah, I guess," I said sitting down.

He got right to the point. "So what are you doing? Kissing off crew?"

"Yes, I've been meaning to tell you," I said. "I didn't earn much money this summer for school, so I need some more dough to pay for expenses. I have this job in the afternoon and no time for crew."

"No time for crew?" he said leaning forward, putting his megaphone on the desk. "Just like that, no time for crew?"

"Right, no time for crew."

"Hey, Allan, if you needed a job that didn't conflict with crew you should have called me first. I can get those jobs for my guys."

Finally, I confessed, "Jim, crew has been a great experience, but I have to move on. I'm thinking about studying in Europe, so I wouldn't be here anyway."

"Junior Year Abroad, huh?" said Lemmon, raising an eyebrow.

"Maybe," I replied.

"Well, let me tell you something, Allan. Crew is more important than any trip to Europe. You can go to Europe any time in your life, but you can only row in college crew once in your life. Here you are, planning to blow off the remaining two years of crew. Not a smart decision. We need you and the rest of you men from the frosh boat. You are all naturals. I had to do what I had to do last season. This year you fellows will have a chance at being in the first boat. Remember there is still the Henley Regatta in England. That could be your trip to Europe."

"I'll think about it," I said.

I did for a few days and was tempted to return until I talked to other members from our original frosh crew and discovered that nearly all had dropped out as well. Tony or "Goose", as we called him, summed up his situation. "I'm in a tough major, Al. Electrical engineering. I don't think it's worth my time to continue to row on crew, especially now that our chance at the Olympics is past. It's just one of those things. However, some of the guys are rowing on their own in the two-man shells on an intramural basis. You interested?"

"Nah, I don't think so. Like you, I have other things to do," I said.

As it turned out, the Cal crew never competed in the Olympics again. Harvard's crew was the last intact college crew to represent the United States in the 1968 Olympics. After 1968, the U.S. Olympic Committee decided to recruit a national team from the best rowers in the U.S. regardless of college. Now and then, Cal contributed an oarsman or two, but the glory days of a single college crew rowing in the Olympics were over.

However, all of that was in the future. At the end of the 1960 spring semester, I was preoccupied with the reality that I was halfway through UC Berkeley, disillusioned with crew, still unfocused in my academics and just bumping along with a C average. About all I knew in early June was I wanted to get out of the Bay Area. I wanted the mountains again. I wanted some fun. I wanted to hang out at Lake Tahoe.

11. LAKE TAHOE

Lake Tahoe is a gem. High, blue and cold. Ringed by snow-covered mountains, an alpine Shangri-La. Despite years of development around the lake, man's dirty footsteps are still dwarfed by this vast body of water. My first encounter with Lake Tahoe was at the age of ten in 1950 when my family spent a week at a public campground in South Lake Tahoe. We endured wall-to-wall tents, squalling babies, mosquitoes, dust and dirt. My mother hated it. She had to set up housekeeping and do all the cooking. Although we tried to help, she nearly had a nervous breakdown. Her only relief was escaping to a nearby beach with a book, while my father, Don and I went fishing.

It was clear to me then that this camping business was déclassé. Don and I would watch with envy as beautiful, mahogany Chris-Craft speedboats streaked across the lake, often pulling a leggy blonde on water skis. We drove by log cabin mansions overlooking the lake in settings, so peaceful and serene. We constantly nagged our dad to rent a cabin, so we could live like human beings.

"Pretty expensive, kids," he would reply. "Perhaps someday."

A year or two later my dad did start renting a cabin and that was a vast improvement. We lounged around all day on the cabin porch reading cheap paperbacks or headed off to the local beach for a swim. Sometimes we rented a rowboat with an outboard motor and chugged around the shoreline. Don and I felt that we had arrived.

***

Now here it was the summer of 1960, and I was headed back to Lake Tahoe and back to camping with my old high school friend, Jan Meirs, a short, stocky guy with dirty-blond hair. Jan had been attending Contra Costa Junior College in Pleasant Hill and was planning to go on to San Francisco State College in the fall. Five years earlier, Jan and I had traveled together to Canada to visit his uncles in Winnipeg. It was an ambitious, month long trip with highs and lows, but we managed to survive. Now, Jan wanted to spend a summer at Tahoe. So more out of convenience than anything else, we decided to go up together.

The Greyhound bus dropped us off at Tahoe City, on the north shore. We each had a knapsack and one big duffle bag that contained a tent and other camping gear. We planned to camp out until we found jobs. Although it was mid-June with snow still on the ground in some spots, the state campground at Tahoe City was already crammed with families, tents, coolers, folding chairs, bicycles and cheap aluminum boats with tiny outboard motors. All the comforts of home.

Jan and I found an unoccupied campsite back from the beach that nobody wanted. It was dank without much sunlight, located in a depression among the pines. It was sure to be wet if it rained and no doubt overrun by mosquitoes. There was a picnic table and a fire pit, but no wood. A bundle at the ranger gate cost fifty cents. The latrine was fifty yards away. Trying to make the best of it, we put up Jan's old army tent, unrolled our sleeping bags and managed to arrange a decent camp.

***

A local bus ran every half-hour along the main highway that hugged the north shore of Lake Tahoe. Unlike the south shore, this stretch was still pristine, populated only by scattered resorts and a few sleepy towns: Carnelian Bay, Tahoe Vista and King's Beach. Jan and I spotted one attractive looking resort past Carnelian Bay. It was here we began our job hunting.

The main lodge was set back, overlooking the lake. Towering pines whispered in the morning breeze and the scent of tamarack was in the air, promising a warm day despite the remnants of snow found here and there in the shadows of trees and buildings.

Inside, in the reception area, an attractive girl worked the front desk. She looked up as we approached. "Can I help you fellows?"

"Could we speak to the manager, please?" I asked.

"Sure," she said. "He was around here a few minutes ago. Wait. He'll be back soon. You boys looking for jobs?"

"Well, yes, as a matter of fact," I said.

We chatted while waiting for the manager. Lena was a student at University of Nevada, Reno. Her family had been coming here for years. Now that she was grown, the owner had hired her as a desk clerk.

A few minutes later, the manager showed up. He was a tall, in his forties with a well-trimmed beard. Jan and I introduced ourselves, explaining we were looking for summer jobs.

He nodded, looked us over and then said, "Sorry boys, we've already hired our help for the summer. Check back in a week in case somebody doesn't show up. In any event, fill out an application so I can have it on file."

"O.K. thanks," I said.

Jan and I went out on the lodge sundeck and sat down at a picnic table. As we filled out our applications, we sipped Coke and looked out over the lake.

Gee, we thought, it would be great working here. It seemed a relaxed, friendly place, but we sensed it wasn't to be, so we handed in our applications and moved on.

King's Beach was the last resort town in California before the Nevada state line. The town dribbled along Highway 28 with scattered homes, stores, gas stations and real estate offices until it stopped abruptly at the border. Here, the knotty pine architecture gave way to the glitz and glamour of the Nevada gambling scene. The Crystal Bay Casino was one of the more striking casinos. Constructed in steel, glass and decorated in aquamarine colors, it reminded me of a giant cruise ship at sea.

Jan and I got off the bus and walked through the casino parking lot. Even at this early hour, the lot was jammed with cars and tour buses. We entered the casino through large sliding glass doors, passing row after row of slot machines, followed by various gaming tables of blackjack, roulette and craps. Though it was only 10 AM, the dealers were dressed in white shirts with spiffy bow ties and vests with the casino logo on it. In contrast, most of the customers looked as if they had been up all night in their wrinkled pants and shirts. The men with chin stubble and dark bags under their eyes, the women, hair askew and make- up smeared. A few customers were in shorts and sandals, ready for the beach after a morning session at the slots.

Jan and I spotted a large breakfast buffet laid out in the restaurant area near the back and noting a price tag of only one dollar, we began helping ourselves. We piled our plates high with scrambled eggs, sausage, pancakes, toast, orange juice and fresh fruit. As we began to eat, the thought occurred to us the Nevada gambling zone might be a better area to hang out in than the more sedate resort areas. At least we could eat cheap.

I struck up a conversation with a tall, skinny kid who was also stuffing his face. Steve was a student at Pomona College in L.A. He was up here for the summer. Between bites, Steve filled us in on the area.

"Yeah, it's great around here. Cheap food, a lot of summer employment."

"So where do you stay?" I asked.

"That's the problem," said Steve. "There are a few employee dorms, but you have to work for the casinos to get in. Until you find a job, you might try camping at Crystal Bay Beach about a mile farther on. You're not supposed to camp overnight there, but the rangers hardly ever check. I spent a week on the beach before I had a place to stay."

Jan and I looked at each other and decided on the spot that we would definitely relocate to the casino area. We chatted with Steve some more. He said he had a job on the grounds crew at Cal Neva Lodge and was staying at the Cal Neva employee's dorm.

"Check out Cal Neva," he advised. "I think they are hiring carhikers right now."

"Will do. Thanks for the tip," I said.

After breakfast, Jan and I took the bus back to Tahoe City, gathered up our gear and returned to Crystal Bay.

By the time we made it to the beach, it was about two in the afternoon. This beach was a beauty with its soft, powder white sand and clear blue water lapping gently at its shore. Unlike most lake water in June at Lake Tahoe, these waters were warm, probably because of its southern exposure and shallow bay. A string of large boulders about thirty yards offshore enclosed the beach in a semicircle.

We were in our bathing suits in a flash and swam out to the boulders. Looking down with my swim mask, visibility was spectacular. I could see the rocky bottom, clear as day with several large trout swimming around and here and there, a submerged log. Later, Jan and I stretched out on one of the boulders and sunbathed, taking in the surrounding mountain peaks, the pines lining the shore and as always, the clear, blue lake.

By early evening, the beach was deserted. It was all ours. The setting sun cast a shimmering pink across the water as the last rays sank behind the mountains. The lake darkened from pink to black. The temperature dropped and Jan and I crawled into our sleeping bags and read by flashlight, now and then looking up at the swirl of stars overhead. Soon we fell asleep, lulled by the gentle wave action of the lake water.

***

I awoke with the sunrise. It was cold, somewhere in the low fifties, but I was cozy and warm in my down-filled sleeping bag. When I finally got up and made my way to the latrine, it was a painful task. I was sore and stiff and the cold bit at my skin through my thin T-shirt. My bare feet on the concrete floor of the latrine sent chills up my spine as I pissed into a smelly urinal. I returned to the warmth of my sleeping bag and watched the brightening day. Jan slept on. I could hear fish jumping and see hawks swooping down for breakfast. A lone fisherman was fishing off the rocks near shore. A peaceful, quiet scene.

Boring actually. I didn't think I could last long on a beach like this. While it was nature at its best, I needed more action. I couldn't amuse myself for hours on end as Jan could.

When Jan awoke an hour later, he threw on his windbreaker, took a pee in the weeds and then started beachcombing, picking up one interesting rock after another. He even dug up an old iron artifact. Jan was a scavenger. He was always finding something of value that he often converted into cash.

"You would not believe what people throw out," he often said. "Their junk is my gold mine."

Jan had told me that he didn't want to spend his time here working at some dip-shit resort job. He wanted to scout out the antiques and artifacts of the Lake Tahoe area.

"You know, Allan, many wealthy people live around here and that means they probably have interesting throwaways."

"Do say," I said.

In addition, Jan was a rock hound and was always looking for precious stones, even gold.

"There was a lot of mining in this area," he continued. "You might be surprised what you can find in the tailings. I want to be like those Chinese miners who moved in after the Americans had exhausted a vein and could still find gold.

Hmm, I thought, I as sat up in my sleeping bag watching Jan pick his way up and down the beach. Where does he get the energy? Why does he know so much? He was always telling me he came from a long line of Dutch traders and had uncles living in the Far East and Indonesia. I remembered hanging out at his house in high school, looking at all his stuff: gold coins, foreign paper money, an Indonesian butterfly collection, Japanese Army artifacts — patches, bayonets, a sooty cooking pot for rice, a ceremonial Samurai sword…and one shrunken head from Borneo. Well, that was Jan, a Dutch trader at heart.

Soon, all I could think about was food. My stomach was growling. I wanted to return to the breakfast buffet at the casino. So I prodded Jan to give up his scavenging. We put on clean shirts and pants and broke camp, hiding our gear in a grove of trees at one end of the beach. We caught a ride back to the casino and soon were stuffing ourselves at the breakfast buffet. Later, we washed up in their restroom and then freshly groomed, we were ready for the job hunt of the day.

Cal Neva Lodge was right across the street from the Crystal Bay Casino. Jan and I hadn't noticed it at first because of the blinding glitz of the newer casinos, but there it was, sedate in its Alpine-Tudor architecture, set well back from the road. It looked more like an overgrown log cabin than a gambling casino, but a casino it was with the California-Nevada state line running right through the middle of it. The California side had the restaurants and the hotel. The Nevada side had the gambling. It struck me as a cozy arrangement.

Jan and I walked through the parking lot to the main entrance, where a doorman in a blue cap and blazer was making notations in a logbook.

"Excuse me," I said. "My friend and I heard that Cal Neva was hiring car-hikers."

He looked up, gave us the once-over and sniffed. "You have to check with Sammy. He runs the car-hiking crew out of that shack," he said pointing to a little shack at the edge of the parking lot. "He should be there around two this afternoon."

"Oh, O.K." I said.

Jan chimed in saying, "Say, mind if we go inside and take a look around the casino."

"Yeah sure. You fellows can take a look around, but forget the gambling unless you're twenty-one or over."

"Sure thing," Jan said as we headed off into the lobby.

The reception area was filled with overstuffed leather chairs and couches. Moose heads and antlers lined one the wall. This was your basic mountain lodge décor with high overhead log-beamed ceilings and a granite fireplace ablaze even though it was warm outside. To the right was a coffee shop, a newsstand and beyond that ornate double doors that led to the main restaurant.

To the left, a big fat white stripe ran along the floor designating the state-line. Beyond this was the gambling casino. It didn't appear to be anything special, a few slot machines, a roulette wheel, several blackjack tables and one craps table. The Crystal Bay Casino was much newer and more inviting. It seemed to me that Cal-Neva had seen better days and was due for an overhaul.

Jan and I exited the Cal Neva and wandered around the area for an hour or two, checking out the tourist traps along Highway 28. Then we killed some time at King's Beach before returning to the Crystal Bay Casino for the lunch buffet where we proceeded to stuff ourselves again and play the nickel slots machines. Nobody bothered to ask our age.

Finally, we hiked back over to Sammy's shack around 2 PM and sure enough there, through an open door we saw Sammy hunched over a high desk, reading a racing form. He was a short, squat man with a head of carefully coiffed steel-gray hair. Bulging arm muscles stuck out of his white short sleeve shirt with the requisite black bow tie. He looked up as we approached.

"Can I help ya kids?"

"Are you Sammy?"

"Fuckin' eh." Sammy had what sounded like a New York or Boston accent to me, but as I was to learn, it was really a Chicago accent.

"My friend and I heard that you were hiring car-hikers for the season," I said.

"Yeah, ya heard right. You both got valid drivers' licenses?"

"Sure do."

"Well lemme see," he said motioning with his index finger to hand them over.

I produced my driver's license. Jan hesitated and then said that he had left his at home back in Martinez.

"Too bad, kid, 'cause no driver's license, no job. I got enough troubles as it is without getting nailed by the cops or the insurance companies," said Sammy as he turned my driver's license over in his hand.

"Oh," said Jan, not seeming too upset. "I understand."

"So," said Sammy handing my driver's license back, "got a good driving record, Al? No accidents?"

"No, I'm clean," I responded.

"Cause, you see, Al," Sammy continued, "we hike expensive cars around here—Caddys, Lincolns, some foreign jobs like Mercedes, Jaguars, a Rolls now and then. Don' want anything to happen to them. The deal is you get a single scratch on one of them and you're gone. No second chances. *Capeesh?*" Sammy shot me a glance.

"Ah...yeah, sure I understand," I said. "Does that mean I'm hired?"

He laughed, "Sure kid...fer today. I'll try you out. See how ya do. But you're going to have to get yourself a white short-sleeve shirt and black bow tie and some khakis. We don' want no jeans around here. If it gets cold, we have Cal-Neva windbreakers you can wear. I'll see you at five. You'll be working to midnight or so."

"Sure, Sammy. That's fine," I said, my head spinning. I had brought a pair of khakis along, but I had no white shirt and no bow tie.

As if reading my mind, Sammy said, "Go see Sal at the reception desk. He can probably dig something up for you, leftovers from the hotel staff."

As I was about to return to the lodge, Sammy said, "Oh, by the way, Al. The pay is two bucks an hour. It comes out of tip pool that we collect every night. Many of these guys tip big. Hold any back and you're gone. It's all share and share alike."

"Yeah, sure," I said doing some quick arithmetic. Two-dollars per hour seemed to me to be enough to survive on up here for food, but not lodging. Where was I going to sleep? Then the thought occurred to me that if I were at home surveying, I could be making $3.00 per hour and have free room and board. But hey, then I wouldn't be on my own up here at Lake Tahoe.

Jan hung around the parking lot while I went in and was fitted with a freshly laundered short-sleeve white shirt and black bow tie. I was now ready to launch my car-hiking career. Back outside, Jan looked on, trying to put a brave face on things.

"I'm sorry, Jan," I said. "You should have brought your license. Maybe your parents can mail it to you."

"Nah, Allan. That's O.K. I can barely drive anyway," said Jan already plotting his next move. "I think I can do better just riding the buses and snooping around. You never know what you can find. I guess we better go back to the beach and get our stuff."

We hitched a ride to Crystal Bay Beach and picked up our gear. At Kings Beach, I said goodbye to Jan. He was going to take the bus down to South Tahoe to see what was happening there.

Lugging my gear, I went back to Cal Neva to find that employee dorm where Steve was staying. Sammy had said nothing about lodging for car-hikers, but I thought, why not? I'm an employee now, even if I am off the books.

The Cal-Neva employee dorm was located in a secluded grove of pines, a block from the lodge. It was a ramshackle two-story affair. Steve had said he was on the second floor at the end of the hall. I lugged my stuff up there and knocked on the door. Nothing at first and then a stirring.

"Whaa...,"came a groan. "Who's there?"

"Allan Brown, Steve. Remember? From the Crystal Bay Casino?

"Oh, yeah, just a minute. I was taking a little nap."

A few seconds later, the door opened and there stood Steve, shirtless in his Levis. "A late night, you know. Day off, I think," he said, groggy. "Shit what a head. I hate beer hangovers. Come on in."

I went in. His room was a mess—clothes, books, a guitar and junk piled everywhere. But I spotted what I needed, an empty bunk.

"Fuck, you wouldn't believe the chick I met," said Steve, rubbing his temples. "Drank like a fish. Couldn't keep up. Jerri. What a trip."

"Jerri? I know a Jerri who lives around here. I met her skiing this winter. Boy could she drink! Maybe it's the same Jerri."

"I don't know, but she's a wild one. Except I don't think she screws that easily. Anyway I was too drunk to find out." Steve sat down on his bed and looked at me. "So what brings you here?"

"Well, I remember that you said you stayed in the Cal Neva employee dorm. I got one of those car-hiker jobs that you mentioned. So now I need a place to stay."

"Yeah, that's cool," said Steve scratching his head. "Except, the guy who runs this dorm says car-hikers aren't regular employees of Cal Neva. That's bullshit. He never checks anyway. Half this place is empty, though it might fill up with more help in a couple of weeks when the tourists start coming in. Meantime, you can stay here, if you don't mind the mess."

"You sure?"

"Shit yes, man. I have an extra bed. I don't want to share it with some dishwashing spic who can't speak English. You seem cool. By the way, the bathroom is down the hall."

And so it was that I shared a dorm room with Steve at Cal Neva. The place was a dump, the bed had a smelly mattress and weak springs, but it was a bed. I stashed my stuff and took a cold shower in a rusty shower stall down the hall. Then, I put on my khakis, my fresh white short-sleeve shirt and my black bow tie, combed my hair and was ready for my first day as a car-hiker at Cal Neva Lodge.

***

The main parking lot was only a quarter full when I arrived back at Sammy's shack. Sammy was on the phone talking about some horse race. He nodded to me as I checked in. "See Joey about the drill."

I introduced myself to two guys sitting on the car-hiker bench. One was a surfer looking dude with bleached blonde hair, acne and a vacant stare as if he had ridden one wave too many. The other, a wiry, dark haired kid with a big 1950s pompadour drenched in oil. I assumed this was Joey.

"So, Al, here's what we do," said Joey in the same Chicago accent that Sammy had. "The car drives up to the main entrance where the valet sign is. The hiker opens the driver side door first, the rear passenger door second if somebody is in back on the driver's side. The concierge will take care of the passenger side. You give the customer a greeting like, 'Welcome to Cal Neva, sir. Allow me to park your car.' He usually leaves the keys in the ignition with the car running. You slip in and drive away to the reserve lot around the corner. Remember before you drive off to check out the dash, the gearshifts, the brakes and so on. Drive slow and park careful like. Most of these cars are big and expensive. That's all there is to it. Give the keys to Sammy and he'll return them when you fetch the customer's car later in the evening."

"How does Sammy know which key is for which car?" I asked, curious. "Are they labeled or something?"

"Jeeze. I dunno know," said Joey. "Sammy just has a pile of keys in front of him, but he always knows which key goes to which car. He never makes a mistake."

"No kidding."

Joey was Sammy's nephew, and he too was from Chicago. This was his third season parking cars at Cal Neva. He was vague as to what he did the rest of the year.

Soon, I had my first car to park, a big steel-blue 1960 Cadillac with sweeping tail fins. I slid in behind the wheel, studied the layout, checked the automatic gear stick and inched out from the reception area while luxuriating in the plush leather seats. I drove down the drive about a hundred feet and turned into the special reserve lot for valet customers. I carefully eased the Caddy into a spot between two other Cadillacs, took the keys out of the ignition and hustled back to the reception area, handing over the keys to Sammy, who was now out by the bench directing operations.

And that's how it went the first night. Every few minutes or so, a car drove up. One of us three would jump in and drive it off. I had never driven so many luxury cars in my life. In addition to Cadillacs, I drove Lincolns, Oldsmobiles, Mercedes, Jaguars and one Austin-Healey. The Healey was hard to drive. I ground the gears moving off, but nobody seemed to notice. Towards the end of the evening, we reversed the process, hustling off to the reserve lot to fetch someone's car. The owner, often half-drunk, would squeeze a few bucks into my hand for a tip, apparently grateful that his car was still in once piece. As the night progressed, I dutifully handed over my tips to Sammy who stuffed them all into a big manila envelope at his side.

When I finished at midnight, Sammy gave me my wages and told me, "Not bad for the first night. Show up tomorrow, same time."

I thought, 'Hey, this is pretty good. I have fourteen bucks in my pocket. I can afford to eat.'

Having had no dinner, I went inside Cal Neva to the coffee shop, which was open twenty-four hours. I ordered a big cheeseburger and a milkshake and then sat in the reception area for a while digesting my meal. Even at this late hour, couples were coming and going. I noticed that most were short, balding men accompanied by tall, buxom, young ladies with large bouffant hairdos. Now and then, some younger, sharp looking dude with slicked back hair and a checkered sport coat would come in with two women on his arms. Who were these people?

A few days later I spotted someone that I definitely recognized — Frank Sinatra. Yes, the real Frank Sinatra. The rumor was that Cal Neva was in the process of being bought by Sinatra, some say as a front for Sam Giancana, the Chicago mobster.

Each time, Sinatra arrived with a different woman on his arm. Sammy always made a big fuss when Sinatra showed up in his Cadillac convertible. He personally greeted Sinatra, opening his driver's side door. (Sinatra drove his own car.) Sinatra would get out, leaving the motor running, straighten his tie, adjust his fedora and march on in with his bimbo of the evening trailing behind.

Joey usually had the honor of driving Sinatra's car. He would slip in behind the wheel and tool off to the reserve parking lot where he parked the car in a special, oversized slot. Later when Sinatra was ready to leave, Joey would fetch the Caddy. Rumor was that Joey always got a $100 tip from Sinatra, but Joey never said a thing and Sammy didn't probe him.

Sinatra was a skinny guy, about 5' 7" or so. Of course, his custom-made sharkskin suits fit him like a glove, making him look taller; plus, he may have had lifts in his shoes. Anyway, he always walked in as if he owned the joint — which it turned out would soon be the case. As far as the mobster Sam Giancana was concerned, I don't know if I ever saw him. I might have, but then he was rather nondescript looking and there were so many short, fat, little middle-aged Italian men that they all looked alike to me.

That summer of 1960 saw not only Sinatra and Giancana hanging around Cal Neva, but according to Joey, Jack Kennedy was spending time with Marilyn Monroe in one of the honeymoon bungalows with heart-shaped beds and mirrors on the ceiling. The story was that Kennedy, while campaigning for President in Nevada, had come up to Cal Neva at Sinatra's invitation to dally with Monroe, who was then filming *The Misfits* in nearby Reno. Who is to say? I never saw either one of them. I was just parking cars, oblivious to all but the obvious. I was making money; I was eating well at the Crystal Bay Casino across the street; and I was having a good time in an alpine paradise with a crystal blue lake.

***

"What's this Jerri look like?" I asked Steve one morning while stretched out on King's Beach catching some rays.

Steve looked up from me from his beach towel, with only one eye open. "I dunno, Allan. Tall, skinny you could say. Auburn hair and a chipped front tooth."

"Yeah, that fits," I responded. "That's the chick I knew up skiing at Squaw last winter."

"No shit?"

"Yeah, that's her."

"Like, I told you Allan. She's crazed. Drinks like a fish."

"Yeah, I know."

"Well, if you want to check her out again, there's going to be a beach party at Crystal Bay Beach Friday night. She might be there."

"Beach party?"

"Yeah, everybody chips in for a keg of beer. Some bring hard stuff for their personal use."

"What time?"

"Well, the early birds get there around midnight after they get off work. The rest drift in after that. It goes on until sunrise," said Steve nonchalantly, as he turned over to tan his front. "It's fun. The locals are a hoot. Sometimes they get into a fight."

A couple of nights later, I found myself at Crystal Bay Beach at two in the morning with the party in full swing, drinking keg beer while shivering in a thin sweater. The smart ones like Steve had brought parkas and others sleeping bags. The partygoers were mostly local kids with a few college kids in and about. I felt out of place, but they seemed friendly enough. Most worked for the resorts in housekeeping or grounds, some in the kitchens. From snatches of conversations I overheard, many of these kids had moved up here from Reno for jobs; others lived with their parents, who ran small businesses or resort services. All the same, it was a lively group supplementing the beer with shots of Wild Turkey.

Right in the middle of this scene was Jerri, the same Jerri with whom I had hung out at Squaw Valley, but now she was in Levis and a baggy sweatshirt instead of svelte stretch pants. Her long Auburn was hair still tied up in the Heidi knot. Yet, she looked and acted like a hick.

"What, the fuck, Al," she exclaimed half bombed when she saw me. "Big surprise. You tired of San Francisco or something?"

"Jerri, I hardly recognized you out of your ski costume," I said giving her a hug.

"Yeah, Yeah. What are you doing up here, Al? Vacationing?"

"No, I'm hiking cars at Cal Neva this summer."

"Oooh, one of Sammy's boys," she said making a rat-a-tat-tat sign with her index finger.

"No, nothing like that. Just trying to make a few bucks and enjoy Lake Tahoe," I said sitting down on a log with her. "So what do you do up here?"

"You don't remember, Al? Like I told you at Squaw, I live with my mom here in King's Beach. She's a housekeeper, a caretaker for rich people with big homes up here. I help her during the summer. They pay good."

"Oh yeah, that's right," I said, not really remembering.

"Here, have a slug of this with your beer," said Jerri as she handed me her pint of Wild Turkey.

I took a slug, feeling the warm burn of the whiskey as it slid down my throat. Suddenly, it didn't seem so cold anymore.

Jerri and I chatted for a while, but soon the conversation petered out. She kept glancing over to the group of locals she had been with. Whatever had worked between us at Squaw wasn't going to work here. This was her scene. Not mine. I was the outsider. I was the college kid on a summer lark up here, not like these locals whose whole lives would probably be spent in this area.

We made vague promises to meet later with her explaining that she always had a case of beer in the trunk of her car and that we could drink beer here anytime by ourselves. With that, I drifted away and drank some more beer with Steve. Soon, I was bored and tired and not wanting to sleep on the beach, I hiked back to Cal Neva and crashed in Steve's dorm room, wondering if I had made the right decision to spend the summer here.

***

Eventually, what had seemed like a good deal — hiking cars, getting paid two bucks per hour, staying free with Steve, eating cheap at the Crystal Bay Casino — got old. By week three of this life, I was tired of it.

However, I still enjoyed hanging out at Crystal Bay Beach during the day and paddling around with my swim mask and snorkel exploring the nooks and the crannies of the boulders offshore. Also, I was fascinated by a stunning, tall leggy brunette who came over to Crystal Bay every afternoon by herself to sunbathe, read and swim around the rocks. I watched her for several afternoons from afar. She would spread her beach towel on the sand about fifty yards from me, slather on some suntan lotion and then lie down, stretching out her long slim legs with feline grace. Once or twice, she glanced over my way as if she was surveying the lake and the mountain horizon. At first, I kept my distance, thinking this striking brunette wouldn't take kindly to an approaching college boy. She had most certainly come here to get away from people; otherwise, she would have gone to King's Beach.

One day, I spotted her sunbathing on one of the boulders off shore. She was lying on her back, her black one-piece bathing suit taut on her body, her straps hanging off her shoulders. This was too much. I had to meet this chick, but how? A crude direct approach wouldn't do. Instead, I resolved in my twenty-year-old mind to swim nonchalantly out in my snorkeling gear in a zigzag pattern, examining rocks and logs along the way, ending up at her boulder. This I did and when I reached her boulder, I grabbed a small ledge and slid up my mask breathing heavily as if I were out of breath. She peered over and with a slight smile said, "See anything interesting?"

"Some rocks and logs, a fish or two."

"It looks like fun. I'd like to try that someday."

Thinking fast, I said, "Give it a try with my gear. The mask can be adjusted."

She peered down at me. "No, maybe another day. I've seen you around the beach. You live up here?"

"No. I'm here for the summer. I live in the Bay Area."

"Oh, yeah. A college boy, I bet?"

"Well, as a matter of fact...," I said. "Say, mind if I join you on the rock. I need to warm up."

"Sure, why not. It's public property," she said flipping her hair back.

"Well, I don't want to intrude."

"Nonsense. It's a big rock."

I was up on top of the rock in a flash, dripping wet, my surfer trunks clinging to my thighs, all muscled up from months of rowing on crew.

She gave me a look and I felt X-rayed.

As I sat down, cross-legged, a few feet from her, she asked, "So what do you do around here? I've seen you on the beach every day for the past week."

"I'm a car-hiker at Cal Neva for the summer." I answered. "I have a lot of free time during the day. It's mostly a night job."

"Yeah, I know how that is," she said turning over to sun her back.

I stayed in my cross-legged position wondering who this babe was. She struck me as older than me, but not by much.

"I'm Allan."

"Hi, Allan, I'm Alice," she said, not turning over. "Nice to meet you," she mumbled, half-drowsy in the sun.

I sat there for a minute wondering what to do. I had the feeling that I had been dismissed. "Well, Alice, I have to get back to the beach to dry off and get over to Cal Neva."

"Yes, sure. Maybe I'll see you around."

And with that, I swam back to the beach, collected my stuff and hitched back to the dorm to get ready for another night of car-hiking, all the time wondering who was this Alice? A cocktail waitress? No, too classy for that. An entertainer? A singer? No, I hadn't seen her around at all, nor had I seen any advertisements for her. However, that didn't mean anything. The casinos only headlined the big stars. The unknowns simply showed up unannounced, unheralded, singing their hearts out or doing their comic routines at the side lounges away from the main casino traffic. Some were good, others mediocre. I myself had listened to a few unknown singers at one of the Crystal Bay bars late at night.

Alice remained an unsolved mystery for a few days. The next time I saw her at the beach, I boldly sat down beside her. She seemed glad to see me and we started chatting. She said she had come out to California after graduating from a school back East with degrees in drama and music. She said she was interested in getting into movies, but that her standby was singing.

"Hollywood is a tough racket unless you know someone," she said. "I beat my head against the wall for a year before I decided to take a break and come up here. Some agent I met at a party said Tahoe was a good place to get some singing experience."

"Yeah, it seems there are plenty of 'unknowns' around here," I said undiplomatically.

"Well, I managed a few gigs but nothing steady."

"What do you do the rest of the time?"

"Oh, not much. Sometimes I try to meet the right people who come up here, producers and the like."

"Like Frank Sinatra, maybe?"

"I wish...but no. I haven't run into him, but I met a few of his friends."

Hmm..., I thought. I couldn't imagine her hanging around with Frank's so-called friends, those short swarthy Italian types in loud sport coats and oily hair. The image was too painful, so I dismissed it from my mind.

Meanwhile, Alice and I had fun on the beach. We swam to the boulders together and dove down into the clear blue water. Alice tried my swim mask and was delighted with it. "I can see all those fish swimming around, so peaceful."

One day I brought a small rubber football and we tossed it around. Mostly, though, we simply lay on the beach in the sun together. As I surreptitiously checked out her long elegant body, with full high breasts in the black one-piece bathing suit, I thought about making a move on her, but I sensed she only thought of me as a friend, maybe as a younger brother.

"Say, Alice," I said one sleepy afternoon, "why don't we see a movie on your day off?"

"What's playing?"

"I don't know. Does it matter?"

"Look, Allan, I'm tied up."

"Even on your day off?"

"I don't have a regular day off. My work schedule keeps changing."

"Well, what do you when you're not singing? You said you don't get that many gigs. I never see you around the casinos."

"Ah, I'm kind of involved in an escort service on my off-hours."

"Oh? An escort service?"

"Yes, I'm only an ornament on some guy's arm when we go out. That's it."

"That's it?"

"Yeah, that's it."

I didn't quite believe her, but I couldn't see Alice as a hooker either. It was hard to imagine her with those mob types that hung out at Cal Neva. Yet, I knew if I pursued this line of questioning, she would continue to insist that it was all innocent and above board. Anyway, Alice stopped coming to the beach, and I was left wondering how such a nice girl became involved in such a scene. Then I would think of her long, sleek body in that skintight black bathing suit and the answer was obvious.

***

A week later, I was fired from my car-hiking job at Cal Neva. I had banged into a Cadillac while parking another Cadillac. I had become too cocky, jockeying these big cars around and squeezing into tight slots. The result wasn't one, but two slightly dented Cadillacs. A double-header. One was enough to get you fired. That was the rule. Two were the jackpot, and I feared some sort of mob retribution, but Sammy was decent about it.

"Don' worry, kid," he said. "The insurance will take care of it. These things happen, but like I explained to ya at first, I'm going to have to let you go."

I gulped. "Ah, O.K., Sammy, whatever you say," I responded, relieved that I wasn't going to have my legs broken. "Nice working with you."

"Yeah, kid, see ya around," he said returning to his racing form.

Except there was no "around" around here as far as I was concerned. I had had one of the best summer jobs on the North Shore. I didn't want to bus dishes, clean rooms or pull weeds. I decided it was time to go home. It was only mid-July. I still had time to make real money surveying back in the Bay Area.

***

High noon on I-80 at Truckee. I stood on the shoulder of the freeway with my thumb out, trying to hitchhike back to the Bay Area. I could have taken the Greyhound, but I was sick of buses and didn't want to spend my last dime on a bus ticket. I felt confident that I could catch a ride.

Sure enough, a turquoise Ford Fairlane hardtop with a blonde at the wheel zoomed by, then it slowed, pulling off to the side of the freeway about fifty yards away. An arm beckoned, as I approached the car. An attractive, thirty-something woman with bleached blonde hair looked me over and nodded. I'm stood there in my cut-offs jeans and T-shirt with my high altitude tan, still buff from rowing.

"Where are you headed, young man?" she asked.

"Berkeley."

"You're in luck. I'm driving to San Francisco."

She wasn't bad. Probably in her late thirties, but tan, trim, although her face was lined from too much sun.

"I'm Sue. I deal at Harrah's in Reno. I'm going to see my sister."

"Hi, Sue. I'm Allan. I was up at Tahoe for the summer, but my job didn't work out, so I'm going home."

"Too, bad. But then there is no place like home," she smiled.

Zoom. She drove fast over the summit with her car radio pumping out the latest Country and Western. Soon we were flying by Soda Springs, heading down the western slope of the Sierras towards Sacramento.

"Say, Allan, would you mind if I stop for a few minutes at Auburn? I have to check something with a Realtor. Some investment property I might buy. It'll take a minute."

"Sure."

As we approached Auburn, Sue pulled into a strip mall and disappeared into a Real Estate office. She came out a few minutes later.

"Say, the realtor isn't around. He's gone for a few hours. Hey, why don't we have a beer and a burger? I'll bet you're hungry, a big guy like you."

"Sure."

We entered a nondescript bar/restaurant in the strip mall. I had a beer and a cheeseburger. Sue had a daiquiri but nothing to eat.

"Where did you get that tan?" she asked, running her finger around the rim of the daiquiri glass.

"I had a lot of beach time up at Tahoe. I worked nights."

She stared at my bare arm. "Hmm, nice arm. You work out?" she asked.

"I row on crew," I answered.

"Great sport," she said reaching over, her hand squeezing my arm.

Pause.

"You know," she said, now caressing my arm. "You're a good-looking kid. I'll bet you have a girlfriend."

"Not at the moment."

"I'm sure you have a nice little girlfriend somewhere," she said teasingly.

"No, I don't. Really."

"That's too bad."

Then, I felt her other hand on my thigh under the table. Boing. Hey, I finally got the idea.

I took another look. In the half-light of the bar, she was not bad. Breasts firm, ass trim. Her face, a little hard but now softening with a glint in her eye.

"Say, I noticed a little motel up the road," she said coolly. "Why don't wait there until my realtor gets back. Freshen up, you know." She winked.

"Sure, Sue. Whatever you say."

***

It was nearly dark when we finally left that motel room. We got back in her Ford Fairlane and drove on to Berkeley, where she let me out at my fraternity house. Sue gave me her phone number and address in case I was ever in the Reno area. I put it in my wallet, thinking older women were a trip. They didn't want your whole life. Just your body. Something to think about.

I lugged my stuff up the steps of Alpha Kappa Lambda, said hello to a couple of brothers who were going to summer school and then crashed for the night on the sleeping porch, glad to be back on the college scene.

12. WALKABOUT

The next day I wandered around a fog-shrouded Berkeley soaking up the scene. After the high altitude heat and crystal blue skies of Tahoe, the fog was a relief. Berkeley was often foggy during the summer until the late afternoon when the sun broke through. Then a few hours later, the evening fog would come rolling in through the Golden Gate. The fog often meant cool summers for the Bay Area from mid-June through July. Yet, the fog had its charm. It enveloped the body and the mind and created a world unto itself—a world that I enjoyed now and then.

I also enjoyed hanging out at the fraternity house during the summer when it was nearly deserted. I loved the living room with the red leather couches and large central fireplace, the dining room and its long oak tables and hanging banners, the entrance hall with its glassed-in bookcases full of old yearbooks, trophies, drinking mugs and photos of long-ago fraternity brothers. Old Freddies standing in various poses in their cardigan sweaters, bow ties, tan slacks and white bucks, their hair parted in the middle, leaning against their prewar Chevys and Fords. A few had gone off to World War II, never to return. Most graduated, went into business and made a fortune in the booming California economy. Now and then, one of these older brothers showed up at the fraternity house for Big Game or other special occasions.

I loved the winding staircase up to the second and third floors. The third floor was my favorite. The rooms on the west side had great views of the campus running down the hill to the bay. Looking out, I felt like a lord in a Tudor castle overseeing his realm

Only three summer students from back East were boarding here, in addition to Neil, a premed student with thick glasses who never went home. He lived in the fraternity house year-round, taking courses fall, winter, spring and summer. Neil explored the worlds of microbiology, organic chemistry and physics. He also took courses in Greek, Latin and Ancient history. Neil was the total student. He studied for hours on end. Occasionally, he mentioned his father, an international businessman, who was constantly on the move. Neil had little contact with him except for the checks that arrived monthly in the mail with a few cryptic notes wondering when he would graduate.

Neil was already a fifth-year student and planned another year to get a master's degree in microbiology before he went off to medical school. When Neil wasn't studying, he drank. In fact, he was one of the big drinkers in the house and an enthusiastic member of Phi-Phi, the drinking fraternity. Occasionally, he went out with some sleazy, non-college chick with whom he would relieve himself and then summarily dump.

Neil was a man with a mission: to become a top doc. This was in contrast to most of the premeds I knew who proclaimed they were pre-med, but usually bombed organic chemistry and wound up in business administration. Getting into medical school from Berkeley was tough. The premed student had to graduate with a B average for even a prayer of being admitted to a California medical school. Of course, as I later learned, the smart, strategic premeds went to smaller private liberal arts schools such as Santa Clara College, Saint Mary's College or even Stanford where they earned an easy A or B average and then attended medical school.

The three students from back East constantly complained how cold the Berkeley summer was. "Shit, I could be at the Cape now soaking up rays," said Paul, a student at Boston University. "I went over to Stenson Beach last weekend and froze my ass off."

"Hey, welcome to sunny California," I said while picking at a bowl of Cheerios for breakfast.

"If I hadn't paid my tuition to go here this summer, I'd be gone," he whined.

"Cheer up, Paul. You're at Berkeley, the Harvard of the West Coast. Come mid-August, the fog goes away, the sun will shine brightly, and you'll be sweating your ass off," I responded.

"That doesn't help me now," he said working on his own bowl of Cheerios. "I'll be gone by then, back to a real New England summer."

"So you will. In the meantime, drive over the hills to Orinda. It's plenty hot there. Try the municipal pool."

***

Actually, I needed something warmer myself. All my clothes including my windbreaker were filthy from my stay in Tahoe. I decided to buy a cheap sweatshirt to keep me warm throughout the day. After breakfast, I trudged over to Telegraph and Bancroft Avenue to Roos Atkins, a men's clothing store that catered to the preppy college crowd, featuring Brooks Brothers knockoffs, imported tweeds, blazers and khakis. A well-dressed salesman sporting a crew cut approached me and asked if he could help.

"I'm looking for a sweatshirt."

"Oh, we have a rack of them in the discount room," he said eyeing me in my dirty Tahoe jeans and rumpled T-shirt. "Say, you wouldn't be interested in a light wool suit would you? We have an early fall sale. Excellent savings. Up to 40% percent off."

"Sounds good, but I'm not in the market for a suit. I only need a sweatshirt to ward off the chill."

"Very well," he said turning away. "I'm sure you will find something suitable on the discount rack."

'What a snot,' I thought as I pawed through the sweatshirts, eventually picking out a midnight blue one with a large yellow "C" on the front.

Mark, a fraternity brother who used to work here, would never be so condescending over a sweatshirt. Mark would have helped me pick out a snazzy sweatshirt. He was a super salesman. Mark understood that every sale was important, no matter how small. It was the first step to larger purchases.

The men of Alpha Kappa Lambda dressed well while Mark worked at Roos Atkins. Mark outfitted us with suits, shirts, coats, casual wear, shoes and then put the merchandise on his own personal account at a 30% discount. Later, he would deliver the goods to us for cash. It was a sweet deal and everyone in the house was looking sharp. However, our sartorial splendor lasted only a year.

Mark came back to the fraternity house in a panic one day and started emptying his closets and drawers, handing out Roos Atkins merchandise to anyone who would stash it in their car trunks or somewhere out of the house. "A little snafu at work," he said. "I have to clear this stuff out for now. I'll explain later."

"Okay, Mark. Whatever you say," said the brothers hauling the merchandise off.

A few hours later, the police arrived with the Roos Atkins store manager in tow. The cops had a search warrant, but found nothing but empty closets and drawers in Mark's room.

"You boys know where Mark is?" asked the store manager.

"I dunno," said one.

"I think he went home," said another.

"What's he done?" asked a third.

"Well, we suspect him of stealing merchandise from our store," said the store manager gravely. "You fellows know anything about that?"

"Nothing at all," said one brother playing stupid.

"O.K.," nodded the manager. "Well, when Mark shows up, tell him that I'll not press charges if he returns the merchandise in pristine condition or at least compensates us for the loss."

"O.K." said someone else.

The cops shook their heads at the leniency of the store manager. One commented that Mark was "one lucky son-of-a-bitch."

When Mark came back a day later, we told him what happened. He nodded and said only, "Not to worry. I'll fix it up with the manager. That little prick owes me."

Owes him? What could the manager possibly owe him, we wondered? Shrug.

Eventually, Mark made amends with the Roos Atkins manager. The manager didn't want any bad publicity and was willing to forget the whole thing if the clothes were returned. Mark went around, collecting the garments from the brothers and returned them with their tags still on. We also discovered that the clothes that we thought Mark had sold us at a discount were in fact stolen from Roos Atkins too, but the store manager never got wise to that because these garments had dribbled out of the store over a period of many months. As a result, Mark came out clean. No charges were pressed, no bad publicity and no record for Mark. The only downer for him was that he lost his job at Roos Atkins and his ability to dress himself and his fraternity brothers at the height of campus fashion.

***

Now snug in my new, warm sweatshirt, I wandered through campus on a little walkabout. The main UC entrance was a construction mess. The university had razed a block of businesses and shops along Telegraph Avenue to make way for a new student union building and a plaza in front of Sproul Hall, the main administration building. Farther on, Sather Gate was deserted as discarded *Daily Californian* newspapers fluttered about. Gone were the cardboard tables manned by student activists touting various causes such as the abolition of the House Un-American Activities Committee and the Young Socialist Alliance.

I walked through Dwinell Plaza, past Wheeler Hall and over to the Campanile, a 307-foot clock tower jutting up into the fog. The Campanile used to be a favorite jumping off spot for would-be suicides. The university had since put up a thick grating around the observation deck and those prone to suicide from high places now had to trek over to the Golden Gate Bridge.

A few steps away was the Doe Memorial Library, the main campus library. I entered and climbed the wide marble staircase to the main reading room on the second floor. This was a magnificent room with a high, barrel-vaulted ceiling, arched windows and skylights. The shelves along the walls were stocked with every reference work imaginable. Down the center of the reading room was row after row of reading tables mounted with old Beaux Art light stands. I often studied here because there were so many distractions at the fraternity house. The chairs were comfortable and the table lamps emitted just enough light to focus on studying rather than on the many cute co-eds also at the table. There was no noise at all except the occasional squeak of a chair or the muffled sound of footsteps. A perfect study environment.

It was here in the main reading room that I ploughed through my American history textbook learning about Frederick Turner and his thesis of westward expansion forming the American character. It was here that I memorized long lists of French verbs in their various conjugations until my eyes glazed over. It was here that I handwrote many of my papers before I typed them up back at the frat house. And it was here that I seriously wondered if I was smart enough to make it through Berkeley.

I envied those students with near photographic memories like Neil, who just looked at a page and got it. Underlining text, taking notes on the reading and later reviewing my lecture notes helped but when it came to coughing up that knowledge in a blue-book test, I could hardly remember anything. So I would blunder through my blue-book essays, trying to remember enough scraps of information to get at least a C and sometimes a B.

Whatever my academic shortcomings, I was in awe of the main reading room and the library in general. It housed the written repository of the Western world along with a good chunk of the Asian and Middle-

Eastern worlds. Of course, the understanding and dissemination of that knowledge depended on someone reading it. Scholars and students might read some of those works, but they were generally unknown to the public.

I recalled the science-fiction book, *Earth Abides,* by George Stewart, in which all but a few humans perish in a worldwide plague. The novel is set in the Bay Area in the near future. The hero, Ish, a former University of California geology professor, makes periodic trips to the Doe Memorial Library over a forty-year period. Despite rats, floods and fires that have destroyed most of the Berkeley campus, the library remains intact—its volumes still waiting for eager readers. But there are no readers. The young men and women in Ish's tribe have never learned to read or write because it wasn't relevant to their hunter-gatherer existence—a mode of life that has evolved in less than two generations. Even Ish no longer reads, realizing it is futile. Ish concludes that the preservation or the destruction of the library makes little difference in this new Neolithic world.

I felt even without the plague, we were headed in the same nonreading direction. Aside from reading a few bestsellers and the newspapers, most, people watched television. After an hour of browsing in the reading room, I too grew tired of reading and continued my journey through campus.

***

I followed a winding path through lush vegetation and a grove of redwoods until I came out at North Gate, the north side entrance to UC. Then it was up Hearst Avenue for several blocks and back to the fraternity house. There, I fixed myself a baloney sandwich in the kitchen and later crashed for a nap.

When I awoke around four, I could see the sun through my window blazing brightly in a clear blue sky. All traces of the fog had disappeared. I got up, splashed my face with water and rushed out of the fraternity house. I hiked up Hearst Avenue, which turned into Cyclotron Road, the main road to the Lawrence Radiation Lab. My destination was the lab parking lot with its view. When I arrived, there it was—a vast panorama of cityscapes, bridges, islands and water, water everywhere sparkling in the afternoon sun. No honking horns. No squeal of traffic. Only a soft quiet wind, full of the scent of eucalyptus leaves.

After a while, I turned my attention to the Radiation Lab itself—a rotund, bomb-shelter looking building squatting on the hillside. Although it appeared deserted, a few cars in the parking lot indicated that somebody was working. I imagined earnest graduate students in there slaving over the latest atomic find, trying to figure out how to blast sub-atomic particles into even smaller particles using the cyclotron.

This was essentially the same cyclotron that had unleashed the nu-clear secrets, which allowed the scientists at Los Alamos New Mexico to build the first atomic bombs. Many of those scientists had come from Berkeley. Ernest Lawrence developed the Berkeley cyclotron in the 1930s. His assistant, Glenn Seaborg discovered plutonium and deter-mined that it was fissionable. Robert Oppenheimer, a UC Berkeley physicist, was tapped to head the Los Alamos project by Army General Leslie Grove in 1942. Then there was Edward Teller. Teller had joined the atomic bomb project at Los Alamos during the war, but sulked most of the time because Oppenheimer ignored his plans to build an even bigger bomb, the hydrogen bomb.

In 1960, Teller still taught at UC Berkeley and was affectionately known as the "Father of the H-Bomb." Years later, I saw a photo of Teller standing proudly next to an H-bomb casing on display at the Strategic Air Command Museum in Omaha, Nebraska. The look on his face told you the H-bomb was indeed his baby.

We knew some of the Lawrence grad students by sight. They all wore a concentrated, worried look on their face as they trudged up Hearst Avenue by our fraternity house. Their shirt pockets were stuffed with pens and slide-rules hung in holsters off their belts like six guns, ready to be whipped out for a quick calculation. Many were going bald even though most were in their mid-twenties. All were pale as ghosts in the California sunshine. We used to joke in the fraternity that it was the radiation emanating from the lab that caused their pallor.

I ended my Northside walkabout down on Euclid Avenue, a small commercial district consisting of a drugstore, a café, a Laundromat, a used bookstore, a corner grocery, the Afro-Cuban jazz joint, Northgate Theater and La Vals, my destination.

I sat down at one of the picnic tables in the courtyard and ordered a half-pitcher of beer and a small pepperoni pizza. Then I picked up a *Chronicle* lying about and settled down to read it as the sunlight filtered through the leaves of the overhead arbor and sparkled in my mug of beer.

I loved this little enclave around La Vals. It encapsulated everything that I thought should constitute an ideal lair for a student—beer, pizza, film, books and interesting people. As I mellowed out, I felt that I could spend the rest of my life around here, drinking beer at La Vals and being a student forever.

Eventually though, reality intruded. After paying for my beer and pizza, I was broke. Here, I had pissed away half the summer on a lark up at Tahoe. It was time to face facts. I needed to find a surveying job and save some money before school started in the fall or I would be poor all year. I phoned my father to come pick me up.

13. CONTRA COSTA

I waited for my father on the fraternity house steps feeling like a small, needy child counting on his daddy to get him out of jam. Dad finally pulled up in his Chevy station wagon around 6:30 PM. He got out and waved at me, a smile breaking over his face. It had been a month since he had seen me. He shook my hand and then hugged me.

"Back from the wilds of Lake Tahoe, I see," he said looking me over.

"Yeah, that's right. Ready to go home," I said. "How's Mom?"

"Oh, fine. Everyone is fine. Don is still working at Dow. Kenny is running around as usual," he said putting my knapsack and duffle bag in the back of the wagon.

Dad appeared to have gained some weight. He was always fighting weight. He joked it was all those mashed potatoes that Mom fed him. In addition, he spent all day sitting at his desk or hunched over a drafting table as he went about his civil engineering work at the Contra Costa County Department of Public Works. He also seemed a few hairs balder, making him look older than his forty-eight years. I couldn't imagine what I would look like when I was forty-eight. I hoped at least I wouldn't be bald. Still, he was strong from all those years of tromping around the California outdoors as a land surveyor for the state. Several years ago, we had hiked up to Vernal Falls in Yosemite, a steep rocky climb along ledges of granite. Dad was wearing his old leather shorts, which he used to wear surveying in the desert. As he climbed ahead of me, his calf muscles bulged with the power of a young man. Although he smoked heavily, he was barely out of breath when we reached the top.

I got into the station wagon and we drove off along Gayley Road, passing by Memorial Stadium, the International House and Greek Row, where most of the fraternity and sorority houses were located. Farther on, we hit a stretch of well-groomed mansions belonging to the Berkeley rich and a few well-off professors. Winding along Claremont Boulevard, we came to the Claremont Hotel, that white gingerbread landmark, which catered to old East Bay socialites with tea parties and gracious dining. Finally, we turned off onto Tunnel Road and drove through the Caldecott Tunnel, the main route through the East Bay hills to Contra Costa County.

We came out of the mile-long tunnel into a burst of bright sunlight and hot air. The evening temperatures jump about twenty degrees. The warm breeze felt good on my arm as I hung it out the window.

"How hot was it over here today?" I asked.

"Oh...I don't know," Dad answered absent-mindedly as he noted some ongoing repairs along the freeway. "In the nineties, I guess. Not too hot."

The old station wagon seemed to be surviving the hot weather. Some of the newer luxury cars had air-conditioning, but for Chevy owners open windows were good enough. It was hard to believe that our station wagon was already five years old. We bought it new in 1955, a two-tone, tan Bel Aire station wagon with a white and beige interior. Dad tried to keep it in good shape, but being the main family car, it was constantly subject to abuse.

After a few minutes of driving in silence, Dad broached the subject that I knew was coming: a summer job.

"Did you manage to save any money up there at Tahoe?"

"Not really. Just enough to meet day-to-day living expenses."

"Are you ready for a real job?"

"Yeah, I guess. I thought I would hit up Leptein and Cronin for some surveying work."

"Yes, give them a try. It's a little late in the season, but you never know. In any case, if Leptein doesn't pan out, I know they're looking to add another survey crew at the Sanitation District. They have a big sewer project going on."

"Yeah, that might work," I said. "What do they pay?"

"I'm not sure," said Dad. "I know it's not the union wages you would make at Leptein, but it isn't bad."

Surveying was a tradition in the Brown family. That's how my father had started in road construction. He got a job as a chainman (a surveying assistant) with the State of California when he was seventeen in 1929. Dad was good at mathematics, especially trigonometry, which was essential to surveying. Soon he was an instrument man, the person who made the calculations, established lines and turned the angles. In short order, he was the brains of the survey party. Dad worked all over the state: the Mojave Desert, the Sierras, the Pacific Coast and the Bay Area, surveying the bridge approaches to the Bay Bridge then under construction.

Outside of work, he and the other young surveyors were a happy-go-lucky bunch always looking for a good time. Dad met my mother, Virginia, in 1935 at a beach party when he was working in Oakland. She was in nurses' training at Merritt Hospital. They hit it off immediately and were married six months later. My mother gave up nurses' training and traveled with my father as he moved from job to job until he was finally based at headquarters in Sacramento. There he took night courses in civil engineering and eventually became a licensed civil engineer. They bought a little house on the outskirts of Sacramento and settled down. By and by, I was born in 1940, followed by Don, eighteen months later.

Then came the World War II and everything was disrupted. My father quit his job at the State to work for Bechtel and Kaiser, two large Bay Area engineering firms. We moved from Sacramento to Mountain View on the Peninsula where my father commuted to San Francisco. Two years later, we moved to Oakland and then Concord. At one point, Dad was about to be inducted into the Navy as a construction engineer to build landing strips in the South Pacific. However, at the last minute, the Navy decided they didn't need him and Dad continued to float from one job to another.

After the war, we settled in Martinez and Dad went to work for the Department of Public Works in Contra Costa County, where he has remained ever since. It had been fifteen years of designing roads and bridges at a time of unprecedented growth in the Contra Costa County. And it was still going strong. Dad worked six days a week, often ten to twelve hours a day. He had to give up his sideline surveying work because his main job consumed him. He often said he should return to surveying full-time because he would make more money and have half the headaches of his county job.

***

We turned off the freeway onto Pleasant Hill Road, which wound its way through the hills to Martinez. Don and I used to play up in these greenish-brown hills. We sometimes went on hunting expeditions with our bows and arrows with the idea of shooting a cow, but we never had the nerve. Instead, we shot at squirrels and birds, always missing.

Pleasant Hill road ran into Alhambra Valley Road, which in turn, morphed into Alhambra Avenue, the main drag into town. We passed the John Muir Mansion, now being restored to its former glory and slated to become part of the National Park System. It was here years ago that Don and I broke into the old Victorian mansion when it was dilapidated and on the verge of collapse. At the time, we knew little about John Muir, the conservationist who created the Sierra Club and put Yosemite and other national parks on the map.

Finally, we passed by Alex's, the local drive-in and the Donley Chevrolet Dealership. Turning left on G Street, we arrived at 3410 Ricks Avenue and the modest little house where my family lived.

Back in Martinez. Good "ol' Tinez" town as we called it. It was only eighteen miles and a half hour from Berkeley but it might as well have been on the other side of the moon. Whatever university cool and sophistication I had at Berkeley dissolved while driving through the hot, rolling hills of Contra Costa County. By the time I got home, I was just another Martinez lug ready to get a summer job, ready to hang out with old high school friends and eager to locate the most nubile Martinez maidens that I could find.

***

As we pulled into the driveway, I noted that our house looked smaller than ever. A one-story, wood-frame ranch with three small bedrooms and one bathroom, built during the war when materials were scarce. About the only amenity it had was a brick fireplace. The kitchen was tiny, the dining room and living room marginal. With three growing boys at home, it was bursting at the seams. My mother was always complaining about the lack of space. A garage that father had built helped a bit. It had his office, a laundry room, a workroom and space for one car. It also had attic space for storage.

Even so, it was crowded and my mother was relieved when I went to college and a year later when Don went off to the Air Force Academy. Suddenly the house became livable. They had a den now and Kenny had his own room. But with my return home for the rest of the summer and Don living at home, we were going to be back to the same crowded living conditions for at least a month and a half. Despite the impending overcrowding, my mother was happy to see me.

"Allan, you grew!" she exclaimed.

"I did? Maybe it's my tan," I said. "I spent a lot of time on the beach at Tahoe."

"Whatever, you look healthy. I guess you ate well."

"That I did. Those casino buffets are cheap and filling. I never ate so much roast beef in my life."

"Well, I guess there is some good that comes out of gambling," she said reaching out giving me a hug.

"Yeah, it's not all that bad. If you don't gamble much, you can make out. You and Dad ought to hit Reno or the north shore sometime."

"Well, maybe. We'll see. Come on in."

My mother fixed me a sandwich, which I washed down with a beer. Don came home an hour later. He had been working late at Dow Chemical on a big rush project. He was mellow even though he now had to share his bedroom with me. Kenny was his usual annoying self, jumping around and demanding that I play some esoteric game with him, which he knew he could beat me at.

As my father had predicted, Leptein already had their survey crews lined up for the summer, but the job at the Contra Costa Sanitary District was still open. When I called, it was as if they were expecting me and I was told to report to work Monday. So there it was. I was back in Martinez after a day in Berkeley playing "student-for-life" and a month up at Lake Tahoe living the high life. It should have been a downer, but for the moment, I was happy. After all, I was home.

14. SEWERS

"Remember, Al, the shit has to flow downhill," lectured George as he peered through the transit in an effort to establish the line and elevation of a sewer line that was about to go in.

"Got it," I said as I wrote digging instructions on a guard stake before I drove it into the ground.

"Yeah, remember that and everything will come out all right," continued George. "If we're off a tenth or so in line or a few tenths in closure, it doesn't matter. It's close enough for sewer work, but if we are off that much in elevation, we're fucked," he cautioned. "The sewer will back up continually and eventually there will be investigations and law suits."

"Bad shit," I said as I tied a red ribbon around the guard stake to keep it from being knocked over by a bulldozer.

George and I were laying out the main branch of sewer line to a new, upscale subdivision in Walnut Creek. A hundred yards away, a large backhoe was already digging a ditch into which sections of the sewer pipe would be laid end to end. These were large concrete pipes, about six-feet in diameter, designed to carry a lot of sewage and storm water. Once the ditch was dug to the precise depth and width, flatbed trucks loaded with sewer pipe would arrive along with a crane to lift the pipes into place.

Next, a team of fitters, working in the ditches, would seal the pipe joints with blowtorches. Every few hundred feet, a vertical manhole shaft was inserted to provide access to the sewer line. Later, the contractor would come in and tie his residential sewer lines into the main sewer line. Once that was done, the line tested and inspected, a bulldozer would fill in the ditch and a few weeks later, the road crews would pour curbs and gutters and pave the street. The job would be complete.

Laying out sewer line wasn't very challenging work as far as surveying went, but it was a decent summer job and it paid well, about $3.00 an hour. In addition, there was a lot of slack time. I often spent two or three hours out of the workday reading in the back of the survey truck while we waited on the contractor to get organized so we could forge ahead and lay out more sewer line. Sometimes, I just stood around and watched the backhoes gouge out huge chunks of dirt from the sewer ditch. I would marvel at the laborers down the ditch with picks and shovels, doing the fine earthwork after the big earthmoving job was done. There was one little black laborer, Duke, who worked non-stop all day long, always digging, always shoveling, always laughing, often saying he worked hard because if he stopped, he would drop dead. As he put it, "Shit. I'm fifty-five. Mos' of my friends are dead at fifty-five. I gotta keep going."

I wondered about these laborers. How did they dig all day at that pace? I was bigger than they were and strong, but definitely not in their league. Although small, Duke was built like a piece of pig iron, solid, indestructible. A real ditch digging John Henry. I felt guilty as I lounged about tossing dirt clots at tin cans or reading while these laborers worked. What I did physically was nothing compared to what these laborers did, but I was paid more and was able to use my brains occasionally. I guessed surveying wasn't too bad.

Other times, when work was slow, George ran errands to the bank or went shopping at Capwells in Walnut Creek. For a surveyor, George was a sharp dresser; always wearing pressed khakis with a new polo shirt or sometimes a bright Hawaiian shirt he ordered special from Honolulu. "No reason to arrive dirty on the job," he often said. And he did his best to stay clean throughout the day. I was the one who had to climb down into the ditch to take the measurements, amid all the dirt and dust.

Then there were the coffee breaks. The first thing in the morning, we headed to George's favorite coffee shop down the road where he would say hello to Sally, a buxom waitress in a tight fitting uniform and order coffee and rolls. Sometimes we ordered a full breakfast. Arriving at the job at nine thirty or so, we would work two hours and then it was time to think about lunch. Often, we drove over to the Walnut Creek Shopping Center and dined in an outdoor garden restaurant, ordering gourmet cheeseburgers and ice tea. In my six weeks at the Contra Costa

Sanitation District, I don't think I worked more than four or five hours during an eight-hour day.

This was a vacation compared to the surveying that I had done with Leptein, Cronin & Cooper the past two summers. I used to run my ass off for a full eight hours, sometimes ten hours laying out roads and subdivision lots from dusk until dawn. As a chainman, I had to pound stakes all day, one after the other, all carefully marked and set precisely on line and elevation for streets, sewers and curbs. I worked mainly with Jasper Cooper, the most hard driving of the bunch. A wiry, little man, he would run up hills carrying his transit, setting up in a matter of seconds. I would barely have time to get out of the survey truck before he was shouting orders to find the line and measure the distance. I learned a lot at high speed, but by the end of the day, I was exhausted.

After work, on the way back to the office, Cooper often cracked open a can of beer he kept in his cooler and sipped it as he drove home, saying things like, "That wasn't so bad, was it Al? You did great. Remember time is money around here. Working hard, the time passes quickly. Help yourself to a beer."

In addition to laying out sewer line for the Sanitation District, we surveyed for an expansion of the District's sewer filtration plant located on the mud flats of Suisun Bay. This plant with its vast settlement ponds, rows of aerators and other filtration systems treated the sewer water until it was pure enough to drink. One of the highlights of a public tour of the plant was watching the guide gulp down a glass of freshly treated sewer water.

The water may have been pure at the end of the filtration process but the place stunk. Not shit stink but an odor more like some giant mildew monster — warm, moist and pungent. Actually, over ninety percent of sewage was water. The few times I had to climb down into a sewer manhole, I never saw remnants of fecal matter, nor did I smell it. Only pieces of soggy toilet paper congealed to the sides of the sewer told me that defecation had actually occurred. After such an excursion, I always made sure to shower with disinfectant back at headquarters.

The District headquarters building was a plush, low-slung, rambling structure — all glass and steel — located on Pleasant Hill Road near Highway 24. This was the administrative center of the Sanitary District, as well as the engineering and maintenance center. Out back were platoons of maintenance trucks manned by crews who constantly repaired and cleaned out the sewers of the county, day and night.

Contra Costa County was booming. New subdivisions were going in everywhere. The nearby towns of Concord, Pleasant Hill and Walnut Creek were spreading out so fast that it was hard to distinguish one town from another. Demand for new sewer lines was high. Most of the people moving into the county worked in the Bay Area and there was talk of building a high-speed commuter train line from Walnut Creek through the hills to Oakland and under the bay to San Francisco. The proposed name for such a transit system was the *Bay Area Rapid Transit* or *BART* as it later came to be known.

Despite the volume of work, the pace was leisurely at the Sanitary District. Most employees were lifers. Many had gone to work for the District when it was first formed back in 1946. They had fourteen years in and planned to go for at least sixteen more and receive a nice pension. All were covered by Civil Service, so their jobs were secure. Of course, sewer work wasn't considered the most glamorous construction work around. For civil engineers, building bridges and six-lane freeways was much more challenging. Nevertheless, building and maintaining the sewers was vital to the county and the men of the Sanitation District did their job well and kept the shit flowing.

However, the slow and settled pace was mind numbing to me. Sometimes, George and I ate in the lunchroom at headquarters where we overheard conversations from the minds that ran this place. It usually went like this:

"How was your camping trip up to Lake Amador?
"Great. I caught a five-pound trout."

"I've been looking at a house trailer. Of course, that means that I'll have to get a pickup truck to go along with it. I can't haul a trailer with my Chevy station wagon."

"Marge is driving me nuts about adding a second bathroom. I'll get around to it someday, but now she is threatening to hire a remodeler to do the job."

Others ate their lunch quietly, looking over some of magazines that lay scattered about — *Field & Stream, Popular Mechanics, Hot Rod, Playboy* with the centerfold usually missing.

Only three or four of these employees had an engineering degree. A few had a two-year degree in drafting. The maintenance men were high school dead-enders. There were two engineering students working as interns for the summer. All were mystified that I wasn't an engineering student.

"So, Al, what are you majoring in?"
"History."

"History? What? Are you going to do, teach?"

"Maybe. I don't know."

"So how did you get into surveying?"

"Family tradition. My father was a surveyor."

"Oh. Who's that?"

"Ray Brown."

"No kidding, Ray Brown at the Public Works Department?"

"Yeah."

"Oh, I see. O.K."

As I said, this was a dull bunch. The world of the Sanitation District was light-years away from the heady, intellectual, hip environment of Berkeley, but I kept telling myself it was only for six weeks. Six short weeks and then I would be back at Berkeley. Meanwhile, I read several James Bond novels (*Casino Royale, From Russia With Love* and *Doctor No*), ate gourmet cheeseburgers and surveyed hundreds of feet of sewer line.

By the end of my tour of duty, I had saved up five hundred dollars for school. I had lived at home peacefully with my family. I had relieved the overcrowding by spending most weekends at the fraternity house. I had had my fling at Tahoe. Overall, I judged it a successful summer. Now I was ready for another full year at Berkeley. Or so I thought.

15. RUSH

Mid-September meant summer in Berkeley with the fog long gone. Endless days of eighty-degree weather and crystalline views throughout the Bay Area. Everybody was going around in T-shirts and sandals, laying out on sundecks and rooftops and hitting the new pool up in Strawberry Canyon. Mid-September also meant rush week, the time when fraternities and sororities recruited new members.

This was my third year of living in the fraternity house. I now had a room on the third floor by myself with a view of the campus and the bay. It was quiet and peaceful. I could actually study here. This was good for me but bad for the fraternity since my single room meant we were down members and housing fees might soon go up. We were trying to recruit more members through rush week, but they were elusive because the competition was fierce from the other fraternities and the University had recently built several new dorms, which had lured many freshmen.

All of this was weighing heavily on the mind of Bill Singleton, the rush chairman, who noted my arrival for the fall semester in Gerard's MG. As I got out of the little MG in my cutoff's and T-shirt, he said, "Jeeze, Brown with that tan and those muscles, you look like a Greek god."

"Surely, you jest," I said.

"Yeah, a real god."

"Stay away from me you faggot," I replied, brushing by him.

He laughed, beer bottle in hand, following me. "No, what I mean is you look like a real asset to the house for rushing. I plan to make you one of my top recruiters."

"Yeah, we'll see. I'm going to be busy next week setting up classes and looking for a part-time job."

"Hell, we're all busy, Al. But as you well know, recruiting new members is vital. You owe it to us to do your part. That's what being in a fraternity is all about. Fulfilling your obligations. Frat life is not all fun and games," he lectured.

"I guess."

Actually, when I got into it, I enjoyed rush. It was a constant round of cocktail parties at alum homes in the Berkeley hills and in Orinda. We usually had a beach party at Stenson Beach, a trip or two to San Francisco to take in a play or hit a couple of night clubs such as the *Hungry I* or *The Purple Onion.*

The prospects, all fresh from high school, were usually impressed and at the end of the evening, I and a few other "closers" would put the hard sell on them to consider pledging Alpha Kappa Lambda.

Not everybody who went though rush week was chosen. After we had seen a rushee a few times, we had a house meeting and voted on whether to offer him membership. The obvious losers were the dorks, the Jews and the occasional black who showed up. They were always a "bong" right up-front. The rationale went something like this: A "dork" was a dork. Always socially unfit. Other than his grade point, he would be no asset to the house. However, if he were the son of an alum, he would of course get in. Jews were considered too loud and obnoxious. In addition, there were plenty of Jewish fraternities at Berkeley that would gladly take them in. Blacks were out of the question. A few of the fraternity brothers had grown up in the Central Valley, which was like being raised in the Deep South with all its attendant racism.

Basically, it was "no" to anyone who wasn't similar to us. What we were looking for were smart, clean-cut, personable white males who were not wimps and who would be able to attract other recruits sometime down the road. It was a plus if their family was well off, if they had a car a brother could borrow now and then and if they had a knack for getting women.

Sometimes to help the "closing" we had a few sorority co-eds who were going with a frat brothers act very friendly. Sometimes we fixed the rushee up with a loose girl. Of course, there was plenty of booze to grease the sales pitch, especially at the pool parties.

The favorite "closing haunt" was an alum's house in Orinda. It was a spacious, rambling modernistic ranch pad in the hills. It had sliding glass doors along the patio side of the house that looked out on a well-landscaped backyard with a gigantic kidney-shaped pool. The party usually ran from late afternoon until ten in the evening and featured a barbequed pig. After a swim and a sauna, we would lounge around the pool in recliners pouring a lethal punch concoction into the prospect's glass and rattle off our pitch.

"John, did you know that Alpha Kappa Lambda was the first and only national fraternity founded on the West Coast?"

"No, I had no idea."

"Yeah, it was founded in 1907 by a group of Cal students. It was originally called the *Los Amigos Club*. Later in 1914, it became officially known as Alpha Kappa Lambda. AKL is now nationwide with chapters at over twenty colleges and universities."

"You don't say."

"All true, John. But you know it takes more than a great history to make a great house. We are still doing it. We have scholars, athletes, campus leaders and all around good guys. For example, I row on crew. Rich here is a campus rep and Neil, the one with his nose in a book all the time, has a straight A average. He's bound for medical school."

Neil would then launch into the academic advantages of belonging to a fraternity, such as the exam files, the class experience of the older brothers, the study halls and the help writing papers.

I would hold forth on how to be a jock and a student at the same time, talking about crew and some of the other sports, also stressing that we were active in the inter-mural leagues. "We have a couple of brothers on the rugby team who take delight in outfoxing the off-season football players. Nobody takes the matches that seriously and they always end in either a fake brawl or a beer bust, sometimes both."

Topping that, Gerard, the social chairman, would describe the great parties we had and all the opportunities there were to meet girls if you were a member of our fraternity. "I can say from personal experience, we put on some of the best bashes around, especially our jungle party with all the vines and fake steaming volcanoes. The brothers wear loincloths and the girls, skimpy 'Me Jane' costumes. Everybody has a great time."

By this time the prospect was so snowed he would often pledge on the spot. Then we would drink a toast to him and made sure he had a nice little girlfriend to keep him company until the party was over.

***

Of course, once the pledge was living in the house, life wasn't quite as rosy as we had depicted during rush. Oh, there were parties aplenty, exchanges with sororities, football game bashes and so on, but the pledge was a second-class citizen in the fraternity and was required to do many house chores and run menial errands. In addition, he had to take part in a mandatory study hall in the Engineering Building across the street. When I was a pledge, I escaped most of that because I was rowing on crew. Jocks received special consideration. Despite their second-class status, most pledges hung in there because they liked the fraternity life, the comradeship, the sharing and the feeling of belonging to a group in the midst of a massive, impersonal, bureaucratic University where you were only a number.

The most critical thing that first semester was to make sure the pledge maintained a C average, hence the enforced study rule. Usually one or two pledges wouldn't make it and they had to remain pledges for a second semester. That's what happened to me. I was a year-long pledge. It was humiliating but, as I said, since I was on crew, I was exempt from many pledge duties. As described earlier, I managed to bring up my grade point average to a C average for the year, so I was eligible to become a member. However, before any pledge could become a full-fledged house member, he had to go through the initiation process.

Yes, the initiation process. Sometimes known as *Hell Week*. A prospect most pledges faced with fear and trembling. This is when otherwise reasonable house brothers acted like Nazi storm troopers and put the poor pledges through their paces of harassment, intimidation and outright terror.

First, let it be said that Hell Week at our fraternity wasn't a full week. It was barely three days and two nights starting on Friday and running until Sunday afternoon. Second, our initiation wasn't as bad as many other houses where the pledges had to go onto campus in an assortment of bizarre costumes. Nor did we force pledges to drink to excess. All in all, our Hell Week was rather mild.

It started Friday with a scavenger hunt that took the pledges hither and yon over the East Bay. Then, once they had obtained the proper object—usually a valued antique beer mug—and had deposited it at the feet of the Grand Inquisitor, who sat on a beer-barrel throne in a cape and a mask, they were ordered into their "poop" costumes. These costumes were burlap bags with holes cut for the arms and legs. The "poops" were allowed to wear sneakers and a t-shirt under the bag if it was cold. Additionally, they had to wear a salted cod attached to a string around their neck, which was tucked inside their burlap bag. This was a simulated dick. At the order, "Show your codpiece, Poop" the poop had to produce his fish. The fish hanging down near the crotch soon smelled and constantly chafed the poop's skin, but it had to remain there. That was an ironclad rule.

Four or five overseers were assigned to an eight-hour shift. Many dressed up in intimidating costumes to further exert their authority, such as US Army fatigue jackets with boots and helmets, biker jackets with leather and chains. One brother, Carl, went out and rented an SS uniform. Brother Gary simply wore a white hood and sheet with the KKK written on the back. I was always amazed how eager some of the brothers were to play overseer. Usually, the sophomore overseers were the most enthusiastic since their own memories of being a poop were so recent and they were motivated by revenge. I remember how enthusiastic I was during my first Hell Week as an overseer.

After a meager dinner on Friday night of "poop food," usually two-day old macaroni and cheese, washed down with water, the work detail began. This was an all-night work marathon of washing down the fraternity walls, painting and most importantly, stripping the hardwood floors of old wax by hand and applying new wax. At various intervals, one of the overseers ordered the poops to stop what they were doing and go through a series of exercises such as push ups while singing fraternity songs or special pledge songs designed to humiliate them. If a poop screwed up, he had a raw egg cracked over his head and he had to clean up the mess. This went on hour after hour until the work detail was done. Then the poops were allowed to rest, but not in a bed. No, the poops had to sleep curled up in closets. True, there were blankets and pads in there for some minimal comfort.

The next day, Saturday, it was more of the same. Window washing and kitchen cleaning. This was the ugliest chore. Our cook never did basic cleaning and so it was a dirty, disgusting job scrubbing the stove, the walls, the kitchen floor and redoing all the pots and pans. Other chores included a thorough scrub-down of the basement rec room, the upstairs hallways and the sleeping porches. In short, the poops performed all fall and spring-cleaning chores under a constant barrage of harassment. Saturday night it was back into the closets.

Sometimes a poop broke down and announced that he had had it and wasn't going through any more of this. This poop was gently taken aside by one of the "sympathetic" overseers and given an hour or so to unwind and decide if he really wanted to opt out of initiation. Nearly all regained their perspective and plunged back into the fray. Occasionally, a pledge truly decided he didn't want to be a member of the fraternity and quickly took a shower, packed his belongings and left, usually winding up at one of the university dormitories.

Sunday was more work, although at a slower pace. By mid-afternoon, the hazing phase was officially over. The poops were allowed to shower and dress for the evening banquet, which was a catered extravaganza of prime rib, shrimp, mash potatoes, vegetables, deserts and many bottles of premium Napa Valley wines. All held in the refurbished dining room by candlelight. Following the feast, the pledges were inducted into the fraternity as full-time members. Some grinned ear to ear. Other's broke down and wept. All felt great and later most said it was the best experience of their lives. A few remarked that they couldn't wait until it was their turn to be an overseer during Hell Week.

So what was this initiation process all about? Many University officials were appalled by it and actively campaigned to end the practice. Others laughed it off as *boys will be boys*. (By the way, the sororities had their own initiation that lasted a day or two, but wasn't nearly as brutal as a fraternity initiation.) Occasionally, a pledge suffered some mishap during initiation. A few had even died while undergoing initiation rituals at Berkeley. Still, it went on. It was an intrinsic part of the fraternity culture. You had to suffer both physically and mentally before you could enjoy the benefits of belonging. Membership would mean nothing if you simply joined up.

Those brothers who had studied anthropology likened the initiation process to that of the manhood rituals in New Guinea and Africa. You didn't simply become a man when you hit puberty. You had to undergo agonizing physical ordeals, often including circumcision and sometimes gang rape by other males. This was supposed to toughen and prepare you for the rigors of war and to give you the iron will to rule others. Whatever. Initiation was what it was. After going through it myself once and acting as an overseer twice, I found the process tiresome and demeaning. After my sophomore year, I didn't take part in it anymore.

16. SCHOLAR?

As a junior, I was now able to take upper division courses in my history major as well as other classes. This meant that the classes were smaller and more intimate, and that I would probably get more individual attention. The fall semester of 1960, I was taking *Twentieth Century British History, Modern French History, U.S. History, English Composition* and *The English Bible as Literature*. While it was a heavy course load—a full fifteen units—I felt I could handle it. I had fulfilled my chickenshit ROTC requirements, and I was done with French, the two areas in which I had suffered D's. Somehow, I felt more confident about my academic abilities. After all, I had survived four semesters at Berkeley, and I heard that the grading wasn't so tough in upper division. It was upward and onward.

Twentieth Century British History was held in a small classroom in Dwinnell Hall. The course, which had only twenty students, was taught by Dr. E, a visiting history professor from MIT. It struck me as odd that the Massachusetts Institute of Technology had history courses, but Dr. E. assured us that it did.

"Oh yes, yes, MIT does have liberal arts requirements. They don't want to produce only technologists," explained Dr. E., a heavyset man with a baldpate and a cheery countenance. "These are brilliant kids who can write as well as they can figure out math problems. However, I'm sure many at Berkeley can match them I.Q. point for I.Q. point."

I didn't know quite what to expect from the course at first, thinking it might be a hardcore history of places, dates and wars. Dr. E. assured us that this was to be more of a cultural history with an emphasis on the British colonial legacy. Great! This was right up my alley. The white man's burden. Steaming jungles. Remote desert outposts. Kipling on an elephant. Lawrence of Arabia stuff.

Dr. E. did touch on all the major British historical events from Boer War on: World War I, the expansion and rule of the empire, World War II up to the present-day status of the empire. In addition to the basic historical text, we read selections from Kipling, Forster and Orwell. Dr. E. was especially fond of George Orwell's essay, *Shooting An Elephant*. "This essay sums up the conundrum of colonial rule."

Orwell, a young British officer in the Burmese service in the 1930s was charged with putting down an elephant that had gone on a rampage. By the time Orwell, showed up on the scene the elephant was peacefully munching on leaves. Orwell was ready to let the whole thing pass, but the villagers were watching him intently, waiting for him to act. After all, the elephant had demolished several of their huts. Orwell felt the will of the crowd. He could not turn back. As a representative of the British Empire, he would lose face. So he reluctantly shot the elephant dead. The villagers cheered. Duty had been done. However, Orwell was left wondering who was ruling whom.

We also explored the Zionist movement, the Balfour Declaration, India's independence movement, British rule over East and West Africa with a quick look at the commonwealth countries of Canada, New Zealand and Australia and the "special relationship" with the U.S. This was a wide-ranging and eye-opening course on how the British considered themselves enlightened rulers of their empire. They had brought civilization to the unwashed. They had built the infrastructure of its many dominions, set up democratic institutions and educated the local elite. Already a few of its colonies had achieved independence, notably India in 1947, Palestine (Israel) in 1948. Many African nations such as Ghana and Nigeria had already become or were in the process of becoming independent from Britain.

Of course, Dr. E. explored the downside to British colonial rule: the exploitation of resources and indigenous people, the rigid social caste system that separated the British rulers from the locals that left a bitter legacy in the mind of many. Nevertheless, the conventional wisdom was that these countries were better off with British rule than without. I studied hard and received a B+ for my efforts.

Modern French History was a bit more complex. It started with the lead up to the French Revolution in 1789. Professor W., a small bespectacled man, was a bore, droning on and on about this date or that date, this French assembly or that French assembly. Even the more colorful aspects of the Revolution such as storming the Bastille, the Paris mob riots and the Reign of Terror were dulled down and de-emphasized. It was all a confusing mess to me. One interesting side note: Professor W. mentioned that Thomas Jefferson was the American Minister to France at the beginning of the French Revolution and helped write *The Declaration of the Rights of Man* in 1789. Jefferson later declared, "The tree of liberty must be refreshed from time to time with the blood of patriots & tyrants."

The rest of the course made more sense. Professor W. hit the highlights of late nineteenth century and early twentieth century France: Napoleon, the restoration of the monarchy, the 1848 Revolution, the Second Empire, the Franco-Prussian War, the Third Republic and the Dreyfus Affair. He skimmed through twentieth century France, touching on World War I, the interwar years, World War II and the ascension of Charles De Gaulle as president. The final was a multiple-choice test with a few short essay questions. Somehow, I managed to score a B.

U.S. History from the Civil War on was a required course for history majors. This was familiar territory for me because my old high school teacher, Fitzy, had covered it so well and so compellingly. Professor M. focused on the economic motivations for the Civil War. He lectured on the perceived economic necessity for slave labor, the lucrative markets for Southern crops of cotton and tobacco in England, Europe and in New England. He also covered the Southern rationale for seceding from the Union: States' Rights. The South had argued that each state had the right to chart its own course, which included the right of secession from the Union. Professor M. further pointed out that Abraham Lincoln was not necessarily against slavery where it existed in the South, but rather against the expansion of slavery to the newly formed western states. Finally, he wrapped up the Civil War by showing that the Northern victory was a foregone conclusion because of its superior strength in men and material, and because England failed to back the Confederacy. Then, it was on to Reconstruction, the opening of the West, the Panic of 1893, the Spanish American War, the Progressive Movement, World War I, the Crash and Great Depression, World War II, the Cold War and the ascension of the U.S. as one of the two great superpowers left in the world. The other, of course was the Soviet Union.

I felt I had this period of U.S. History down pat, so I didn't study much. Then Professor M. threw in some obscure historical curve balls that I hadn't caught, and I wound up with a C.

Next up was an English Composition course. Why was I, a history major, taking a lower division English course at this late date? I had skipped English in my freshman year, taking Speech instead. As a result, I was feeling self-conscious about my writing and I wanted to improve it.

I had hoped for an upper-division English composition course, but when the English department advisor glanced over my transcript, he sniffed and said, "Mr. Brown, you cannot possibly take an advanced composition course without the basic freshman course."

"I can't?"

"Of course not. We reserve the upper-division courses for English majors."

"Oh." I said, thinking how tough can it be? Here I am, a big-time junior. This should be a breeze. An easy B, if not an A.

The class met three times a week. It was small, about fifteen students, all freshmen except me and mostly women who wanted to be English majors. Our teacher was Arnold, a poetic, longhaired dude in English tweeds who spoke in a mid-Atlantic accent. Arnold was originally from Kansas, but he had spent time at Oxford.

"We shall write. We shall endeavor to construct the classic English essay, a lost art if I may say so. We shall also read the best in American literature such as *On Walden Pond* by Thoreau, essays by James Russell Lowell and *Life On The Mississippi* by Samuel Clemens, otherwise known as Mark Twain. Perhaps some of their literary expertise will rub off on you."

We dutifully plowed through selected works, and I wrote the required four essay papers. I thought they were well done, but Arnold didn't appreciate my style or point of view.

"Mr. Brown. You make light of these works, especially *On Walden Pond*. Whatever you may personally think about David Thoreau, you must admire his style."

"I heard that he lived at home when he wrote Walden Pond and only occasionally retreated to his cabin," I said. "Doesn't that strike you as odd?"

"Well, perhaps, but he wrote rather well unlike you and hence your C."

I could tell Arnold didn't like me much as he continued to give me C's on my essays. I put myself out on the *Life on the Mississippi* essay because I truly liked the book. It was a masterpiece of humor, autobiography and travelogue. That essay came back with a D and when I asked why, Arnold simply said, "Come see me in my office and bring the essay in question."

So I did. He was sitting there, feet up on his cluttered desk, reading a slim volume of Wadsworth when I arrived at his office.

"Sit down, Mr. Brown. Now, what is that you wanted? Oh yes, no doubt you want to dispute the D I gave you on your last essay."

"Well, yes. I wondered why. I thought it was my best essay so far."

"Indeed it was. Indeed it was. That is why I gave you a D and probably should have flunked you outright."

"What! I don't understand?"

"You see, Mr. Brown, I don't believe you wrote that essay. It was so far superior to your other work, that I suspect you plagiarized it."

"What, not at all," I insisted, plopping the essay down on his desk. "Where did I plagiarize?"

Arnold leaned forward, scanning the essay. "Here, for instance, take this sentence describing the unfolding of the Mississippi from the deck of the riverboat. I would have sworn Mark Twain wrote that. I did check the work. That sentence was not in there, but similar sentences were. In any case, you don't write that well, so you must have stolen it from somewhere, some other essay or article on the work."

"Hey, Arnold," I said defiantly. "This is my work. All of it. Occasionally, I write a good sentence. Of course, I was influenced by his style. How could I not be? Even so, that sentence is mine."

"If you say so," sniffed Arnold. "In any case, I'll not change your grade for that particular paper. If you do well on the final, we will see. That is all, Mr. Brown."

I felt like turning his desk over on top of him or shoving his little book of poetry down his throat. Little arrogant, fake-English prick. Boy, I thought, what a mistake it was to take this course. I could get a D in it, but I managed to restrain myself and stalked out wondering if I should complain to the head of the English department. However, I knew if I did, it would prove futile. They always backed their teachers when it came to grades.

I did O.K. on the final and got a C in the course. I vowed no more undergraduate courses for me, no matter what. They graded only to weed people out. Anyone deemed not worthy of being an English major was dumped on. Fuck English majors. Most of those I knew couldn't write well anyway. All they produced was pretentious garbage.

***

The English Bible As Literature, taught by a Dr. K., was a completely different story. I had been urged to take the course by Neil. He said it was easy and fascinating, and a great way to meet Jewish chicks. The course sparked my interest in several ways. First, was the Bible itself. Being raised Protestant and not a regular churchgoer, I considered the Bible a collection of fairytales, with perhaps some historical truth behind it. Yet, references to the Bible were everywhere and as a history major, I felt I should have a detailed acquaintance with the number one book in Western civilization. Second, I was indeed fascinated by some of the Jewish women I had met. They all seemed smart and hip with none of the self-consciousness or pretentiousness of the Protestant sorority girls I knew. Many had a wild dark beauty about them and the word from Neil was they liked to "play" with no strings attached, especially with *goys* whom they would never marry, but with whom they certainly would have dalliances. O.K. We would see.

After the first lecture by Dr. K., I was hooked. He began by describing the many versions of the Old Testament including the Hebrew text, the Greek Septuagint, the Latin Vulgate and finally the King James Version, the one we were using. Then he noted the course focused primarily on the Old Testament. The New Testament was to be treated more like a text of propaganda rather than literature or history. The major course themes would be the history of the Jewish people via the Bible, the evolution of the concept of God and the string of prophets heralding the coming of the Messiah. We noted the historical setting and learned how the selected books came to be included in the Old Testament. Dr. K. also pointed out major discrepancies between different versions of the same book. Finally, we marveled at the sheer literary and poetic brilliance of several books in the King James Version such as the *Book of Psalms, Song of Songs* and *Ecclesiastes.*

Our text was the bible itself, the handsome *Reader's Bible.* Although the Bible was pure King James with the *thee-s* and *thou-s*, the text was organized in conventional paragraph form rather than in a string of numbered verses, making it easy to read. All the historical and literary background came from the lectures, which were well organized and thorough. (What a relief!) These were the best lecture notes that I had ever written. I read each assignment thoroughly, taking careful notes and when test time came, I got a B on the two midterms and an A on the final. My first A at Berkeley. Dr. K. wrote a note on my final saying he liked my essay on the evolution of God from a god of wrath to a god of mercy. But alas, I received only a B+ in the course. So close, yet so far. Nevertheless, I felt I was conquering Berkeley at last. I had finally gotten into the swing and felt I knew how to write a bluebook final. I had three B's and two C's for the semester, giving me a B- average for the semester. I felt in high gear. I felt in the moment.

17. POLITICS

"So what's the big deal about Kennedy?" I asked Rich Petrillo one day in September as the 1960 presidential race was heating up.

"He's the man for our time," Rich responded.

"Seems to me he spends a lot of time chasing ass," I said.

"Excuse me? *Chasing ass?*" Rich blinked.

"Yeah, when I was up at Cal Neva this summer, the rumor was he was shacking up with Marylyn Monroe, among others," I explained.

"I don't know about that, Al, but don't you think eight years of a Republican administration are enough?"

"I don't know. I think Eisenhower has been a good president."

"Good God, look at all the social programs the Republicans have been dragging their feet on," said Rich. "Harry Truman proposed the Fair Deal back in 1948, which included programs such as universal health care, higher minimum wages, anti-discrimination laws and so on. All Eisenhower has done is worry about the Cold War."

Rich, myself and three other fraternity brothers were seated in a booth at the Rathskeller on Telegraph Avenue drinking beer on a Friday night. We were giving Rich moral support because he was about to go on stage and sing a few folk songs. But for the moment, we were focusing on politics.

"Hey, Rich," I responded after a few seconds of thought, "Eisenhower launched the Interstate Highway Program. That's a social good."

"Sure it is," answered Rich, "but the real reason he did it was for national security, so military convoys could roll across the nation in record time, to say nothing of the pork it provides for various Republican controlled states. Do you think it's an accident that Wyoming, Utah, Montana and Nebraska have the best highways in the nation? Look at the crap we have to put up with here in the Bay Area."

"My dad says all of that is about to change. There's going to be a big federal road building program around here," I said. "Anyway, I still don't know what's so hot about Kennedy. I see his face plastered on every magazine around, *Life, Time* and *Post.* Everywhere."

"Kennedy is sharp," Rich insisted. "He's smart and liberal when it comes to social issues. Furthermore, he's as tough on national security as Nixon is."

"From what I read he doesn't have much experience," I countered. "Nothing like Nixon, who has been Vice President for eight years."

"Nixon is a sneaky liar," said Rich defiantly. "He'll resort to any dirty trick to get elected. You ought to read about the stunts he pulled to become elected as a congressman in 1946 when he ran against Jerry Voorhis."

"Like what?"

"Like printing Voorhis' voting record on pink paper, implying he was a communist sympathizer."

"Oh…that's politics," I responded. "At least Nixon is from California and has been tough with the Russians. You remember that kitchen debate he had with Khrushchev last year. Sticking his finger in that fat Russian's face. We need a tough guy like that."

"Brown, you'd better start reading some real newspapers such as *The New York Times* instead of that right wing rag, *Oakland Tribune.* You're a political moron."

And with that, Rich picked up his guitar and went up on stage to sing old Kingston Trio tunes.

***

Rich was right. I was a political moron. I never thought much of politics. To me, politicians were a bunch of opportunists who promised anything to be elected. I also had to admit I was influenced by my father, who was a big Eisenhower supporter and who thought Nixon would do a good job as President. He was suspicious of Kennedy.

"Here's a politician who comes from Boston known for its corruption and machine politics," Dad said. "He talks with a funny accent and he's Catholic. How can someone like him be elected? Even worse, he's just a rich kid."

"What's bad about being rich?" I asked.

"Nothing, if you've earned it. His money was handed to him by his father, Joe. Also, what has Jack Kennedy done? I never heard of him doing anything as either a congressman or a senator. Give me Nixon. At least he's a known quantity. He has experience. Most importantly, he'll look out for California." So sayeth my father.

My mother echoed my father sentiments except she did allow that Jack Kennedy was youthful and handsome.

"What's being handsome have to do with running a country?" asked my father.

"Oh...nothing I guess, but..." said Mom dreamy eyed, looking at a big close up of a smiling Jack in a full-page *Life* spread. She also admired Kennedy's wife Jackie, now visibly pregnant, but still charming and fashionable. Jackie appeared to be a perfect mate for Jack. She had given Jack a beautiful daughter, Carolyn, and now had another on the way. An ideal family image. No wonder Mom was smitten.

Even so, the Brown family stood behind Nixon.

Of course, my problem was I couldn't vote in the November election. I was only twenty. There had been talk in Congress about lowering the voting age to eighteen at some point in the future, but for the 1960 presidential election, I was out of the picture and slightly pissed that I could not vote for Nixon.

***

Another reason I didn't pay much attention to politics was that in small town Martinez, politics were generally a squalid affair. Basically, Italians ran the town. They controlled the city council and the mayor was usually Italian. With names such as Sparacino, Castanza, Amato and DiMaggio, the Italians owned most of the restaurants, bars, car dealerships and assorted other businesses. They also controlled what was left of the waterfront and fishing industry. It was the fishing in the Carquinez Strait that had drawn many of them here directly from Sicily around the turn of the century.

All the city contracts went to Italian friends and relatives with rumors of city council members pocketing large sums of cash. With all the nepotism and corruption, it was always a mystery how things got done in city government, but they did get done and Martinez prospered.

The Italian kids walked around town as if they owned the place. They were always the best dressed and had the nicest cars. Few went to college. Most went into the military after school and then worked for their father or an uncle when they came back.

"What do I need college for?" one said to me once. "After the Army, I'm going to take over my dad's construction business and make some real dough."

As I learned years later, the real key to their success was land. Much of the empty land near downtown Martinez and out in Alhambra Valley was owned by the Italian families. Over the years, they sold it off acre-by-acre for subdivisions, for shopping centers, for whatever, becoming rich in the process. Even Guido, one of the dumbest kids in school, who worked on the county road crews, inherited his father's land in Alhambra Valley and sold it for a fortune. It made me wonder.

***

Politics in Contra Costa County were on a larger and more tainted scale because there was more money involved, but at least the Italians didn't control it. The controlling group was an elected Board of County Supervisors who appointed all the county department heads, set the tax rates and heavily influenced which contractors got which contracts, including the lucrative road building contracts and other infrastructure jobs.

My father, as Assistant Director of Public Works for Contra Costa County, sometimes complained bitterly about the politics involved in letting a road or bridge contract. It wasn't decided strictly on who had the lowest bid. Other, more intangible factors were at play such as the company reputation, its history of doing business with the county and whether it came highly recommended by the Board of Supervisors.

None of this was a small matter because throughout the 1950s and 1960s, Contra Costa County was experiencing unprecedented growth and millions of dollars in contracts were being let. Most of the money came from the federal government. As a result, the competition was fierce for contractors striving for a piece of this pie.

Much of the federal money that flowed to Contra Costa County was due to the efforts of Congressman George Miller Sr. He was an elusive figure, but the local politicians loved him because, as they said, "He brought home the bacon." My father was especially fond of Miller because he was a former civil engineer and understood the county's needs.

Politics on the state level were even more complex. Edmund (Pat) Brown took office in early 1959. Although Pat Brown was a Democrat, my father thought he was a good man with an understanding of the problems of fast growing California that now had a population of almost sixteen million. The family rumor from L.A. was that Pat Brown was somehow part of our Brown clan. I never could figure out if there was a connection except he did vaguely resemble my father. Maybe that's why my father voted for him.

No sooner had he taken office than Pat Brown launched his *Master Plan for Higher Education for California*, which called for a major expansion of the university, state and community college systems in California. The idea was that any California kid who wanted to go to college should be able to do so. If the student didn't have the grades or the money to go to a state university or college, he could enroll at his local community college, earn the equivalent two years of regular college, and then transfer to a four-year school as a junior. Even so, going to a four-year school wasn't very expensive. There was no tuition at California universities and state colleges. They had only an "incidental fee" that hovered around one hundred dollars per semester in the late 1950s. The major cost of going away to school in California was room and board, typically from $1000 to $1500 per year.

Governor Brown's other project of interest to my father was his State Water Project. It included a proposal to build a 444-mile aqueduct along the length of the state to carry water from the northern California rivers down to ever-thirsty Southern California. Most of the water would go for agricultural irrigation, but much of it would also quench the thirst and water the lawns of the L.A. basin. The most spectacular part of the project was a "pump lift", which would carry the water two thousand feet up and over the Tehachapi Mountains and down to the L.A. basin. My father thought the aqueduct would also help industry and farmers along the bone-dry, eastern edge of the Contra Costa County that bordered the San Joaquin Valley.

***

The other political force gathering strength throughout the state was the John Birch Society. This was a group of right wing nuts who thought Democrats were communists in disguise and even called President Eisenhower a "dedicated agent of the communist conspiracy." The Birchers were especially strong in Southern California and campaigned strenuously against John Kennedy. They figured that a moderately conservative Nixon was a lot better than a "pinko" Kennedy. In 1960, none other than movie actor and pitchman Ronald Reagan campaigned as a Democrat for Richard Nixon. He offered this smear of Kennedy:

> *Shouldn't someone tag Mr. Kennedy's bold new imaginative program with its proper age. Under the tousled boyish haircut is still old Karl Marx...*

Reagan was referring to Kennedy's plan for nuclear arms reduction that was anathema to the Birchers. There was also talk that someday Reagan might make a run for public office himself. Although he had started out as a liberal Democrat in the 1940s, by the early 1960s, Reagan had shifted his allegiance to the Republican Party and had begun seriously flirting with the Birchers. The rest, as they say, is history.

***

The other realm of politics with which I was familiar was student politics at Cal. Rich Petrillo was a Campus Rep and took it very seriously. When I asked exactly what he did, he explained, "I represent Greek interests to the University." Still, I thought mainstream student politics were a joke. It was all about one fraternity or another dominating student government and distributing perks to their brothers such as free football tickets, travel to student conferences, even deals to tour European universities. The only interesting political group was SLATE, a student group, which was considered radical, even communist by some of the more conservative students. SLATE's focus at the time was on the House Un-American Activities Committee. HUAC was conducting ongoing hearings in San Francisco to sniff out subversives in the Bay Area. In May of 1960, SLATE staged a mass protest at the hearings being held at the San Francisco City Hall. The protestors were summarily washed down the steps of City Hall by fire hoses. Out of this came the HUAC propaganda film *Operation Abolition*, which accused the students of being inspired by communists.

SLATE was also promoting free speech on campus. UC had a policy that prohibited gatherings, rallies and demonstrations on campus for "off campus" causes. At one point in 1959, SLATE organizers bucked that policy and proceeded to hold a rally focusing on "off campus issues" under an oak tree on Dwinell Plaza near Sather Gate. Later, the leaders were called up before the Student Faculty Committee on Student Conduct, but no disciplinary action was taken. Emboldened, SLATE vowed to hold more unauthorized rallies on campus.

***

During September and October of 1960, many in the fraternity watched a series of televised presidential debates between Jack Kennedy and Richard Nixon on our small black and white television set. I saw the first debate and was unimpressed. Both candidates were fuzzy on our house TV, which had bad reception. Kennedy and Nixon stood at separate podiums like statues. In the close-ups, Kennedy, with his bulging cheeks, looked like a chipmunk with a tan. Nixon appeared sallow-faced with a five-o'clock shadow covering his jowls. His gray suit disappeared into the background of the set. I thought neither looked particularly presidential.

The debate was dull. I found Kennedy's Boston accent annoying, as was his phony cadence, "Let me say...blah blah." While Nixon was visually less impressive, he seemed the more informed on the issues of the day whether domestic or international. Kennedy, by contrast, seemed less sure of himself, although he put up a good front and had a better-tailored suit. In the end, it was hard for me to imagine that a television debate could change anybody's mind. Either you were for Kennedy or for Nixon.

The November election was a squeaker with Kennedy winning by some 113,000 votes nationwide, less than half of one percent of the votes cast. Four states—California, Michigan, Illinois and Minnesota—were up for grabs throughout election night. The Illinois vote was especially controversial. Nixon won downstate, but Chicago carried Illinois for Kennedy. Of course, it was widely assumed that Chicago Mayor Richard Daley had rigged the city election in favor of Kennedy. Nixon took the high road and never challenged the election results.

Years later, the debates were seen as the great turning point for Kennedy in the race. Further, it was realized that television was a valuable tool for delivering a candidate's message to a national electorate. However, at the time the debates weren't relevant to me or most of those that I knew except for Rich who was gloating over the Kennedy victory. "It doesn't matter how he won it, Al. The important thing is that Kennedy is our next president, and he'll get this country back on the right track."

Welcome to the New Frontier.

18. FLIES

Kennedy's "New Frontier" wasn't the only one opening up. Big changes were also afoot in the world of genetics. How did I know this? I wasn't a biogeneticist. Rather, I was a lowly bottle washer in a genetics lab. I dealt with fruit flies. Thousands, maybe millions of them. I didn't know. But I did know that when the little buggers escaped from their bottles and buzzed around my head, they drove me batty.

So what if this place was on the frontier of science. The lab was hot, steamy and smelly. I had hundreds of bottles to wash and sterilize. Then I had several gallons of fly food to mix, a disgusting concoction of barley yeast and molasses. Stripped to the waist and sweating, I would swab out each bottle with a stiff brush, trying to get rid of the remnants of fly food. Once I had cleaned the bottles, I would place them in a metal rack and shove the whole mess into the sterilizer for twenty minutes or so. This washing and sterilizing operation took most of Saturday morning. The last hour of my day was spent mixing the yeast and molasses in a giant bowl with an electric mixer. Once that was done, I stored the food in a refrigerator. Later, a lab assistant would come along and insert a precisely measured gob of the yeast into each bottle, along with several fruit flies. Officially known as *drosophila melanogaster*, these flies ate, shat and fucked and within a matter of days, their offspring flew around like mad in the bottles, desperate to get out. The geneticist, Jim, would then pick out a bottle at random, spray the flies and examine them for possible mutation.

Again, what was I doing here? Working in a genetics lab was way off my liberal arts track. I had inherited this job from premed Neil who used to work here. It was a ten-hour a week gig, a job that I needed because my summer earnings weren't enough to get me though the academic year, thanks to my goofing off at Lake Tahoe. I was also vaguely interested in the science of genetics.

"You see, Al," said Jim in his Okie drawl, "what you're doing here may not be glamorous, but it is vitally important. Those bottles have to be sterile and the food has to be mixed precisely. These have to be constants if we are going to be accurate in tracking genetic variation."

"I see. Well I will do the best I can."

"You're doing a great job," he continued. "Here, take a look at this Petri dish."

As I peered through the microscope at two dead flies, Jim offered a running commentary: "The fruit fly or the *Drosophila melanogaster* can reproduce every thirty hours. The larvae spend five or six days feeding on the yeast then finally hatch. That's when we nail them and examine their genetic make up. The ones we don't kill can live for eight days breeding like gangbusters. We never run out of fruit flies and have plenty of genetic variation in a very short time. If we used rabbits or mice, we would spend forever waiting for their offspring."

"Jim, that's all very interesting," I said bored, "but all I see here are two dead flies."

"Yes, but look closely," said Jim. "The fly on the right with the red eye is the normal fly. The one on the left with white eyes and short wings is a mutant, the product of a significant genetic change. Someday, we hope to apply this knowledge of genetic variation in fruit flies to other species. In the distant future, we may be able to create genetic variation on the molecular level. In effect, we will be able to tailor the genetic make up of plants and animals."

"Including humans?" I asked, looking up from the microscope.

"Possibly," he responded.

"Sounds like Frankenstein science to me."

"Yeah, there will be many ethical issues to work out," he replied nonchalantly as he put away his Petri dish of dead flies. "But someday it will happen,"

I found Jim fascinating. He was an assistant professor of genetics now in his mid-thirties. You would never know it from looking at him. He looked like a regular blue-collar guy, with a crew cut, a gut and an Oklahoma twang. Jim had graduated from the University of Oklahoma many years ago in biology and had spent time in the military working on biochemical stuff. All very hush-hush. Then he had decided to go back to school. He bounced around at various universities as a teaching assistant until he landed at Berkeley, which was on the forefront of genetics. It was here he received his doctorate.

Jim was similar to many of the academic types that I encountered at Berkeley. Very bright, but repelled by the outside world. They preferred to spend their lives in the ivory towers of major universities scratching out a living as assistant professors or teaching assistants. Though it paid little, the academic life did have its compensation. Hang loose living, willing co-eds bucking for a grade and plenty of beer. Jim especially liked beer. His gut was proof of that. His comrade in arms as far as beer drinking was concerned was Ollie, the lab manager in his fifties, who was a German immigrant and a connoisseur of beer. Short, squat Ollie sported an even larger beer belly than Jim did.

"I do not drink the piss that passes for beer here in the states," Ollie declared. "I drink only the finest German brew. I know where to buy it by the case, Dortmunder, the best German beer in the Bay Area. I also know where it's served on tap at a few select restaurants and bars in San Francisco and Marin. I am sorry to say that Berkeley has little to offer in that area, although I hear that La Vals may soon be offering imported Lowenbrau on tap, a mediocre German beer at best."

"Do tell," I said mildly interested. "I once had a bottle of Dortmunder at Squaw Valley."

"Ya, Al. If you want the real German beer drinking experience, you must come with Jim and me to the Mountain Home Inn on the road to Mt. Tamalpais. They serve Dortmunder on tap in the proper mugs at the proper temperatures in the proper mountain setting."

"Sounds interesting."

"Ya. And as you may know, October Fest is underway. Jim and I are planning to take a little hike up Tamalpias this Sunday and then afterwards go to the Inn to quench our thirst."

"Sounds good. Count me in," I said, mentally blowing off my planned study schedule for Sunday. I was eager for some outdoor exercise. Since I had quit crew, I felt out of shape. I was also eager for some good German beer.

***

Sunday morning, the three of us piled into Ollie's little Volkswagen Beetle and made our way over to Marin County, weaving our way up the Panoramic Highway to the base of Mt. Tamalpais where the hiking trails began. As far as mountains went, Mt. Tamalpais, at 2,500 feet in elevation, wasn't much of a mountain, but it did dominate the other costal range hills and valleys in the area. The two-mile hike up to its summit was pleasant, with open areas of low, brushy chaparral punctuated by groves of Redwoods and scattered maples with burning red autumn leaves. The trail also offered stunning views of Marin County and San Francisco Bay beyond.

I was in better shape than I thought. I kept up a steady pace as I climbed in elevation. It was Ollie and Jim who were puffing along, complaining about the steepness of the trail and vowing to lose weight. A couple of times on the hike up, Jim and Ollie stopped and sat down on a log, announcing they needed a rest. "No need to rush, Al. Let's enjoy nature for a while," said Jim while examining a fern.

"Whatever," I said, sitting down on a decayed stump. I broke off a few pieces of the dead wood and examined the termites slowly dismantling the long dead trunk. I pointed this out to Jim, asking, "Who's in charge here? Man or bug?"

"Insects... of course," said Jim. "Humans are merely a passing phase, a moment on earth. Insects in one form or another will control the planet. It's a simple mathematical certainty. Their genetic make-up allows for infinite variation, infinite adaptability. Humans, like other large mammals, change too slowly and will eventually perish."

"Such pessimism," I said.

"Of course, the human race is speeding up the process with the nuclear arms race and its destruction of the earth's environment," concluded Jim.

"Ya," said Ollie. "That's why it's important to drink as much German beer as possible. We must be happy while we are still here. Like that film *On The Beach*, the last people on Earth partied until the end when the radiation reached them in Australia." Then jumping up, Ollie said, "Let's climb to the top of this damn mountain and drink some beer."

We hiked up to the summit and found ourselves in a parking lot full of cars and camper vans and a closed ranger's station. We scanned the views through coin-operated telescopes on the periphery of the lot and then hiked back down the paved road to the Mountain Home Inn, having had our fill of backwoods nature.

The Inn was a ramshackle roadhouse done up in a vaguely Swiss alpine style with a sundeck out back hanging over the hillside. Jim and I sat down at a picnic table under a large umbrella while Ollie went inside to fetch the beer. He came back a few minutes later with a pitcher of foaming Dortmunder and three mugs. Ollie expertly poured the beer into the mugs with a minimal head of beer, and we each took a healthy draught to quench our thirst.

"Not too bad, this beer, huh, Al?" said Ollie licking the foam off his lips.

"Nectar of the gods," I said, swallowing a big slug of the mellow Pilsner. "Why can't they brew beer like that in the States?"

"Oh...they could and once did," said Ollie. "Nineteenth and early twentieth century brews in America were similar to the ones in Europe, but because of mass marketing the taste of beer went flat, so to speak. Anyway, enjoy the Dortmunder and the view."

"This is great," I said looking out over the hills at the Marin County panorama, breathing in the warm fall scents of redwood, sage and grass. "You know how to pick the spots, Ollie."

"Ya, well, you can't live by fruit flies alone, right Jim?"

"Sure, sure, Ollie," said Jim, "even geneticists need a break now and then. Yet, when you delve into it, it's compelling stuff. Hard to let go."

"Yeah, I'll say, Jim," said Ollie. "Look at you. Mid-thirties, no girl-friend, just a studio apartment and your research. I'm the only friend you have."

"Well, I'm happy. I 'm doing what I want. After I become famous, there will be plenty of time for women."

In the midst of this conversation, a flustered waitress came up and asked us in a German accent if we wanted anything to eat. We ordered knackwurst and sauerkraut, the perfect complement to a stein of beer. Before we knew it, we had consumed the whole pitcher, so Ollie ordered another.

"Hey, Ollie," said Jim, "you drink that pitcher and you're going to give me the keys to your Bug."

"What are you talking about?" exclaimed Ollie. "You've drunk as much beer as I have and you will probably drink some more."

"Well, somebody has to stay sober here," said Jim.

"I'll drive," I announced. "I'm not drinking any more beer." I had had only two steins and with the food, I felt clearheaded.

"O.K., O.K, Al," said Ollie, tossing me the keys and pouring himself another stein of beer.

I stuffed the keys into my pocket, excused myself while the two worked on the second pitcher of beer and wandered around the Inn. As far as I could tell, it was no longer a functional inn although there were a few rooms upstairs. The place, however, had a history dating back to the 1910s judging by the photos on the walls and a few newspaper clippings. Back then, Mt. Tamalpias had been a big attraction for Bay Area day-trippers. They took ferries across the bay to Marin County and then climbed aboard a small gauge train, which transported them to the base of the mountain. Some hiked up to the summit; some picnicked; others repaired to the inn for food and drink as people do today. Often, local celebrities such as Jack London showed up to spend the day drinking and carousing.

When I returned to the table, Jim and Ollie had polished off the second pitcher and were now drowsy in the afternoon warmth. I sat down and read my James Bond paperback until Jim stirred and announced that we had better get going.

"You sure, you want to drive, Al?" said Ollie as he came to. "I feel fine now."

"Sure, no problem, Ollie. I've driven these Bugs before," I said thinking no way was I going to let Ollie make his way down the twisty, curvy road to Mill Valley half asleep, half-drunk.

The drive back was pleasant. I took it easy on the curves and managed not to grind the gears too much. Ollie and Jim slept most of the way, waking up only when we crossed the Richmond-San Rafael Bridge and the fresh bay breezes blew in through the open windows.

I liked the VW. It was small but roomy and had a certain amount of pep. Heck, you could buy a good used one for only a few hundred dollars. It wasn't glamorous, but it was transportation. It was exactly what I needed. However, my father thought the VW was a dangerous piece of junk. As he pointed out, when a VW got into an accident, it was usually crunched. No matter. It was wheels. It was freedom.

As soon as we hit Berkeley, Ollie took over the driving, declaring he was stone sober now. He dropped me off at the fraternity house. I waved goodbye to Jim and Ollie and climbed the three flights of stairs to my room. I crashed on my bed, worn out from the hike, the beer and the drive. My day with Ollie and Jim was over. My glimpse into their world of beer, genetics and the insignificance of man in the cosmos faded from my consciousness as I fell asleep.

19. TIE-TIE

In the end, bottle washing and mixing fruit fly food didn't do it for me. I needed more money, so I took a part-time job Christmas season. Every year, Sam, an AKL alum in retailing, hired a fraternity brother to keep the shelves stocked at Capwells with his Tie-Tie Christmas products. Sam had to supply several East Bay department stores with hundreds of Tie-Tie items—bows, ribbons, stickers, tags, tags labels, everything but the wrapping paper. This was no menial restocking job. Twice a week, I had to dress up in a coat, tie, and bus down to Capwells Department Store on Broadway Avenue in Oakland. Not only did I stock the Tie-Tie shelves, I also re-ordered stock and arranged the displays. In effect, I was a junior vendor.

I worked in a special Christmas Wrap Center set up for the season. The staff consisted of four salesladies and one temporary department head, who happened to be my fraternity brother, Ron. Ron had recently graduated and was working as a management trainee until he went on six months active duty in the Army Reserves.

Working a month at Capwells gave me an insight into department store retailing. I couldn't imagine how anyone could make a career here. Yet some did. Capwells hired Berkeley graduates by the carload. Usually these people had majored in liberal arts and had no definable skills. The business majors got jobs in the more prestigious corporations. *Crapwells*, as we called it, was definitely down at the bottom of the list as a desirable place to work. Ron, who was aware of my mediocre academic career, used to tease me saying that I would wind up there. "Brown, you'll be selling shoes at Capwells before you know it."

On the other hand, Sam, the Tie-Tie vendor, was a nice guy. He'd had a checkered career after graduating from Berkeley ten years earlier. He had drifted from one retailing job to another until he figured out that the people who made the most money with the least sweat were the vendors, the ones who worked directly for the wholesalers and sold the products to the stores. One day over lunch at a downtown coffee shop, he instructed me in retail markups.

"Here's a general example, Al," said Sam scribbling some figures on a paper napkin. "Figure an item cost $20.00 to produce. The producer maybe marks it up $5.00 and sells it to the wholesaler for $25.00. The wholesaler marks it up about $10.00 and sells it to a retail store for $35.00. A full-service retail store turns around and sells it for $50.00 — marking up the price by $15.00."

"Wow, that's quite a markup!" I said.

"Yeah, the public doesn't have a clue," Sam continued. "They're conditioned to pay those prices. Even if the item is on sale at 20% off, the retailer is still making money. Of course, retail department stores have a lot of overhead and salaries to deal with, so maybe they clear only 10% profit.

"Where do you come in on this?"

"The wholesaler pays me a 10% commission on what I sell to the retailer. In addition to stocking this product, I go around and hustle up business. On a thousand dollars worth of merchandise sold at the wholesale price, I make a hundred bucks. The wholesaler still makes money, about 20% profit. Everybody is happy — producer, wholesaler, retailer and the customer, especially if the item is on sale."

"Whew, what a racket," I responded, severely tempted to ask Sam how much Tie-Tie merchandise he sold.

As if reading my mind, Sam, continued, "Christmas is our big season. Sixty-percent of what we sell, we sell during Christmas. I make most of my money then. Of course, I have a draw against my commissions because the year is so uneven. So you see, Al, it may appear to be low-grade grunt work, lugging this stuff around, stocking it and selling , but it can provide a good living if you work it right. Last year I sold around $200,000 worth of product, wholesale price. That netted me a cool $20,000. Keep vendor retailing in mind when you graduate from Cal."

"That's certainly something to think about," I replied.

***

Once a week, I had to unpack several boxes of Tie-Tie merchandise that Sam had picked up from the warehouse and store it in the cabinets below the display shelves. I spent a lot of time squatting down and rummaging around the cabinets trying to find the proper product to put on the display shelves. The cabinets were in constant disarray. So many little items. Who would have thought that selling wrapping accessories could be so complicated?

Of course, none of this fazed the salesladies working here. They were a cheerful lot, always chatting with the customers as they hustled the various products.

"Oh yes, Mrs. So-and-so. This ribbon is something new. See how it glitters. Very festive. It will add immensely to the fun of giving."

"Now we have these personalized gift cards. If you order in advance, we can have your name printed on them."

The sales staff acted as if wrapping a gift was the most important thing in the world.

I also had to fill out inventory sheets weekly. The inventory sheets listed each item and my job was to tally how many specific items were sold and how many remained. Sam then analyzed the sheets to see which items had moved and which hadn't and ordered accordingly. He had to do this for the six or seven stores he served. What a nightmare of paperwork! I kept thinking there had to be a better, faster way of doing this. There was talk of doing it by computer someday, but that idea seemed as farfetched as putting a man on the moon.

The shoppers were another story. Nine out of ten were women. They came up to the Christmas Wrap Center, weighted down with all their shopping bags. This usually being their last stop in the store, they loaded up on Tie-Tie products and wrapping paper.

Most paid cash, but some used the store charge card — a plastic card stamped with the Capwell's logo and the shopper's personal account number. The card was especially useful for big-ticket items such as furniture or appliances, which the customer could pay for in monthly installments. Of course, Capwells charged a hefty interest rate on balances left at the end of the month and made a bundle of money on the interest charges alone. In the frenzy of Christmas shopping, shoppers seemed oblivious to what they were spending. They wanted their families to have a great Christmas. So what if they would be in debt for the rest of the year!

The salesladies loved the charge cards too because it saved them the hassle of handling cash. Ringing up sales on the clunky registers all day long was tedious. Making sure the right amount was paid and providing the change was a constant headache and often mistakes were made in doing the mental arithmetic to give the correct change. The discrepancies were discovered at the end of the day when the salesladies had to tally up the sales receipts and reconcile the tally with the amount of money left in the cash register. If it was a matter of a few dollars, it was overlooked, but if more, then a recount was in order.

Add to this the general hysteria of the Christmas shopping season — the frantic look in the eyes of women on all-day shopping marathons, running after last-minute sales with their screaming kids in tow. Further, a grumpy Santa was found on every floor causing the little kids to lament, "How come there are so many Santas, Mom? I thought there was just one."

"These are only Santa's helpers," Mom would explain. "The real Santa is back at the North Pole overseeing his elves that are making the toys."

"Oh...," the little kid would say, unconvinced.

This Tie-Tie experience convinced me that I would never take a job in retailing. Promoting, selling and keeping track of all this merchandise — the million little bits of it — would drive me nuts. Yet, Ron, a business administration major, seemed to thrive on it.

"I like the interaction with the customers, Al. I like overseeing the salesladies. We have a good time. I don't mind seeing the monetary fruits of our labor. Checking how much we sold on a daily basis. I get a kick out of tallying it all up at the end of the day. Day-to-day sales give you a sense of accomplishment and also the satisfaction of providing products that are useful to the customer."

"Well then, why aren't you hanging around and making it a career?" I asked Ron one day as we took a coffee break together.

"I thought about it, Al, but it's not in the cards. I have to spend six months in the Army Reserves on active duty and then I'll probably go to work for my future father-in-law. He owns the largest Chevy dealership in the Sacramento area."

"Sounds like a better deal than working here," I said.

Ron nodded.

"All I know, Ron, is I'm done with this gig in a few days, and I doubt that I'll ever return."

But I did return. Two years later, when I found myself short of cash again, I hit Sam up for the part-time Tie-Tie job. Occasionally, I wondered if I was destined to become another captive at Capwells with a liberal arts degree.

20. EURO BUG

It began to dawn on me towards the end of the fall semester of my junior year that I had only three more semesters to go until graduation. Three short semesters and then boom! I would be out in the real world. Of course, the real world meant a job and/or the draft. The draft especially bothered me. I could envision the geezers down at the Martinez draft board licking their chops. You would think we were at war, but in early 1961, there was nothing going on, only a few American military advisors stationed in dink-ass Vietnam.

As noted before, I had done well that fall semester by my standards—three B's and two C's. I felt that I had finally gotten into the academic swing. I felt that I knew what it took to get at least a B at Berkeley, and I was confident that I could achieve a B average for the rest of my time at UC and possibly go to graduate or law school. Regardless of what I did, the key was to stay in school. The draft board would certainly issue another student deferment if I continued in school.

At this point, I was only mildly interested in law school. Several of my fraternity brothers were planning on law school. However, the idea of plowing through legal tomes didn't inspire me. Also, I had heard Boalt Law School was tough to get into. You had to do well on the LSAT (Law School Admissions Test), and you needed at least a B average, an average I did not yet have. Of course, there was always Hastings Law School in San Francisco that took anyone from Cal, but it had a high dropout rate.

A couple of fraternity brothers were going on to study for a master's degree in business administration. Others were going to work for some big corporation such as IBM or Standard Oil. Business held no interest for me. I couldn't see myself as a junior management trainee somewhere.

Then there was teaching. I could spend another year at Berkeley in the Department of Education and earn a secondary teaching certificate. All you needed was a C average to do that. However, I wasn't sure I wanted to teach a classroom full of annoying kids.

Essentially, I had no clear idea of what I wanted to do other than to stretch out my student career for as long as possible and avoid the Army. One way to so was to spend my junior year abroad. I had been toying with this idea off and on. Now the more I thought about it, the more sense it made. A year abroad would mean at least another semester at Berkeley or perhaps another year. I could be graduating in spring of 1963 instead of the spring of 1962. That would work.

The obvious choice for studying abroad was France despite the fact that I hadn't fared too well in French. I realized I had no natural talent for learning another language, but I still wanted to learn French. It was an ego thing. As my former French teacher, Reginald put it last year:

> *Mr. Brown, if you are serious about learning French, consider going to France to study for at least a semester. I know of a great program in the South of France, Aix-En-Provence. It has good weather, beautiful scenery; plus the history — Greek, Roman, medieval cities. If you go, do it right. Total immersion. Don't hang out with English speakers. Bury yourself in the culture...*

The other big attraction of going to Europe for a year was the chance to ski in the Alps. Ever since I had listened to the European students at the Cal Ski Lodge describe the glories of skiing in the Alps, I was intrigued. I could see myself schussing down the wide-open treeless slopes, through blinding white snowfields with jagged mountain peaks in the background. And it was cheap — about half the cost of skiing in California, according to the Swiss student, Rolf.

Also, last fall, I had gone out with Meg, a Chi Omega, who informed me in her high-tone way that she planned to study next year at the Bryn Mawr program in Paris. Meg was from the upscale Oakland suburb of Piedmont. She came off as the archetypical Eastern college girl who happened to be going to Berkeley.

"You ought to go, Allan," she declared one night at a cocktail party. "It would broaden your horizons."

"No doubt. Still, there is the question of money."

"Yes, I suppose it is costly, but perhaps there are scholarships," she said with a hint of condescension.

"With my grade point average, I don't think scholarships are likely," I responded.

Nevertheless, even with my mediocre grade point and my lack of funds, I forged on exploring this idea, an idea that was rapidly becoming an obsession.

***

My research consisted of perusing the bulletin boards of the French Department that were plastered with brochures of study abroad programs. They extolled the glories of studying in Paris, Tours, Grenoble and Reginald's favorite, Aix-En-Provence. Most carried heavy price tags, which amounted to the full tuition at a private university, some $2,500 to $3,000 for the academic year. However, one little mimeograph sheet on the bulletin board did inform me that the Foreign Institutes run by the French universities were free. This sounded enticing, but the catch was that even with a certificate of successful completion, there was no guarantee of transferring credits back to Berkeley. I needed something more certain because I did want some credit for spending a year abroad.

As it turned out, the Institute for American Universities in Aix fit my needs. It was fully accredited, meaning I could earn at least unit credit. It was relatively cheap. About $1500 for one year's tuition. In addition, the Institute accepted students from a variety of colleges not only a few snobby eastern schools. Of course, despite a reasonable tuition, the $1500 was still a hurdle for me. I also needed another $600 or so to travel to and from France along with money for room and board. This was money that I had to earn by next fall. It would mean dropping out of Berkeley spring semester, finding a job, living at home for seven months and trying to save at least 25-hundred dollars or so.

As far as room and board in Aix was concerned, I thought I could persuade my parents to kick in monthly expenses, which would be no more than they were now spending on me, about $125 a month. All of this would total about $ 3,700 for the year. Was the money and hassle worth it? I decided yes and drew up the following budget:

JUNIOR YEAR ABROAD

EXPENSES

1. Institute tuition	1,500
2. Room and board	1,125
3 .Travel	600
4. Misc.	500
	$3,725

INCOME

1. Six month earnings (March-Aug.)	2,600
2. Parents:	1,125
	$ 3,725

***

"Are you sure, you want to do this, Mr. Brown?" asked my advisor, Mr. Marks when I met him in his Sproul Hall office. I had seen this guy only twice before in my academic career at Berkeley.

"Yes, I think I do," I answered.

"Well, consider it carefully. We want to see you back here. We want to see you graduate."

"I'll be back. At worst, I'll have to spend an extra semester here"

Mr. Marks was a chemistry major advisor and theoretically still advised me although I had long since abandoned chemistry and chemical engineering. He was one of scores of advisors at Berkeley who simply rubber-stamped whatever students wanted to take as long as they were fulfilling requirements. Until now, it was merely a formality, but now his advice was crucial. I wanted to know if I went to the Institute of American Universities at Aix, would I receive full credit.

"Well, according to our list, the Institute is accredited, so I don't see why not," he explained. "Of course, we will not be able to give grade credit, only unit credit, which will not be averaged into your Berkeley grade point."

"What if I get all A's and B's over there?" I asked.

"It would be meaningless. Those grades will only translate into a unit credit as if you received C's."

"Gee, thanks," I said sarcastically, as I left the office.

"Good day, Mr. Brown."

***

When I finally revealed my plans to my parents a few days later, my father was horrified.

"Allan, here you have the chance of a lifetime to graduate from Berkeley, even if it is a major in history. Don't throw it away on a fool's errand."

"I'm not, Dad. I plan to continue at Berkeley when I return. In the meantime, I need to earn some dough so that I can go to the Institute."

I showed them the brochure on the Institute, which stated that it was fully accredited. I told them about my meeting with my advisor who confirmed that it was indeed accredited and that if I took the right courses, I could receive a full year's worth of credit.

My mother was enthusiastic. "Oh Ray, don't worry. This is a chance of a lifetime for Allan. After all, he is a history major. He should see Europe. I do think its part of his education."

"Humph...probably just a chance to chase French girls," Dad mumbled.

After another few days of discussion, my father finally came around. "O.K., Allan, here's the deal. We will pay for your monthly up-keep over there, if, as you say, it will be around $120 a month."

"That's what their brochure says," I responded.

"Yes, well we'll see. It could be more, and you'll need some money for traveling around Europe. As far as the tuition is concerned, you'll have to pay for that. I can't afford that now, especially with Don at Berkeley too."

"I know, I know. I plan to earn that money during the seven months I have off from school," I said.

"Yes, that's another thing," Dad continued. "If you don't find a job or are unable to save up the tuition, then you're going right back to Berkeley next fall, which is what I think you should do anyway. No *ifs, ands,* or *buts.* Is that a deal?"

"Gulp. Yes. I guess that's a deal," I said, now wondering what I would do if I didn't get a job. I had assumed I would find a surveying job and make some real money. But what if I couldn't? What then? I didn't want to think about. I wanted to plunge ahead.

***

A few days before I withdrew from Berkeley, I paid a visit to Reginald at his office.

"So Mr. Brown, you decided to take the plunge. Bravo. You will never regret it," he said leaning back in his swivel chair, chewing on a pencil.

"I hope you're right. This Aix seems too good to be true."

"Well, it's not perfect, of course. During the winter months, the Mistral does howl, cutting through alleys, windows and even heavy clothing. Take a down ski parka, if you have one. Also, don't believe the bit about the South of France being warm in the winter. That's a lot of drivel. It gets cold, especially with the Mistral. Be aware that indoor heating is almost nonexistent. The cheapskate landladies barely turn it on. Be prepared. Bundle up. Of course, don't expect a personal bathroom. It will no doubt be down the hall. As far as showers or bathes are concerned, be prepared to hike to the bathhouse once or twice a week. That's about it. That's the downside. Don't worry. You will survive."

***

And so, one cold, foggy morning at the beginning of spring semester in February of 1961, I took a deep breath, walked into the Registrar's office and officially dropped out of school. The lady at the window said nothing, but I thought I detected a little smirk indicating to her that I was only one more sucker who couldn't hack it at Berkeley and who would probably never return. As I walked out of the Sproul Hall, I felt as if I had stepped off the edge of a cliff into the unknown.

I wandered down Telegraph Avenue, asking myself over and over again if I had done the right thing. I had a cappuccino at the Mediterraneum to ponder the situation. As I sipped the foamy cappuccino, I watched the scruffy, beatnik types aimlessly drift in and out. Maybe in a few months I would be like them. But no, I reminded myself. I had a plan. I was going to find a job, make money and then fly off to Europe. I wasn't going to be a bum.

By the time I finished my cappuccino, the sun had come out and the day was warming up. As I walked through campus on my way back to the fraternity house, for some reason, I was greeted with smiles by several co-eds and a nod or two from a couple of fraternity guys. Maybe it was my imagination, but I felt light, I felt free and the sun felt warm on my back. And I knew everything would be all right.

***

However, this buoyant mood didn't last long. Back at AKL, I told an incredulous Bill Singleton, now house president, that I was dropping out for the semester and would be going to Europe in the fall.

"How can you do this, Brown?" said Singleton. "We were counting on you to become Rush Chairman."

"Yeah," said Gary, the house manager. "You're being selfish, Brown. You don't care about the house. We need your dough."

Pre-med Neil nodded and, with a little smile and a wink, he said, "Here, I line you up with a bottle washing job in the genetics lab, and you chuck it all. Make sure you come back to Berkeley. No trip to Europe is worth fucking up your college career.

Only Jean-Paul truly understood what I was doing. Little Jean-Paul with a broken front tooth had grown up in France but had emigrated with his family to the U.S. when he was fourteen. Jean-Paul had gone to a Catholic school in Burlingame on the Peninsula. He was bright as a tack, speaking English, French, German, Spanish and reading and writing Latin. He had joined the fraternity last fall, the beginning of his freshman year, because as he put it, "I wanted to be around guys who had fun, not stuck in a dormitory or at International House with its foreign losers."

"What you are doing is great, Al," said Jean-Paul. "Never mind what these guys say. More American students should study in Europe, especially France because my country has much to offer. Who knows, you might learn some French."

"Maybe, Jean-Paul. You never know. At least enough to order a café," I said.

With that, I went upstairs to my room and packed my bags. That evening, my father picked me up and we drove home to Martinez, where I was to spend the next seven months trying to make my year abroad become a reality.

21. LIMBO

A month later, I was sitting at my little desk writing in my journal, occasionally gazing out through my open bedroom window at the green rolling hills, smelling the honeysuckle in our backyard and hearing the drone of the dragonflies. It was one of those balmy mid-March days that sometimes arrive between rainstorms in the Bay Area with the temperatures in the seventies. The skies were clear blue and the scent of growth was in the air. All was well, except I had not yet been able to land a job.

I should have been deeply worried. After all, I had pissed away four weeks since dropping out of Cal. Aix-En-Provence was only six months away, but I wasn't too concerned. I felt something would turn up. I had already done a few days of surveying for Ferguson & Company, a civil engineering firm in Pleasant Hill, and they had promised a long-term job was coming up. Of course, that had been two weeks ago and since then nothing. I needed something more certain than a day here and there. Dad was becoming antsy.

"Nothing yet, Allan?"

"No, Dad. Something will turn up."

"You hope. Remember what I said. If you don't earn the tuition, it's back to Berkeley next fall."

"Yes, Dad. I remember."

"Well, get out there and keep knocking on doors."

"I will, but maybe as a safeguard, you could see about getting me hired on a survey crew for the county."

"I can't do that son," he said. "It would look bad. In addition, they hire only engineering students. Just keep hitting those surveying firms. They know who I am. Maybe they can do something for you."

"Sure, Dad. Thanks."

To cover my bets, I put in applications at Shell Oil in Martinez, Monsanto Chemical in Avon and Dow Chemical in Pittsburg. I didn't want to work in an oil refinery or a chemical plant, but it was better than nothing. At least it would provide steady employment. The pay averaged about $2.50 per hour, less than the $3.00 per hour I would get surveying, but still respectable. I figured my best shot would be Dow Chemical since Don had already worked there and knew people. When I handed in my application at Dow, the gray-haired personnel lady, Mrs. Spenser, told me that they would be hiring vacation replacement workers in April.

"Don was a fine worker, a fine lab assistant. He went into engineering, didn't he?" she asked. "How is he doing?"

"Oh, he's doing great."

"Good. Now let's see," she said turning to my application. "You're not in engineering are you?"

"That's right. I'm majoring in history."

"Oh, yes," she said adjusting her spectacles. "Right here on the application."

"But I have had chemistry and math," I continued. "Perhaps you have something as a lab assistant."

"Well, we usually reserve those jobs for engineering or chemistry majors. I will see what I can do, but normally we put liberal arts people out in the plant for general duties. You will hear from us soon."

***

To keep my mind from rotting during this period, I enrolled in three night classes through UC Berkeley Extension: *Greek Literature*, *Marxist Philosophy* and *Conversational French*. Three nights a week, I borrowed Dad's car and drove over to Berkeley for a three-hour-long session in each of these classes. I didn't expect these courses to be hard. They were designed for the casual student, the bored housewife and the retiree. I would receive no credit for these courses.

Conversational French was indeed elementary, but it did provide an opportunity to speak some rudimentary French, at which I was terrible. It made me rethink my position about France. Why was I going there when I was such a klutz in French? I could barely spit out: *Bonjour, Monsieur. Comment allez-vous?* Our book, *Basic Conversational French* by Harris and Leveque, followed the trials and tribulations of Robert Hughes, a young American studying in Paris. Robert learned French the hard way, chasing around Paris, conversing with his landlady, his teacher, the postmaster, whomever. However, he never hooked up with a *jeune fille*, someone he could court and learn French from at the same time. That was my goal. Learn French through pillow talk. I was tired of this classroom stuff. I was tempted to drop the course, but my mother pleaded with me to persevere, so I hung in.

Marxist Philosophy was dense but enlightening. We read selections from *Das Kapital* and *The Communist Manifesto* that declared: "The history of all hitherto existing society is the history of class struggles..."

The professor traced how the Communist philosophy was implemented and distorted by Lenin and Stalin. Under their rule, the dictatorship of the proletariat became a permanent state rather than the temporary, transitional process that Marx had envisioned.

The professor did note that workers owning the means of production made sense up to a point, but that it would be impossible in the capitalist U.S. The next best thing, he said, was workers organizing in unions to secure wages and working conditions. Although tough battles had been fought in the early twentieth century, unionization had proven workable and even profitable in the postwar years. Everybody made money—the investors, the corporate executives and even the rank-and-file union worker who had moved into the middle class. He could now afford a small house and a car and could send his kids to a state college.

I had some experience with unions. I joined the Retail Clerk's Union when I worked at U-Save supermarket in high school. It paid well for a bagboy job. Then I joined the Operating Engineers Union when I went to work for Leptein, Cronin & Cooper as a surveyor two summers ago. I had made good wages for 1958, around $2.50 per hour. So far, unionization had worked for me.

Greek Literature was the best course of the lot. We read excerpts from Herodotus, Thucydides, Homer and several playwrights including Sophocles, Euripides and Aristophanes. The professor told us that, although this was an extension course, he expected us to do the readings, come to class prepared for discussion and write two short papers if we wanted a certificate of course completion.

Herodotus' *Histories* was an entertaining, anecdotal history, much of it based on hearsay and rumor with tall tales of gold digging ants, bizarre sexual practices and a race of one-eyed giants. Thucydides, on the other hand, was the father of serious historical analysis. In his *History of the Peloponnesian War*, he analyzed the causes and effects of the war. His stated goal was to explain why things happened the way they did and how they might reoccur in the future. He ascribed nothing to divine intervention and instead relied on cool, rational observation.

And then there was Homer. The legend of a blind poet who wandered around ancient Greece reciting the epic tales of Greece's war with Troy that evolved into *The Iliad* and *The Odyssey*. Historians weren't even sure if Homer was a real person or a composite of several ancient poets. I plowed through Richard Lattimore's translation of *The Iliad* and *The Odyssey*. I grew tired of *The Iliad* with endless exploits of Achilles and tedious battle scenes, but I loved The *Odyssey*. It was a brilliant, mythical travelogue of the Aegean, replete with Sirens and Cyclops forever distracting Ulysses as he tried to make his way home.

The Greek playwrights were also amusing with their pithy, satiric and sometimes tragic works. I thought their tragedies were somewhat contrived and their bloody ends a bit much. In Sophocles' *Oedipus Rex,* Oedipus gouges his eyes out and his wife Jocasta hangs herself all because he (Oedipus) had unknowingly married his mother (Jocasta) to preserve the kingdom. The family relationships of the royals in those days were always confusing. Nobody kept good records.

I thought the best antiwar comedy was Aristophanes' *Lysistrata*, in which the women withheld sexual favors until their men found a diplomatic way to end the Peloponnesian War. I thought some of that spirit could be applied to the idiotic little military incursions going on such as the recent invasion of Cuba in the Bay of Pigs. Thinking back to Lake Tahoe and all the girlie rumors of Jack Kennedy, I thought U.S. policy towards Cuba might change overnight if the president was cut off from sex.

***

My other connection to Berkeley during those days of limbo was Ana—little, cute, sweet, sexy Ana. I had met Ana at the Sierra Club Ski Lodge over Christmas break. With her raven dark hair, cream complexion, disarming smile and a luscious body all set off in a snow-white cable knit sweater and black stretch pants, I was immediately hooked.

She was new to skiing so I showed her some skiing techniques on the Sierra Club ski hill that she gamely picked up. One night after a polka dance at the nearby German Ski Lodge, we made out on the veranda while the bright moonlight shimmered on the snow.

Back at Berkeley, we started going out regularly in early January and before I knew it, we were more or less going steady. Within weeks, she was already hinting for the fraternity pin. I was torn. I still wanted to fly the coop, to explore the world. Ana had her own ambitions as well.

She wanted to go to medical school. She claimed she was ready to give up her dream for me, but I knew I couldn't do the same for her. My planned escape took on more urgency than ever.

Although Ana was extremely upset at me for dropping out of school, we kept going out because we couldn't get enough of each other. Our favorite rendezvous spot was the architects' shack—a little, brown-shingled building shrouded in growth and trees on a far corner of the fraternity property. Crammed with a drafting table, chairs, desk, lamps and a space heater, it was used by two architect majors for their late night projects. It also had a narrow, sagging bed and mattress topped by somebody's old sleeping bag. The door locked from the inside. Perfect. It was in this setting in the firelight of the space heater that Ana debated whether it was love or lust. Lust was good enough for me, but maybe love was involved too.

Despite all of this carrying on, there were serious problems. Ana was still upset that I was dropping out of school. You didn't just drop out of college. She was the first person in her family to go to college in the U.S. You don't throw away an opportunity like that.

"It's a beautiful dream and all of that going to Europe," she said. "I want to do that someday too. But look at you. You have no money. You're going to have to work like a dog to earn enough to go away for a year. You are going to miss a year and a half of Berkeley. Why don't you go only for the summer, huh? Work for a few months and then go. You'll be back in time for fall. And we can continue on as if nothing ever happened."

Ana, for all her sexual liberation, was quite conservative at heart. As she was fond of pointing out, her family was from a long line of Spanish nobility in Mexico. They were not *Mestizos.* They had kept their Spanish blood pure. Her father and mother had come to the United States as legal immigrants under a quota program. Her father was a supervisor at Bethlehem Steel in Antioch. Her mother was a dental assistant. Both were well educated. She was an only child and her parents had high expectations for her.

In addition, her mother's sister was a doctor. The aunt had gone to medical school in Mexico and was able to become certified to practice in this country. She was a gynecologist and was quite successful in her San Francisco practice. Ana wanted to do the same.

"Talk about dreams. That's one dilly," I remarked. "A woman doctor! Wow!"

"Well, I know that it's nearly impossible for a woman to become a doctor in this country, but a few do manage it. I don't see why I can't," she insisted. "I get straight A's in science. I'm especially good at chemistry. I know I can ace organic chemistry. That's the usual downfall of most premeds."

"Medical school is going to take years," I countered. "What am I supposed to do?"

"We can work it out, Allan. My Aunt said she would help me out financially for medical school. You can work part-time and go to law school."

"Ana, I still want to go to Europe. It won't be forever. And when I return, we can pick up where we left off. How's that?"

"Well, maybe, but don't count on it," she pouted. "My girlfriends at the dorm say I'm stupid to get involved with you this way. I shouldn't tie myself down. Also, I'm thinking about joining a sorority next year. I'm tired of dorm living."

Good god, I thought. A sorority will ruin little Ana for sure.

And that's how we left it for the time being. Nothing decided. Everything hanging.

22. BLUE-COLLAR

There it sat—a 400-pound drum of some noxious, no doubt poisonous chemical destined for the farms of California. The drum, emblazoned with the red Dow Chemical logo, contained perhaps a weed killer, an insecticide, a fertilizer or some other chemical concoction that would help produce a miracle crop. Better farming through chemistry. My job was to tip the drum up on its edge and roll it into the waiting boxcar along with scores of other drums. George, an old-timer at Dow, showed me the trick.

"See here, Al, you grab it by the lip nearest you and using your body weight as leverage, you lean back, bending your knees and tilt the drum up on its edge where you can balance it." George, in his heavy-duty work gloves, hardhat and steel-toe work boots, demonstrated, neatly tipping the drum on its edge and then keeping it balanced, rolled it the twenty feet into the boxcar. Of course, all the time, I was wondering why they didn't load the drums into the boxcar with the forklift.

"Can't do it, Al. Not enough room to maneuver with this big baby," said George pointing to the idle forklift sitting off to the side. "If they ever designed one small enough to work in these confined spaces, we'll all be out of a job."

"Righto," I said, as I put on my own heavy-duty work gloves, adjusted my hardhat and goggles and proceeded to tilt my own drum up on its edge and roll it into the boxcar.

***

This was my second week as a vacation-relief employee at the Pittsburg plant of Dow Chemical. True to her word, Mrs. Spenser, the personnel lady, had called me late March to start work.

"We would like you to start next Monday, Allan. Is that possible?"

"Sure," I answered, after quickly reviewing my other job options, which at that point were zero.

"Fine, now why don't you come in tomorrow and we can have you sign all the paperwork before you officially start Monday?"

"O.K.," I replied and then asked, "Ah, by the way, this vacation-relief job doesn't entail any lab work does it?"

"Oh no, Allan," she responded. "As I told you, we reserve those jobs for engineering or chemical majors. You will be working as a vacation fill-in at various plant sites. I will probably start you at Distribution first."

"O.K. See you tomorrow," I said as I hung up dazed.

So there it was. This was my best shot at earning enough money to go to France. But the price was high. I had to be a plant worker. A blue-collar dude. This would be a definite step down from being a surveyor. All the plant workers I knew my age were the losers who barely graduated from high school, and who went right to work for Shell Oil or one of the other refineries or chemical plants around here. Of course, most were drafted after a year or two on the job. And when they got out of the military, they went right back to their old jobs, married their old girlfriends and started having babies.

I had grown up with this. This was how life was in Martinez and other industrial communities along the bays and rivers of northern Contra Costa County—communities such as Pinole with its giant Union Oil Refinery; Hercules, the former site of a gunpowder plant, now a fertilizer plant; Crockett with its C& H Sugar Refinery; Pittsburg, home to Dow Chemical and Antioch with the Bethlehem Steel Works. It struck me now and then that living and working around here was a chancy thing to do. Nitrate explosions at Hercules, third-degree sugar burns at C & H Sugar, refinery fires and pollution at Shell Oil and God knows what deadly fumes at Dow Chemical.

Adding to the hazards were the military installations scattered about here such as the Concord Naval Weapons Station at Port Chicago, where they once loaded ships with live ammunition during World War II. In 1944, someone dropped a shell and the result was the largest wartime explosion on U.S. soil ever. Hundreds of sailors died. At the time, we lived four miles away on the outskirts of Concord. The blast knocked in our front door and shattered the living room window.

Then there was the Benicia Army Weapons Depot on the north shore of the Suisun Bay, as well as the Mare Island Naval Shipyards near Vallejo. Mr. Kuntz, a neighbor of ours, was a manager at the Army Weapons Depot. He never talked about his work other than telling us the Bay Area was one big, deadly minefield of secret weapons and munitions. Over a beer with my father, Mr. Kuntz once casually remarked, "If the Ruskies ever attacked the Bay Area, the whole place would go up in smoke."

Nevertheless, the Martinez area had been a big industrial playground for me as a kid. I used to bike through Shell Oil Refinery with its cracking towers, miles of twisting pipelines and silver storage tanks dotting the hills. The smell of sulfur and gasoline was strangely addictive. I would continue out on Waterfront Road to the ruins of the Mountain Copper Company on a hill overlooking Suisun Bay. The smelting plant was long gone, but some of the brick chimneys and ovens were still intact, dominating the hill like remnants of an ancient city. Often I sat in the shadow of a chimney and gazed out over Suisun Bay watching the oil tankers plowing along. In the far distance, a mothball fleet of hundreds of old World War II ships sat in a corner of bay, quietly shimmering in the afternoon heat.

Once, I biked over to Port Chicago itself, which had been partially rebuilt after the blast. Most of it was off-limits because it was still a naval weapons station. But the main drag was accessible to the public with its bars, cheap eateries and tattoo parlors. Later, the Navy completely took over Port Chicago and it disappeared as a town. Such had been my industrial playground around Martinez.

***

Before I could start my vacation relief job, I had to fill out a ton of paperwork and take a physical. I was surprised by the reams of legal documents that I was required to sign, and which probably prevented me from suing Dow if I was injured on the job. The plant doctor, a grizzled old-timer who smelled of gin, had me take my shirt off in his office and gave me a quick check-up. He thumped me once or twice on my chest and on my back and declared me fit enough for Dow. When I was done with that, Mrs. Spenser led me to the public relations office to meet a Mr. Olson. I wondered what that was all about, but dutifully sat in his outer office until I was ushered in by his secretary.

Mr. Olson was standing by a picture window looking out on the plant. He was a tall, rotund man with a thick mane of gray hair. He greeted me and shook my hand.

"Glad to meet you, young man. Welcome to the family of Dow," he said in a deep baritone voice that hinted of his broadcasting background, which Mrs. Spenser had mentioned.

"Thank you," I replied, all the while wondering why I, a lowly vacation-relief plant worker, rated such attention. Mr. Olson soon answered my unstated question.

"Allan, we at Dow meet with all our workers, no matter what they do. Because we feel you are joining the Dow family. We like to know our workers and have the chance to explain why Dow is special."

"I see," I said nodding. "From what I know from my brother Don Brown who worked here last year, it's an impressive plant."

"Yes, well this one of two Dow plants in California," said Mr. Olson launching into his well-practiced spiel. "It's the largest integrated chemical manufacturing plant of its kind on the West Coast. We are here primarily to meet the needs of California agriculture by producing herbicides and pesticides. We also produce other chemical products used for carpeting, paints, shampoo and cosmetics as well as an array of chlorine products used in the manufacture of paper. Our scientists in research and development are always looking for new and better ways to improve our chemical lives."

I was having trouble concentrating on this, wondering what it had to do with me. I found it hard not to stare out the window and daydream as Mr. Olson droned on:

"Now, as a vacation-relief employee, you will be a part of this vast enterprise. You will be contributing to Dow productivity by allowing the regular employees to go on a carefree vacation without overburdening their co-workers. As I said, we want our workers to be happy here. And I believe most are happy here, but we do expect them to work hard and follow the instructions of their supervisors to the letter because a chemical plant can be a dangerous place. We will provide you with all the safety instructions necessary and will supply all the proper safety gear, but you will still have to use your head to avoid danger."

About now, I was wishing hard that I had stuck to surveying. I was already getting claustrophobic about this place. I had visions of steamy, hot bubbling vats of poisonous fumes. I wondered if they provided gas-masks.

"Further, you will be required to join the ICWU."

"What's that?" I asked.

"Oh, it's the International Chemical Workers Union that represents most of the plant workers here. We are, after all, a union shop and we have good labor relations. We will deduct the modest initiation fee and dues from your biweekly paycheck."

"Fine!" I said, eager to get of out there.

After a few more platitudes, Mr. Olson checked his watch and announced he had to meet with a science reporter from the *San Francisco Chronicle* who was doing an article on the latest chemical wonder produced by the plant.

***

The work beat began: Up at 6 AM. Pull on a T-shirt and a pair of dirty Levis and slip into my heavy work boots. After a quick breakfast, out on the front porch waiting for my ride to Dow. My co-worker, Ben Brashler, pulls up around 6:40 and off we go.

Ben, a flaming red-haired dude who drives a hopped-up '55 Chevy Bel Aire, burns up the Arnold Industrial Highway. "I can make this fucker in ten minutes flat from Martinez," he says as he stomps down on the accelerator.

Ben is a good guy. He gives me a ride when he doesn't have to. He carpooled with Don last year. I pay for his gas to make up for his inconvenience. Ben is a lab tech who lives in Crockett about ten miles west of Martinez. Although my age, he is already married with two kids. Ben had knocked up his high school girlfriend and married her. He had managed to go to Berkeley for a year in chemical engineering before he dropped out because of money problems. As he often puts it, "Always use a rubber man. Look what a mess I got myself into. A wife and two kids."

We race along Arnold Industrial Highway, the highway that serves the refineries and plants strung along Suisun Bay and the San Joaquin River. The morning sun is right in our face as we head east, bright and blinding as it bounces off the highway. Off to the right Mt. Diablo sits mute, its peaks and ridges casting long shadows over the surrounding foothills, now cool and brown in the morning light. On the flats, one newly minted subdivision follows another. As my father always proudly says, "Contra Costa County is booming. Everybody wants to move over here from the Bay Area because the homes are cheap." As far as I am concerned, I prefer it the way it used to be—small, sleepy towns with a lot of rural space.

Around 6:55 AM, we pull into the Dow parking lot. Ben strolls over to the R&D building and saunters in. He has no time clock to punch. Nobody in R&D cares it if you are a few minutes late. On the other hand, I have to jog to the plant-worker entrance and punch in at 7:00 AM sharp. Once clocked in, I can take my time getting to my work site. Usually, I grab one of the plant bikes from the bike rack and pedal over. Bikes are a handy mode of travel around the plant; they save a lot of walking. By 7:10 AM, everybody is at his appointed post and the Dow workday begins.

***

After a couple of weeks of rolling 400-pound drums into boxcars in Distribution, I moved on to loading 50-pound sacks into trucks at the loading dock. It was boring, grunt work, but the upside was I was getting back into terrific shape. I was a man of iron again with arm muscles rippling. While the work was dull, my co-workers were not. As I mentioned, there was George, an old-timer, somewhere in his fifties. He had been at Dow for years. He was a tough old goat, lean as a rail and agile. "None of those cushy jobs for me, shutting and closing valves," George often said. "Those guys sit on their asses and get fat. Nah, I'll keep active here until they carry me out."

Then there was Al Sanchez, the forklift driver. Al was the unofficial boss in Distribution. The official supervisor, Dan, stayed in his office all day, letting Al run the show. A tall, good-looking Mexican in his mid-thirties, Al was kind of a godfather around here. He was from the Mexican section of Pittsburg and it seemed all his cousins and old high school buddies worked at Dow. In the lunchroom, they sat around and told stories of the old days at Pittsburg High, how Al ran the show, keeping the Negroes at bay. About how great he was in a knife fight. About how he could cut somebody up and never get a scratch on himself. And about how Al never went in for the kill, but would slice up a guy just enough to let him know who was boss.

Al was also the union shop steward and he approached me the first day on the job and checked out my union credentials. As he looked over my temporary card he asked, "You go to school, Brown?"

"Yeah, Berkeley,"

"So, what are you doing here in Distribution?"

"Just a job, Al, to save some cash up so I can go back to college," I answered.

(I hadn't told anybody at Dow that I had dropped out of school to save money for Europe. My cover story was that I was earning money to return to Berkeley.)

"Yeah, it's a bitch I bet paying for school," Al said thoughtfully, handing my card back. "I tried the local junior college once, but dropped out after a semester. A guy like me can't go to school with an ol' lady and three hungry mouths to feed."

"I understand."

Then Al waxed philosophical, "Yeah, I'm not doing too bad. I have a new three-bedroom house, a pick-up truck with a camper van and a sixteen-foot runabout for fishing."

"Sounds good."

"Yeah, it's a good life working here. It sure beats working in the fields like my ol'man and ol'lady used to do. But what the fuck do you know? You're just a college kid out to make a few bucks. You'll probably be my boss in a few years."

"I doubt that," I said. "You'll probably be running Distribution yourself in a few months the way things are going."

"Maybe," said Al as he got back on his forklift. "Now get back on the job, college boy and start humping those sacks."

After a month in Distribution, the call came down. I was to be transferred to the garage to help the mechanic and to drive the plant taxi. When George heard that, he teased me about having friends in high places. "That's a cushy job, driving the plant cab."

"Yeah, but I like it here," I protested. "I like working with you guys. I like the physical labor."

"Don't be a fool, Brown," Al said. "Get out of here. This is a dead end."

"Yeah," said George, "and remember, around here it's not who you know, it's who you blow that gets you ahead."

"Well, pucker up old man," said Al. "I'm going to be heading this joint in no time."

***

I showed up at the plant garage at 7 AM sharp the next day where I met Ralph, the man who ran the garage. Ralph, a sweaty, heavyset man, asked me if I had any experience as a car mechanic.

"None, other than changing tires," I responded.

"Yeah, well, I figured as much. None of you college kids knows how to fix cars. That's O.K. As a mechanic's assistant, you'll be doing grunt work, probably washing cars, cleaning them out and maybe changing oil."

"Fine. I can do that."

"That's only part of the job. Mostly, you'll be on-call to drive the plant taxi, chauffeuring bigwigs around. Dress nice when you come to work, khakis and a pressed shirt. We have overalls here for the dirty work."

"Sure."

And with that, Ralph showed me around the plant garage. It was big with five service bays and several mechanics working on various trucks and cars. I was introduced to the head mechanic, Sam, who gave me the once-over while Dan informed him that I knew nothing about cars.

"Oh well," said Sam, "we have a bunch of vehicles to wash and clean around here when you're not driving the cab."

The first day I was put to work operating a primitive car wash with a power hose that squirted soapy and then clean water. I had a pile of rags to dry the vehicles off. I used a small vacuum to clean the insides. After ten cars and several pick-ups, I was wishing that I had stayed in Distribution. I was soaking wet, my hands were waterlogged and I ached. I was all but ready to walk off the job when the call came that someone needed the plant taxi. Ralph came out to fetch me.

"O.K. Al, you come with me. I'll take you on a tour of the plant with this guy so's you know what to do when you're on your own."

We got into the plant taxi, a big Chrysler sedan with *Dow Taxi* painted on the side, and drove off to the main administration building where we picked up an executive from company headquarters in Midland, Michigan. He was with Mr. Olson who was also the designated tour director of the Pittsburg Dow Plant. The exec, a stiff uptight man in a white short sleeve-shirt and tie, said nothing, nodding only now and then as Mr. Olson went through his spiel about the state-of-the-art plant.

"I'm proud to say that Dow Pittsburg is the primary supplier of pesticides and herbicides to California agriculture. In addition, we are very active in the manufacture of various chlorine products..."

"I am well aware of all of that," interrupted the executive. "What I'm interested in seeing is your R&D department. As I understand it, you are outgrowing the facility and plan to build a regular R&D center somewhere near Walnut Creek. I would like an update on that and to see the plans."

"Yes, that's correct, Mr. Jones," said Olson. "It has been in the planning stage for some time. As you may know, the founder of this plant, Mr. Hirschkind, was research oriented and it's a tradition that we have been carrying on. With all the brainpower in the Bay Area at Stanford and Berkeley, it's a natural orientation."

I dropped them off at the R&D building, a sleek low-slung brick structure with one-way glass windows and white-coated scientists and lab techs going in and out. This was a section of the plant where brother Don had worked and its labs were off-limits to regular plant workers.

Don had been involved in polypropylene, a plastic that Dow was trying to develop into new products. He had run a pilot plant to test its various applications. Later, Don told me he thought he had lost his sense of smell because of exposure to the polypropylene. I was still disappointed that I hadn't become a lab tech. I knew I could do that testing and measuring. Don said it was simple-ass stuff. You only had to be accurate.

After that initial day of car washing, I was busy most of the time driving the taxi and discovered I liked it. I not only carted VIPs around the plant, but I also delivered packages to various departments. I liked the freedom to come and go as I pleased. As long as I delivered everyone and everything to its proper destination, nobody complained. And I was always reachable by car-radio. Also, I was able to get a good look at the plant and gain some insight into its operation and history.

A boy genius named Herbert Dow founded the company in 1897 in Midland, Michigan. His initial goal was to manufacture bleach, but by the early 1900s, Dow was also into agricultural products, producing such items as sodium benzoate as a food preservative and bug killing sprays. In the 1920s and 30s, Dow started manufacturing magnesium and additives for gasoline. During World War II, Dow made synthetic rubber and developed silicone for the military. By the 1950s, chemicals comprised over half of the Dow products, plastics about a third. It was now an international operation with plants in Canada and Europe. Dow had recently introduced a bunch of new products including something called *Handiwrap* for the homemaker. The executives were hoping that it would be a big seller.

***

The taxi gig lasted only a few weeks, and I was transferred again. I was assigned to being a watchman at one of the truck entrances to the plant. My job was to sit in a little shack with wrap-around picture windows overlooking the truck entrance. On the desk was a microphone for an intercom, which I could activate over a loudspeaker to give instructions to the truck drivers. There was also a big red button on a console that opened and closed the gate. I was given a clipboard with log sheets to note the time of entrance and exit of the trucks. I was issued a short-sleeve gray wool shirt and a security badge to pin on it. I also had a regulation security hat with the Dow logo on it. To top it off, I wore a pair of large sunglasses to cut down on the glare and also to look cool. About the only thing missing was a side arm.

I wasn't sure how I got this job. The regular watchman was on an extended leave of absence for some operation, but there were other regular workers on the security patrol who wanted it. I guess in order to avoid the bickering, they gave it to the vacation-relief worker.

The first few days, I diligently sat at attention and duly logged the trucks in and out, but sometimes only two or three trucks came by in an hour. This was boring, so I read the newspaper between trucks. However, that became boring too, so I brought a few books along with some notepaper for doodling. When the head security honcho came by now and then, he didn't care what I did between truck arrivals as long as I didn't sleep on the job, which apparently the main watchman did occasionally.

I had three breaks a day during which time I was relieved by another security guard. The first was a coffee break that I took across the street at the R&D cafeteria. Sometimes I met Brashler and we would chat and compare notes on how the day was going. Then, there was lunch break at the R&D cafeteria or sometimes I brought my lunch and ate it on the R&D patio. Lunch was usually followed by a volleyball game with some of the lab techs. For the afternoon break, I walked around the park-like grounds of the R&D facility, sipping coke.

The volleyball games were the highlight of my day. The lab techs and research scientists were ace volleyball players; jumping, twisting, tipping off and spiking were all a matter of course. The games were wild and exciting. I held my own, but after an hour of this, I was usually wiped-out and dripping wet. I had to go back to the gatehouse all sweaty, but the techs could go shower up in the R&D locker rooms.

The afternoons were the worst. After eating and the volleyball game, I was sleepy and the hot little gatehouse didn't help even with a fan and an open side- window. Temperatures usually shot up to a hundred degrees. By this time, I was stripped to my T-Shirt. But whatever else I did, I couldn't sleep. So, with a cup of coffee in hand, I read or wrote in my journal. I was currently reading the old English Poets — Wordsworth, Coleridge, Shelly, Byron, Burns — all contained in one little volume I found in the back of my father's bookcase. I had never focused on poetry before, but for some reason the English poets with their lyrical descriptions of the cool, green countryside of the British Isles were especially attractive in his hot little booth with the brown foothills of Mt. Diablo shimmering off in the heat:

> *And on that morning, through the grass,*
> *And by the steaming rills,*
> *We traveled merrily, to pass*
> *A day among the hills.*

The Two April Mornings, Wordsworth.

In a more serious mood, I began reading William H. Whyte's *Organization Man*. It was indeed timely that I was reading this as I sat in the gatehouse of a chemical refinery of a major American corporation and contemplated my future. The passage that caught my eye right away was Whyte's description of the new Organization Man as a modern day monk:

> *They are the ones of our middle class who have left home, spiritually as well as physically, to take the vows of our organization life.*

Whyte further observed that most young men drawn to corporate life had to reconcile themselves to do the bidding of their superiors while believing they were pursuing the corporate good.

Hmm. So according to Whyte, in order to make it in this corporate world, I would have to do what somebody else wanted me to do. I would be obliged to live in a suburban tract home, join a country club and play golf with the right people. All of this struck me as a nightmare right out of a John Cheever short story where the main character plays endless rounds of golf, drinks a lot, commits adultery, and in the end, blows his brains out.

Of course, the irony was that at first glance I looked like the perfect candidate for corporate America. I was tall, athletic and fairly intelligent. In addition, I would be a Berkeley graduate. I fit the image of a young Protestant male on the make. In the fraternity, I constantly heard, "Hey, Al. Forget history. What are you going to do with that? Major in Business Administration. That's where the jobs are." That's what my friend Gerard was doing as well as Bill Singleton, who was now being recruited by Standard Oil.

I once went to the Cal placement office looking for a part-time job. I noted the seniors in their button-down suits, all spiffy and perfect and the corporate recruiters in their more expensive button-down suits, all spiffy and perfect. The gray-flannel uniform. It struck me as another form of indentured servitude. I couldn't get excited about selling toothpaste or gasoline or plastic products. Yet, here were these young men (all men) ready to throw their lot in with the corporation, ready to do what it took to launch a career, ready to move cross-country at a moment's notice, ready to blow off California for the dull landscapes and winters of the Midwest or the congestion and expense of the East. No, none of that was for me.

Working at Dow was as close as I wanted to get to large corporate structures. As I kept reminding myself, the only reason I was here was to earn enough money to escape to Europe for a year. It was five months of blue-collar servitude in exchange for nine or ten months of freedom abroad. There was only one nagging detail. I wasn't saving money fast enough. At my current rate I was going to fall short by at least five hundred dollars, dollars that my father couldn't make up, stretched as he was. Somehow, I had to increase my base wage, so after a month in the gatehouse in early July, I approached Mrs. Spenser and told her that I needed to earn more money.

"Earn more money?" she said in mock surprise.

"Yes, at this rate, I am not going to have enough money to go back to Berkeley in the fall." (An outright lie.)

"My, my, Allan that's a shame. However, I can't do anything about your base rate. That's what we pay all the vacation-relief workers in the plant."

"Well, yes. What about one of those jobs that pay a premium over the base wage, such as at the chlorine plant? Those guys are always bragging about how much they make."

"Normally, we don't have vacation-relief workers work in that location because of the safety hazards. You are around chlorine gas, mercury and various other nasties, although we do provide protective gear."

"What does it pay?"

"Oh, I believe fifty percent over base and double time on weekends."

"Good, that's what I need."

"Well, if you're sure, Allan, I will see what I can do."

***

A week later, I found myself dressed from head to foot in a rubber suit with gloves, goggles and a gasmask. I was standing in the cavernous chlorine plant with a power hose in my hands washing down row after row of chlorine cells. These were massive salt encrusted concrete blocks about sixty-feet long and fifteen-feet high. Exactly what went on inside these cells was beyond me, except they used the process of electrolysis with a liberal dose of mercury to separate brine into chlorine and hydrochloric acid. All of this was supposed to occur in a tightly sealed environment to prevent a major leak of these chemicals, which could prove very toxic. Nonetheless, small leaks were common because the concrete blocks often developed cracks and had a rather short lifespan. Hence, my protective gear.

"This is a critical and dangerous job, Al," Mack, the supervisor explained. "Always use your protective gear. You get a whiff of that chlorine gas or a bad acid burn on your arms, you can call it a day."

"So how bad can it be?" I asked.

"It won't be lethal, but you could feel it for days. You might have to take time off. A lot of guys who work long-term here have to go on disability."

"Swell."

"Oh, the other thing, be careful crawling around under the cells. It's easy to get an electric shock on exposed skin. They're pretty mild, but you will feel it. Stay covered up."

"Swell."

"You sure you want to do this, Al?" Mack asked. "You don't have to, you know. This is not normally a job for vacation-relief workers."

I thought about it for a second. "How bad can it be if I follow the safety rules?"

"Not bad at all," said Mack. "You do it only three times a week. You get done early, and you can goof off out back."

So, with visions of time-and-a-half dancing in my head, I plunged ahead into my job of washing down chlorine cells. Initially, it wasn't too bad. The rubber suit was a pain in the ass and on hot days, suffocating. Nevertheless, I dutifully suited up, donned my gloves, goggles and gasmask and set off to wash down the cells.

First, I climbed up to a catwalk that spanned the cells and with my power hose, sprayed the salt formations off the tops. Then I went down to floor level and sprayed the sides and the ends of the cells. Finally, I crawled under each cell with only a three-foot clearance and sprayed underneath. This was the nastiest part of the job: crawling around in the hot rubber suit, with acid-drenched water dripping down and the occasional electrical shock. After a while, I ignored the mild shocks and continued with my work.

It was also underneath a cell that I encountered my first whiff of chlorine gas. Somehow, a slender fume seeped under my mask. Suddenly, I felt a constriction in my chest and it was hard to breathe. I didn't make a big deal of the gassing. I simply crawled back out from under the cell and went out back of the plant for a few minutes to catch a breath of fresh air. Soon I felt better and went back in and continued my job.

Mack had told me to take my time doing the cell-washing job. It was supposed to be an all-day job, four cells in the morning, four in the afternoon, but I figured the quicker I got it done, the less time I spent in my rubber suit. So I reduced the cleaning process down to a quick three hours.

At first, Mack was incredulous. "Shit, Al. There is no way you can do that in three hours."

"Take a look, Mack. Not a trace of salt on those blocks."

Mack carefully inspected the cells and had to agree they looked good, but still objected. "Look, Al, I know you can do it quick. You're young and strong. But it sets a bad precedent for the regular workers who take all-day. If management finds out it's a half-day job, it could put somebody out of work. That would piss off a lot of people around here."

"Yeah, well. I don't fancy staying in a rubber suit all day when I don't have to and running the risk of electric shock to say nothing of getting gassed."

"Like I told you Al, go sit in back on the patio. Read. Sleep. I don't care. Just stay out of sight."

We reached a compromise of sorts. Mack pretended it was an all-day job. I stretched it out to four hours with a long break on the patio in the morning. It was pleasant out there behind the chlorine plant. The patio was nothing fancy, just a large slab of concrete in the shade with a picnic table and a couple of Adirondack chairs. The San Joaquin River ran about fifty yards away, past a strand of bullrushes, gurgling by without a care in the world. Often, there was a cool breeze to cut the heat. In addition to my morning break, I spent most of the afternoon there, reading and staying out of sight. When I became bored reading, I went over to the next building, an abandoned warehouse and rode my plant bike, weaving through rows of pillars. Sometimes, a co-worker, Roberto Gomez, and I raced to see who could get through the pillars first.

When I wasn't washing the cells, I did general janitorial clean up around the plant with Gomez. He was an interesting guy: a short, pudgy Mexican with an amputated hand. Gomez told me his hand had been crushed in a piece of machinery at Dow several years ago.

"Fucker got crunched just like that," he said. "At first it didn't hurt. It wasn't even bleeding much. I didn't believe it had happened. I just stared at my mangled hand and tried to go on with my work."

"No, shit!"

"Yeah, when my co-workers saw that, they nearly fainted. Mack tied my wrist off with a tourniquet to stop the bleeding and called the ambulance. Before I knew it, I was at the Antioch hospital and the doctor cut the sucker clean off. No he way could have saved it, he later told me. Once I got over the shock of losing a hand, it wasn't too bad. I can do almost anything with this hook," he said raising his arm, "and I don't have to worry about getting it crushed."

I examined his hook. It was a stainless steel claw clamp that looked lethal with its cable wires and hooked point. "Strong, I bet," I said.

"Man, I can do stuff like Superman with it. I can twist stuff, pull stuff, punch stuff in. And I never need a can opener to open a can of beer."

"Even so, losing a hand is pretty bad," I said.

"Yeah, but look at it this way, Al. I have a job for life here. Dow will never lay me off 'cause I promised not to sue. I get all the comfortable jobs in the plant. All I do here is wash down the floor, clean up the lunchroom and in general putter around. And, like you, I spend a lot of time out back."

"Roberto, why don't you go on disability and go to school?"

"Yeah, I thought of that. In fact, I did go on disability for a while, but I was bored, so I came back. I also tried Diablo Community College. But that wasn't for me. Shit, I have eight years at Dow already. Someday I will retire from here. I have a great little home in Antioch with a boat, two kids and a wife. I'm happy. I guess I'm just a dumb Mexican who doesn't know any better. I got all I want out of life."

Gomez was anything but dumb. He was an ace chess player and ran the chess tournaments in the lunchroom. I was astonished when I first saw the set up. Row after row of chessboards, all neatly set with the pieces. Chess in this place! I had always thought it was a game for intellectuals. I rarely played chess myself and when I did, I was mediocre at it. Don, of course, was good, my dad even better. I was always checkmated. I could never see the traps coming.

As I soon learned, you didn't need to be a certified intellectual to play great chess. The guys in the chlorine plant were amazing. They played at lightning speed, polishing off at least two games during the fifteen-minute breaks and at least four during the forty-minute lunch break.

When I first played, I was assigned to the rank beginner's row where I slowly and cruelly learned the rudiments of the game as the other players guffawed in glee at the college kid losing his ass. Then as I improved, I advanced to a higher level of competition until I could consider myself midlevel out of the fifty or so who ate lunch here. The one time, I played Gomez who was the reigning champ. He polished me off in about seven moves.

***

So for about a month, I settled down to a routine in the chlorine plant: washing down the cells, janitoring, reading out back, riding the bike in the abandoned warehouse and playing chess. It wasn't a bad life and the money was piling up. With a few double-time days on Saturdays and my regular pay, I had exceeded my goal by several hundred dollars. It was now the second week in August. I had two more weeks to go. Clear sailing, I thought. Then, as luck would have it, I was gassed big time.

It was my own stupid fault. I had stopped wearing the gas mask when I was washing down the tops and the sides of the cells. I always wore it under the cells, thinking that was the most likely time to be gassed. Well, I don't know how it happened, whether it was a crack in the side of the cell or some overheated, pissed off pipe springing a leak, but I received a blast of chlorine gas right in my face. It felt as if somebody had punched me in the chest. I backed off gasping for breath, my eyes tearing, my face burning and stumbled out of the cell section of the plant and over to the first aid station, croaking to Mack that I had been gassed.

"You dumb shit, Brown. I warned you," said a disgusted Mack. "I've seen you working without that mask. It always happens sooner or later."

Mack sat me down in the lunchroom, squirted a saline solution in my eyes and gave me some water to drink. I could breathe, but it was painful.

"You had better go see the plant doc to get a reading on how bad this really is," he said.

A few minutes later, the plant taxi picked me up and took me to the infirmary. The doctor, the old gin-smelling quack, listened to my chest and my breathing, gave me a shot of oxygen and then informed me there was nothing he could do.

"It doesn't sound too bad, Mr. Brown. Take a few days off and rest. Drink a lot of water. It will dissipate and you'll get over it."

I sat in the infirmary reading my *Organization Man* until Brashler finished work and we rode home together.

"Bad shit that chlorine, Al," he said. "That's what they used to gas soldiers with in World War I. Mustard gas, they called it. It was chlorine-based. Wrecked them for life. You know your lungs never get over it. It can cause permanent damage."

"Thanks for the info," I croaked. "That makes me feel a lot better."

"Aw, you'll be all right. If you were gassed badly, you wouldn't be sitting here now. You'd be in the hospital."

***

I lay around at home for two days brooding about how much pay I was missing out on. But the tightness in my chest did lessen, indicating to me that this chlorine gas was getting out of my system. Nevertheless, my mother was worried.

"Allan," she said, "I don't think you should go back and work in that chlorine plant. I don't think it's safe."

"Well, it does have its problems," I said.

"You've enough money saved. You are leaving in two weeks, so why don't you give them notice? You could use the time to get ready."

"Funny, I was thinking the same thing."

In fact, I was ready to leave Dow. It had served its purpose. In addition, I was antsy about the hazards of the chlorine plant. I wanted to quit while I was ahead.

The next morning instead of clocking in, I went to the personnel office and told Mrs. Spenser that I was quitting.

"Quitting?" she exclaimed. "We have you scheduled for two more weeks of employment."

"I know, but something came up, and I have to go out of town for a couple of weeks."

"Couldn't be a vacation could it?" she said with a sly smile.

"No, not at all, just a family obligation thing," I lied.

"Well, I suppose we will manage, but the powers-that-be around here don't like people resigning before their time. I'm sure Mr. Olson will remember that if you apply for next summer."

"As I said this was a special situation."

"I see, Allan," she nodded. "Well good luck to you. By the way, tell Don we will be happy to have him back should he reconsider Dow."

(Don had taken a summer job with the county as a soil-tester.)

"I'll do that. And thanks again for hiring me on for the five months."

And with that, I walked out of the personnel office, out of the Dow Chemical plant with its toxic chemicals and out of my life as a blue-collar plant worker.

23. MONICA

As I was nearing the end of my blue-collar career at Dow and savoring my impending escape to Europe, I got a call from Monica, a young lady I had been seeing for the past two months. I was sitting on the back patio sipping a beer after a hard day in the chlorine plant, watching the shadows lengthen on the hills behind our house. Mom and Dad were off somewhere. Don was over at a friend's house and Kenny, now almost ten, was zooming up and down the block on his bike. It was hard to lead an independent life living at home but I was trying. All I had to do was check my savings account booklet with $1700.00 neatly inked in by the bank teller to know that I made the right decision. *One-thousand-seven-hundred big ones.* I could hardly believe that I had saved that much since April. Despite its hazards, I was grateful the chlorine plant had put me over-the-top. So as I sipped my brew and squinted into the sun fast sinking behind the hills, I was at peace. I was going to make it. Or so I thought until the call came.

"Hi, Allan. This is Monica."

"Oh yeah. Hi, Monica," I said, feeling guilty I hadn't talked to her for a while. "How are you doing?"

"Not too good, Allan. I'm two weeks late with my period, and I don't feel very well in the mornings."

"Whaa...!"

"Yes, I know. I'm probably being silly. Periods are not always reliable. Still, I'm scared. Can you come over?" she asked in a small little voice.

"Sure. We'll go for a drive and sort this out," I said trying to sound cheerful and unconcerned. "I'll see you in ten."

I hung up the phone in a daze. No period in two weeks? That can't mean anything. Girls are always losing track of their periods. I had always used a condom with Monica. Or had I? I remember once about a month ago, after a swim at the Forest Hills pool on a hot Sunday afternoon, we had gone back to her place to cool off in her air-conditioned house. Nobody was home. Her parents and little brother were gone for the day to San Francisco. Before we knew it, we were both out of our wet bathing suits and on Monica's big feather bed. She was hot to go, twisting and moaning around like a cat in heat. Her brown, suntanned body sucking me in like a vortex. Before I knew it, it was over, and I realized that I had forgotten to use a rubber. The unused Trojan three-pack was still tucked away in my jeans. 'Oh shit,' I thought at the time. When I mentioned that perhaps she should douche, she said, "Don't be silly. I just had my period. I'm not fertile now."

"Oh," I said. "That's good." And I promptly forgot about it and started going back for seconds, but not before I fetched my three-pack.

***

I had spotted Monica at the Forest Hill pool in early June. It was one those blazing hot days that still sizzled in the late afternoon. I had Brashler drop me off at the pool instead of going home. As I came out of the dressing room, I noticed Monica sitting there on the lawn on a red-stripped beach towel, catching the last good tanning rays of the sun. She was wearing a Jack-n-Jill swimsuit, looking cute with her dark hair and long, smooth, legs upon which she was smearing suntan lotion. As I walked by, I caught a glimpse of her full breasts as she concentrated on rubbing the lotion in. I put my towel down a few yards a way and dove into the pool, the cool water feeling great after a day in that stifling plant. I swam around for a while and then got out. As I returned to my towel, I waved at her and she waved back.

"How you doing?"

"Fine," she smiled. "Just trying to keep up my tan. It's hard when you work."

"I know what you mean," I said. "Want some company?"

"Sure."

I moved my towel over to her and continued the conversation, but all the time I was drinking her in. God, she looked sexy. I couldn't keep my eyes off her. Monica didn't seem to mind. She smiled, leaned back and closed eyes in the sun.

I had been in a funk since Ana and I had broken up a couple of months ago. She had gone off to Daly City to live with her doctor aunt for the summer and work in San Francisco. I was definitely in need of some female companionship. As if on cue, Monica appeared on the scene.

I knew Monica from high school. She had graduated a year behind me. She was heavier back then but still cute and had gone steady with several boyfriends. A year ago, she went out with my old high school friend, Bob, who told me she was hot stuff, but that all she wanted to do was get married, something he definitely didn't want to do. He even described the mole on her inside thigh. So I had an idea of what I was getting into. I knew that I should probably stay away and not complicate my life. But I was lonely and horny, so when I saw her there on that beach towel with her tan thighs disappearing into her Jack-n-Jill shorts, culminating into a dark, unseen place, I was besotted. Even so, I tried to keep my cool and carry on a nonchalant conversation.

"What are you doing this summer?" I asked.

"Oh, I'm a receptionist at the Pittsburg Health Clinic."

"Really? I work in Pittsburg too. At Dow Chemical. I'm a plant worker."

"Yeah, I can see that you must being doing something like that," she said checking me out. "You're in good shape."

"Yeah, that comes from rolling 400-pound barrels all day long."

"What are you doing at Dow, Allan? I thought you were going to school. Berkeley wasn't it?"

"Yeah, I was. But I'm taking some time off. I'm going to school in France next fall."

"France. My, that will be nice. I'd love to see France. I have some French blood in me. My father was originally from Montreal. I took French in high school, but I can't say much, just *Bonjour, Au revoir.*"

"That's about as much as I can say. I'm not too strong in French myself, but I hope to gain some fluency over there." I said leaning back on my elbows, admiring her strong smooth back. I knew Monica was a competitive swimmer. She had been on the Alhambra swim team and had the swimmer muscles to show for it. In fact, I had heard she had been offered a swimming scholarship to Oregon State, but for some reason never took it. Instead, she had gone to Diablo Valley Community College, but now from what I gathered, she had given up on school.

"I'm afraid I'm not much of student," she eventually told me. "I can never concentrate. I just want to get on with life, earn some money and buy a new car. Right now, all I have is my mother's old rattletrap Ford, but it gets me to and from work."

"So how do you like working in a doctor's office?" I asked

"Oh, it's neat. I wear a little uniform. My job is to smile at people and do light office work. One of the doctors is cute. He keeps smiling at me."

"Sounds as if there might be an opportunity there," I kidded.

"Oh...don't say that. That's what my mother says. I don't want to get married yet. I just want to have fun. Once I buy my car, my girlfriend and I are going to save up to go to Hawaii. Maybe I'll find a job there. Then I can swim all I want and never have to worry about rain or foggy weather."

So that's how it started. On our first date, I tried to impress Monica with my college status. I took her over to Berkeley. We wandered around campus and then had pizza and beer at La Vals. Next, both feeling slightly tipsy, we went to an "art" movie at the Northgate Theater. I don't remember what we saw because half way through the movie, Monica started running her fingers up and down my thigh. Then as if by mutual, unspoken consent, we left the movie theater and drove up Hearst Avenue to the Lawrence Radiation lab parking lot, which had a spectacular nighttime view of the bay. But we didn't pay much attention to the view. All was going well until I reached for her breast.

"Easy, Allan. I heard about you."

"Heard? What did you hear?"

"I heard you were fast. A big lover man on campus."

"Who told you that? Bob?"

"Well, yeah and others. You know girls talk. I heard something from Judy who goes to Berkeley too."

"All hearsay. I'm always a gentleman."

"I bet," she said, squeezing my crotch.

***

Looking at Monica, you would never suspect. I mean she didn't look slutty at all. She was slim, yet voluptuous in the right places, well-groomed and nicely dressed. And she wasn't at all stupid. I bugged her constantly to start taking classes again at Diablo Valley. I suggested a pre-nursing course. I thought she would make a great nurse. But she complained that she didn't like to study. She only wanted make money and drift along until Mr. Right came along.

After hanging around her house for a couple of weeks, I began to understand Monica a little better. She took after her mother, Delores. Bob had told me a few things about Delores. Even though she was pushing forty, she was still very attractive. Middle-aged men panted after her shamelessly, and she seemed to enjoy the attention. Delores was slim and shapely at a time when most women her age were dumpy. She managed Chic-Vogue, a pseudo-French clothing store on Main Street in downtown Martinez. She was always beautifully dressed and had a chic hairdo and a flirtatious smile. Bob swore she came on to him once and that he could have screwed her if he wished. The husband, number three, was in his late fifties, a thin, innocuous little man who made a living selling industrial steam boilers up and down the West Coast. He was out of town a lot. Once, Delores had a few neighbors over when I was there with Monica. Most of them were men. Their wives were somehow, unable to attend. Delores served wicked rum punch along with Hawaiian appetizers and played South Seas music. Before long the laughter was raucous, and I swear when she passed by some potbelly guy who owned a car dealership, she squeezed his crotch. The guy grinned and patted Delores on the ass. Now I knew where that came from. Like mother, like daughter.

Another time, Monica and I came home late from a date and were sitting on their front room couch. Thinking the parents were asleep, she was giving me the business. Right in the middle of the proceedings, Delores paddled by in her bathrobe and slippers, glanced down, smiled and kept on going. Monica didn't miss a beat. What kind of family was this? I was ready to bolt before the old man was alerted and came out with a shotgun.

"Relax, don't worry, Allan. My mom is cool," cooed Monica

Other than a few of these little idiosyncrasies, the family appeared normal. Their house was lovely with all the latest gadgets, including a big color TV, a landscaped backyard with room for a pool that the old man was going to put in. (He made good money selling those industrial steam boilers.) Monica had a charming little ten-year-old brother, Danny, whom she loved dearly. After being an only child for ten years, she was eager to become a little mother to him. I played catch with Danny and one board game or another. The family didn't appear at all put out that I was hanging around so much. As far as they were concerned, I was the new boyfriend and maybe it would develop into something. The fact that I told them I was planning on going to Europe didn't faze them. Dolores simply said, "Well a year is not forever. What are you going to do when you get back?"

" Graduate from Berkeley, I suppose. Maybe go to law school."

"Oh, yes, law school is a good idea," she said nodding in approval. "Lawyers in Martinez do very well. Of course, that's three years and it's expensive. Many law students marry and have the little wife work to help put them through."

"So I've heard," I said. "But right now I'm concentrating on getting through a year in France."

"So you are, but plans have been known to change," she said with a wink.

***

Slowly, slowly, I was descending into a sexual fog, something like the fog of war. Europe seemed more distant and unreal than ever. Worse, I was starting to feel it might be a big waste of time and money. Maybe her mom was right. I needed to get on with my life. Now and then, I seriously considered forgetting Europe, returning to Berkeley in the fall and settling down with Monica. I had only three more semesters at Berkeley and then I could go to law school. With Monica working, I would have the means to go. Life would be simple. Berkeley girls like Ana were too complicated. They were so ambitious. The allure of a sweet, sexy working wife whose main goal was simply to help her man was tantalizing indeed. Also, I felt there was hope for Monica intellectually. She wasn't stupid, simply not curious. Maybe I could show her the way, improve her *Pygmalion* style. I would be her Professor Higgins.

Monica sensed my change of heart and as if to further convince me, the next time we went out, we did it all night on an old army blanket on a hillside orchard in the moonlight. Monica shone in the moonlight, her smooth tanned skin glowing, her perfect, full breasts vibrant and her crotch warm and inviting.

A week later, we were pinned. I sensed that Monica had been hoping for an engagement ring, but she had to settle for my fraternity pin. I carefully explained to her that in college life, it was an important first step to pin a girl before engagement. I promised her that an engagement ring would follow.

"Well, if you're sure," she said fondling the diamond-encrusted pin that spelled AKL. It's beautiful."

"I'm sure," I said, not being at all sure.

It was about this time we did it in her bedroom, and I forgot to use the rubber. And hence, my problem now.

Monica had just spent a week in Oregon visiting her natural father. I had used the time to clear my head. I had received my final packet of material from the Institute in Aix-En-Provence. After thumbing through it, checking out the glossy photos of ancient Aix, the carefree life of the cafes and the dozens of attractive, exotic looking European women on the main drag, the Cours Mirabeau, I realized I had to go. The departure date was only two weeks away. Monica could wait. I was sure she would listen to reason. I was about to tell her all of that when the call came.

I drove over to her house and we went on a ride in the hills. Monica didn't say much. She was pale and tired looking. I joked that Oregon wasn't a good place to maintain a tan.

"I don't care. I don't want a tan anymore. I won't be wearing a bathing suit anyway."

"Hey, don't jump to conclusions. Periods are often late."

"I know but this time it's different. I know I'm pregnant. I can feel it."

I didn't say anything. I looked at her. "We'll get through this together," I said trying to reassure her, but I don't think she was reassured. I think she was waiting for the "I love you, let's get married" line that I wasn't about utter at this point.

"Why don't you go to your doctor and find out for sure?"

"I was planning to do that. In fact, I have an appointment tomorrow."

"Come here, I said trying to reach over and kiss her. She gave me a little peck on the lips and started crying.

"Shit! Shit! Shit! I don't know what I am going to do. You have your Berkeley or maybe Europe for all I know. I just know I'm going to be left alone."

"No, you're not. I'll stand by you. Now let's not get too carried away and go see the doctor."

I dropped her off and waited anxiously for a call.

Finally, the call came two days later.

"Allan," said a sad little voice. "My period came."

"It did? That's great! See, all that worry for nothing."

"No, it wasn't like that. I went to see the doctor and he gave me something to start my period. It hurt like hell, but boy, did it come."

"What do you mean? Were you pregnant or not?"

"I don't know if I was. He never said. He just gave me this pill and a few hours later, I had these horrible cramps and out came all this bloody stuff."

Hmm... I was wondering if Monica had been pregnant after all. I had heard about Berkeley doctors giving pill to co-eds in the first weeks of pregnancy to abort the fetus. But I didn't want to think about that. I didn't want to think about some blob of flesh that could be part of me being flushed down the toilet. The important thing was Monica wasn't pregnant now. I was still free. "So when can we get together again?" I asked.

"I don't know, Allan. I feel drained. Call me in a couple of days."

I did call a few days later, and we went out on a date as if we had just met. Monica was cool. There was barely a kiss. After a boring movie in Orinda and a milkshake at the local drive in, Monica said, "Allan, I have to talk to you.

"Yes."

"I don't think you're ready to settle down. I think you still want to go to Europe."

I began to protest that it wasn't true but it was. Monica had a good sixth sense.

"No, hear me out. I've been thinking. I think we need some time away from each other. As you said, nine months isn't forever. If what we feel is real, we should feel it nine months from now."

"O.K., yeah sure."

"So I'm giving you your pin back. I want you to be free to decide what to do without pressure from me."

I was secretly relieved, but then realizing that my fine piece of ass would no longer be available, I said. "Well, can't we see each other for the next couple of weeks before I leave?"

"Well, if you want. But don't expect all the hot times we had because I couldn't bear you leaving then. Now I feel strong. Maybe it would be better if we cooled it now. It'll be easier on both of us that way."

"We don't have to decide now," I tried to reason. "I'll give you a call in a few days." I kissed her like a sister before dropping her off.

***

A week later, I ran into Bob downtown after work. He was looking bad these days. He had dropped out of Diablo Valley Community College and was working at Monsanto as a plant worker. Bob was in a dirty T-shirt and torn Levis and he hadn't shaved for days. I thought he had been drinking. "Hey, Al, how's Monica these days?"

"O.K. I guess. I haven't seen her recently."

"Yeah, I heard about you and her. Great piece, huh?"

"Shut up, Bob."

"Oooh. Don't be so touchy. It always ends with her sooner or later."

"Ends? What ends?"

"Oh, you haven't heard? She's been going out with Craig Gordon. Good old Craig—jock, smart guy, going to San Jose State. Wants to be a doctor."

"Gordon?"

"Yeah, she has been going out with him for the past two weeks. Rumor is it's hot and heavy."

"No shit!" I said amazed. Had she been playing a double game? I remember her mentioning something about Gordon's sister being a friend and about Craig, a junior at San Jose State. But I thought nothing of it. After an initial twinge of jealousy and a few flash images of Craig screwing her eyes out, I realized that this was my ticket out of our relationship, guilt free. I thanked my lucky stars that I hadn't been sucked into the Monica trap.

***

A few days later, I received another fateful call from Monica.

"Allan, my little brother, Danny, is dead."

"Dead? What do you mean dead?" I asked, thinking this must be some joke.

"He was hit by a truck yesterday while crossing Arnold Industrial Highway on his bike," she said with a sob.

"Jeeze, Monica. I don't know what to say. That's awful. How did that happen?

"We aren't sure. He was riding with some other kids. Maybe they were racing, not paying attention to the traffic."

"Do you want me to come over?"

"Oh, no. This place is a madhouse with relatives. I just wanted you to know. I still can't believe it myself. The funeral is Friday at the Taylor Funeral Home if you want to come. I have to go now."

I put down the phone. All at once my head was spinning. I had seen Danny over at the Forest Hill pool a few days ago, alive and full of energy. He had asked me when I was coming over to see him. He said he missed me. The thought of that hurt badly. That night I wrote in my journal:

> *Alive one minute, dead the next. Danny ceased to exist. He left a small void in the life stream that will gradually fill in again, but a void, which is still an immense hole in the hearts of the Murels. Still, I believe that Danny will continue to exist in whatever form or wherever. But he was Monica's heart and joy. Her precious only brother. Now she is back to being an only child.*

The funeral chapel was overflowing with family, Danny's little friends and fresh cut flowers. It was a perfect little boy's funeral. All his baseball teammates sat in the front row in their Little League uniforms, like little old men, solemn and understanding. The minister's talk was simple, yet deep. He assured us all that there was another life for Danny. And that God gives back much more than he takes.

Following the funeral, I got in line and gave my condolences to the family, giving Monica a hug and telling her to be brave. She looked at me through teary eyes and gave me a weak smile, but said nothing. I also saw Craig Gordon standing off to the side, looking cool and blond in his blue seersucker suit. I ignored him.

That was the last time I saw Monica before I left for Europe. Danny's death was the fatal and final punctuation to our relationship. It was obvious that she had been going out with Gordon behind my back, but I didn't care. I felt sorry for her losing her little brother like that, but I was relieved that I had escaped the sweet honey trap.

***

A year later, after I returned from Europe, I ran into Monica in the Bank of America parking lot. I hardly recognized her. She was now fat with a spotty complexion and very pregnant. Her left hand sported a big diamond engagement ring and a modest wedding ring. She had obviously hooked Gordon.

"Long time no see," I said.

"Yes, indeed, Allan. As you can tell, a lot has happened in the past year," she blushed.

"How many months?"

"Oh, about seven. We think it's a boy because it's so big."

"So you married Craig?"

"Oh yes. He's wonderful and ambitious. He's a senior now at San Jose State. He comes home on weekends. You know, he plans to go to medical school. I'm going back to work after the baby is born and help him. We're going to have a good life."

"I'm sure you will Monica. I wish you and Craig all the luck. You're a sweet and wonderful person," I said hugging her. "I'm sorry the timing was so bad for us. Also, I still think of little Danny and your loss. Maybe the baby can help make up for that."

"Funny, I was thinking the same thing," said Monica as she stared off into space with a little smile. Then she added, "So did you find a nice little French girl over there?"

"Oh, no. I'm back, unattached."

"I'll bet."

We hugged again, and I walked off down street to run some errands.

24. EUROPA

A few days after my encounter with Monica, I sat on my patio, sipping wine and watching the sunset behind the hills while I pondered if Europe had been worth all the hassle, time and expense. Here, it was August of 1962. I had missed three semesters of Cal, had spent over four thousand dollars and had come down with mononucleosis from which I was still recovering.

On the other hand, I did manage to secure twenty-six units credit from the Institute that Cal had accepted — almost a full year's credit. Although I could theoretically graduate at the end of the fall semester, it would mean taking a heavy course load of eighteen units. I decided to go another full year at Berkeley.

When my mother met me at the Oakland Airport upon my return, she was shocked at my appearance. She said she barely recognized me. I was pale and I had lost twenty pounds. Also, I was listless. She later told me she was sure Europe had wrecked my health. After a visit to the family doctor who prescribed rest and a healthy diet with large doses of vitamins, I began to gain weight but continued to feel listless.

"Mononucleosis takes a long time to recover from," said Dr. Bradshaw. "It could take months."

"Will I be well enough to go back to school?" I asked.

"If you take it easy."

So how did I get mono? I wasn't sure. It was supposed to be a kissing disease. Maybe I had kissed the wrong girl, although I spent the last few months in France hanging out with Bobbie, who was healthy as a horse. I stared at a photo of her taken at the bullfights in the Camargue, the delta region where the Rhone River meets the Med. She had been running around a *corrida* with a small bull chasing her. Her face was streaked with dust, her blonde hair blown askew, but she had a broad smile across her wholesome Midwestern face.

No, the mono was probably not from her. I thought it was a combination of poor food, running around, traveling on the cheap, sleeping upright in stuffy train compartments and bad luck. I knew a few other students who had suffered from mono. The French called it *la grippe*. I had seen a French doctor and after examining me, he shrugged and prescribed some antibiotics. That helped, but I still stayed in bed for two weeks recovering in May, almost missing my finals. My landlady, Madam Vachyran, took care of me, cooking me meals that were healthier than the student restaurant food. The American Institute was so concerned that they considered shipping me home. But I talked them out of it since the semester was nearly over.

Finally, I got out of bed, took my exams and packed to travel to Paris and London before flying home. I hadn't fully recovered, but I had enough juice and enthusiasm to get through my last two weeks in Europe. Traveling with Bobbie and her friend Joan, we hitchhiked to Paris from Aix. With two attractive blondes at my side, hitchhiking was a breeze. Truck drivers screeched to a halt. We preferred trucks because they were usually on a long haul, and we could cover a lot of ground in one ride. Getting to Paris took only a day. We found a cheap hotel with three beds in the Latin Quarter. Then with Bobbie's art history book in hand, we toured the City of Light—the Louvre, the Jeu de Paume, the Eiffel tower and the Champs-Elysées. Paris was impressive, yet I was glad that I hadn't spent my time abroad here. Americans were everywhere and in some places English seemed to be the predominant language.

On our third day, we went to the American Express office so Bobbie could pick up some cash from home. While she was standing in line, a short stocky guy with a crew cut tapped her on the shoulder. Bobbie turned around, went white and then blushed.

"Oh, Tommy!" she shrieked. "I can't believe it." She gave him a hug. Obviously, Tom was an acquaintance.

Bobbie introduced "Tommy" as an old neighborhood friend who was now in the U.S. Naval Academy. I also knew that "Tommy" was an old flame of hers who hadn't paid her the slightest bit of attention. Tom was on a two-week leave touring around Europe with some shipmates. Before I knew it, Bobbie and Joan had invited Tom to join us and he had accepted, unceremoniously ditching his buddies. I had nothing to say about this.

This didn't bode well. Old flame, huh? Maybe that flame was about to rekindle.

Bobbie and I had sort of a relationship. She described it as a "friend-ship" and indeed that was what it was until we took a trip to Greece together in April for three weeks. Initially, Joan was supposed come along, the happy threesome, but Joan decided to go to North Africa with her aunt and Bobbie still desperately wanted to see Greece. We were supposed to go as *friends*. I was to be her protector from Greek men. I protested saying that I didn't have the money to go to Greece and was in fact planning a cheap trip to Barcelona, Spain. But she offered to loan me a few hundred dollars as long as I paid it back when I returned home. So, it was a deal I couldn't refuse. When my French friends heard about the impending trip, they immediately assumed it was to be a *voyage de noces* – a honeymoon. I tried to set them straight, but they would have none of it. They were convinced that Bobbie and I were an item.

Early April, we were on a train to Brindisi, Italy, to catch a boat to Piraeus, the port city of Athens. It was three weeks of touring Athens, Crete, Rhodes and Mykonos. Three weeks of museums, ruins, cool dips in the Aegean, waterfront meals, ouzo, retzina and impromptu parties staged by dancing Greeks crazed by the sight of an attractive, happy-go-lucky American blonde. In addition, it did turn out to be an informal *voyage de noces* for us, which later proved to be a problem for Bobbie, a staunch Catholic who was having trouble reconciling the temptations of the flesh with teachings of the church.

"Not to worry," I would proclaim. "You are too cute to go to hell."

"Ohhh, I know, but I was supposed to save myself for marriage," she lamented.

"Marriage. That's an idea. Why don't we get married and run away and join the Peace Corps after we graduate?" I said half-kidding.

Her reaction: "Ah...Allan. This is serious. You're not Catholic. You would have to join the church and our children would have to be raised Catholic. And I want a lot of children, five or six at least."

Gulp. I dropped the subject. Of course, I didn't want to marry. I simply wanted to cruise along, let things flow and see how it would all turn out. Just enjoy each other while we were here. That was why I was traveling again with Bobbie to Paris and England, trying to recapture some of what we had had in Greece. However, Tom's appearance complicated the situation.

Bobbie was bawling her eyes out once we returned to the hotel. By now, we had split up into two rooms, Bobbie and I in one, Tom and Joan in the other. Tom, being no fool, had immediately realized what was going on and suddenly took an interest in Joan, who was willing and waiting, and had no hang-ups about religion. Now, Bobbie was upset at Joan for being so easy. The old flame was indeed revived.

"He never, ever looked at me," she bawled. "All through elementary school and high school I had a crush on him. He never took me out. I went out with a lot of boys, flaunting and flirting around. He didn't care. Oh, he would come over sometimes as a friend, and we would play cards, ride bikes or whatever. He acted as if we were only neighborhood friends."

"Why are you so upset, then? Let it die," I said.

"I can't. I still care for him," she sniffed.

"Care for him. What about me? You're here in Paris with me, remember? We spent three weeks together in Greece. Remember. What am I, chopped liver?"

"Oh," she sobbed. "You're different, Allan. You're from California. I'm only a passing phase with you. You've been around a lot of girls. We were convenient for each other."

"Is that all?" I said.

She looked at me with her big blue-green eyes, "Well, maybe not," she said as we sunk back on the rickety bed.

And that's how the rest of the sojourn went. We left Paris for London, taking the cross-channel ferry. Tom and Joan appeared to be clicking. Bobbie suppressed her jealousy, and we made it a point to stay at two different bed-and-breakfast places. We met at a local pub before setting off downtown for a round of museums and sights. London was a comfortable town. The pubs were like a second home, but it was all too familiar for me. I was broke by now. I didn't want to borrow more money from Bobbie, so I decided to call it a trip and fly home.

At the last minute, I found out the new "threesome", Tom, Joan and Bobbie, had big plans to tour northern England and Scotland before they returned to Chicago. There wasn't much I could do about that. I had an uneasy feeling that old flames might revive once again, even though I had promised Bobbie that I would visit her in Chicago before school started next September.

That was the end of Europe for me. I took the cross-channel ferry over to Belgium and then the train to Luxembourg where I boarded an Icelandic Airline plane and flew to New York and eventually home.

***

In addition to the twenty-six credits from my year abroad in France, I learned some French and could speak it on an elementary level. *Café français,* I called it.

When I first arrived in Aix, I lived with a family in their eighteenth century villa about four miles outside town. The villa was set off the main road in hot, dry, rolling brown hills that reminded me of the back-country in Southern California. The father, M. Puyer, a professor of Greek and an archeology buff spoke English, but his wife and three small children did not. I had two weeks before school started, so I spent some of the time babysitting and playing with the kids and learning "little kid" French. It was a happy place and certainly picturesque with old ruins about, crumbling walls and a daily gathering of monks outside the walls of the villa where they picnicked on cold cuts, baguettes and drank large quantities of wine. The meals Madame Puyer fixed were simple but delicious with plenty of fresh fruits and vegetables, roasted wild game and exotic cheeses. This, along with beer and wine and my comical attempts at speaking French made for many memorable meals. Under the direction of M. Puyer, I spent my days exploring the local ruins, piles of rocks, really. At other times, I traveled the back roads of the area on a small, motorized bicycle called a Velox that I had bought. For two weeks, I was indeed a happy camper.

However, there were major drawbacks to this living arrangement. First, my room on the third floor was a monk's cell, barely furnished with a lumpy bed, a chair and a rickety table. That lumpy bed was soon giving me backaches. Second, another Institute student had arrived from Alabama two weeks after me. He spoke atrocious French with a deep Southern accent and tried to hog all the conversations in French. He was annoying. I was no longer the center of attention. After a month of this, I decided that it was time to find my own place in town in the center of the student action.

In order to procure a room from the Institute's housing office, I had to undergo an interrogation as to why I was leaving the Puyer household. I told the director, Dr. Maza, that I simply wanted to live in town and have better access to the French students, which I thought would improve my French. He pointed out how embarrassing it was to the Institute since they had assured my continued residence at the Puyer's for the entire academic year. In addition, he pointed out the financial sacrifice the Puyer's would have to undergo until the Institute could provide them with another student. I said I was sorry about that, but I needed to be living on my own downtown. Finally, he relented and let me go.

Once ensconced in a large room off the main boulevard, the Cours Mirabeau, I settled down and studiously avoided hanging out with

American students. Instead, I became involved with a group of *Pieds-noirs*—French students from Algeria. They weren't as uptight as the regular French students and were friendly with Americans. After a few weeks, my ears tuned in to their accent, and I could carry on a simple conversation.

A few who spoke some English also used my presence to justify French control of Algeria. They considered Algeria merely another department of France. After all, France had run Algeria since 1830.

"Just as Texas is part of the U.S., so Algeria is part of France. *La même chose*," they said.

I would diplomatically remind them the native Algerians who had been conducting seven years of guerrilla warfare, had other ideas.

"Remember your own history," they countered. "You exterminated hundreds of thousands of Indians. Then you pushed the Indians onto reservations and took over the West. Algeria is part of France."

I simply nodded.

Remember, this was the fall of 1961. Plastic bombs were blowing up all over France, including in Marseille and Aix. One of the cafes on the Cours Mirabeau had been demolished by such a bomb late one night after it closed. No one was hurt but anxiety ran high.

One day, French President, Charles De Gaulle, came to town and spoke before a crowd in front of the Hotel de Ville (City Hall). The whole town held its breath, certain that something awful would happen to him, convinced that assassins were on the prowl. But there De Gaulle stood, on a podium right out in the open with little apparent security. I was a mere twenty feet away in the crowd. He spoke very slowly in French. I could understand every word. The gist of what he said was Algeria would soon be set free from French rule. He had already granted them the right to vote on their independence.

"Heresy," said the *Pieds-noirs*. However, by the summer of 1962, Algeria had indeed voted for its independence.

Sensing the inevitability of Algerian independence, many *pied-noir* students never returned to their comfortable middle-class homes in Oran or Algiers after the 1961 Christmas break. They were now a bitter bunch and kept to themselves, avoiding me entirely. I began hearing rumors of what had gone on over Christmas vacation. Supposedly, some of the *pied-noir* guys had gone hunting for Arabs in the countryside, randomly shooting them down as if they were rabbits. Later came the stories of torture performed by the OAS, the secret military organization of French elite commandos determined to maintain French control of Algeria.

By this time, I was hanging out with another group of French colonials from Indochina and various African countries. The Indochina group was comprised of the sons and daughters of French military officers and other French officials left over from the days of French glory in Vietnam. They were still bitter about their defeat at Dien Bien Phu in 1954, which had led to the partition of the country into North and South Vietnam. Some of these students were exotic half-breeds, a mix of French and Vietnamese. The woman were beautiful with their Eurasian features but reminded me of miniature little dolls. I wanted someone more robust, and I found her in the person of Madeleine.

Madeleine was the daughter of a French doctor in Madagascar. She was hang-loose, not uptight like the French girls were. Tall, buxom, with ravishing red hair, freckles and small dark classes that she wore on the tip of her nose giving her a sassy look. She looked me over and called me *"Le grand américain,"* apparently deciding I was worthy of her time.

We spent hour after hour at *Les Deux Garçons* while she filled me in on the glories of Madagascar, the climate, the tropical breezes, the beaches, the exotic mix of French, African, Arab and Asian cultures, the unique wildlife of lemurs, chameleons and various other lizards. But despite all of that, she lamented that it was boring to live there and how happy she was to escape to Aix-En-Provence. Also, she spoke passable English, the result of frequent visits to Kenya and South Africa as well as British tourists coming to Madagascar. However, we managed to conduct most of routine conversations in elementary French.

> *"Ça va?"*
> *"Ça va bien."*
> *"On sort ce soir?"*
> *"Peut-être."*
> *"On va au cinéma?"*
> *"Oui, bien* sûr."

Of course, some of these conversations were conducted in my room where Madeleine had no qualms about taking it all off and feeling at home in bed. It was her tropical upbringing, she explained. All of this might sound great for a young man abroad in France. As my old French teacher Reginald said, the best way to learn French was to learn it in bed with a *juene fille* or whomever. Nevertheless, there was some culture shock involved.

First, I noticed that most French women didn't shave their legs or under their arms. Hairy legs didn't look too bad, but when they put on nylons, which most did, their legs looked bizarre, even disgusting, especially if the hair was dark. Blonde hair was better. Madeleine had darkish blonde hair on her legs, but since she didn't wear nylons, it was O.K.

However, the underarm hair was too much. At first, I thought it was gross and tried to ignore any display of such. This coupled with the bathing habits of the French at that time initially dismayed me. Most took a bath or shower only once a week. The rest of the time, they washed up at a sink or the *bidet*. As a result, in a smoky, closed café, the air became pungent. Of course, eventually, I became used to it since I was only showering or bathing once a week myself. To do so involved a trek to the bathhouse about a mile away, which wasn't an appealing prospect during a bitter cold winter with the Mistral howling down the streets.

Anyway, I managed to overcome the hairy aspect of things and in truth, Madeleine was very clean, being brought up in the tropics where daily bathing was routine. During my time with her, my French did make rapid progress, but alas, she went home for Christmas and never returned to Aix because her mother fell ill and her father needed her there. I did receive an exotic postcard inviting me to Madagascar. It depicted a lemur swinging in a tree in the foreground and the old town of Fort Dauphin in the background.

***

After Christmas, I started spending more time with other foreign students—the Germans, the English and the Dutch. All spoke English and were more fun to be around than the French. We had some great parties, because after all, Aix was known as a party school and all were here to have a good time and learn a little French.

My personal party scene started when one of my French friends, Jean-Michel, told me he had some hot records and a phonograph, but he needed a place to party. He suggested my room because it was so centrally located. So, one Saturday night, the word went out and before I knew it, at least forty people were crammed into my room dancing the twist. The landlady later told me plaster was falling from her ceiling and cautioned me about being too noisy. The downstairs bar provided all the wine that we needed.

One group of students was especially party prone—the English. Too stupid or too lazy to go to school in England, they spent a year in Aix having fun. Most were from well-off families, including Toby who always wore a blazer, an ascot and white pants. There was also Elizabeth who was truly beautiful in a peaches-and-cream way. She liked to drink and make out.

All I can remember of one such party was a bunch of English bodies writhing on my big double bed groping one another in intimate spots.

Most of the French watched with a mixture of shock and amusement, except for Jean-Michel who had joined in and was barely visible in the mess. Just as I was about to settle down with Elizabeth, Bobbie and Joan showed up at my door, saying they heard there was a party. At the time, I think I had Elizabeth on my lap and my hand under her sweater. Both Bobbie and Joan looked on in horror at the squalid scene and left. Bobbie later accused me of being immoral for allowing this out-of-control partying. This was a couple of months before Bobbie and I started going around. I was convinced then that she was a prude. Little did I realize that she was probably jealous. Anyway, the cops arrived and the party broke up. Elizabeth was last seen leaving with Jean-Michel. As I noted in my journal, I was left to clean up the mess:

> *I am alone now in a place that two hours before was filled with people, music, wine and laughter. Wine and beer bottles lay about and the cigarettes butts adorn the floor. My bed is rumbled and lumpy. The smell of Gauloise is rampant. I throw open the windows to let the cold night air in to clear the room. I gaze up at the cartoon black sky between the buildings, suck in the air and feel an empty nothingness.*

During those heady weeks, if we weren't partying at my place or someone else's, we hit the nightclubs. One favorite was *Le Hot Club*, a basement affair that you reached by going down two flights of a winding metal staircase. On the weekends, the place was packed with students doing the twist to the Chubby Checker song, *Let's Twist Again*. The nightclub was hot and stuffy and probably a firetrap but fueled by cheap wine, beer, and earsplitting music, it was the place to be. The normally restrained French students, along with the more relaxed foreign crowd, sweated with glee as they danced away the night.

After a few hours of *Le Hot Club*, I would come up for fresh air and wander the streets of Aix on my way back to my room. I always made it a point to pass by the fountain of the Four Dolphins. Aix was full of bubbling, gurgling fountains, but this one with its seventeenth century baroque dolphins spurting water of their gaping mouths was my favorite. I often paused there listening to the musical splash of the water reminding me that I was only one of many thousands of students passing through Aix's glorious history.

Farther on, at the end of the Cours Mirabeau stood the statue of the Roi Rene, the happy-go-lucky King of Provence in the fifteenth century. Rene wasn't much of an administrator, but he always had a song in his heart and knack for poetry. He was a patron of the arts, established various festivals celebrated even today and promoted wine making in Provence. He was considered the guiding spirit of Aix, a good-time Charlie who was always ready for a party.

***

I had initially thought the Institute would be an academic breeze. However, after receiving a D in French and two C's in other courses the first semester, I had to re-adjust my attitude. The French teacher was a real dip from De Paw University. He used a standard French grammar textbook that bore no relation to the French I was learning in the cafes. The "dip" spoke a phony academic French that he must have learned from old Berlitz tapes. While he was grammatically correct, his accent was bad with a flat Midwestern twang. I hated hearing it, although I could easily follow him and indeed would respond in French unlike most of the other students in class. Still, I screwed up in my written French and ignoring my speaking skills, the "dip" gave me a D that I protested, but to no avail. As he put it:

"Mr. Brown, you may have a passing acquaintance with colloquial spoken French as it is practiced in the cafés, but your written French leaves a lot to be desired. That's what this course is focused upon. Café chit-chat is not enough."

Swell.

However, a French graduate student running a course called *Travaux Pratiques*, in which we carried on elementary conversations in French, recognized my practical language skills and gave me a B.

I fared better my second semester of French. For some reason the "dip" had to go back to De Paw and he was replaced by a hip, young French woman who was more interested in exposing us to the glories of French literature than hammering us with grammar exercises. We focused on nineteenth century French literature, reading excerpts from Balzac, Stendhal, Hugo, Flaubert and Zola, all neatly presented in Castex booklets that covered French literature century by century.

I was also taking an art history course in Modern European Painting. Since Aix was the home of Cezanne and, nearby Arles, the brief home of Van Gogh and Gauguin, we focused on those painters with a nod to Picasso who lived in nearby Vauvenargues. Picasso reportedly showed up now and then at the Les Deux Garçons and at the bullfights in Arles. I never saw him, but others claimed they did.

We spent time at Cezanne's home and studio on the outskirts of Aix and hiked around nearby Mont. St. Victoire studying the views that so enthralled Cezanne. We also made a field trip to Arles to check out the scenes that had inspired Van Gogh and visited the sanitarium in St. Remy where he had been hospitalized for a while after he almost cut off his ear.

My medieval history professor, Dr. Smerle, was a Texan who spoke fluent French with a southern drawl. However, he was cool and a walking encyclopedia of Provence. We spent a lot of time with him crawling around the Greek, Roman and Medieval ruins of the area. I did well in his course receiving two B's. For fun, I took a Shakespeare course at the University of Aix-Marseilles proper. No grade here, only unit credit. It was all in French except for the English text. We spent a whole semester reading and studying *Othello* until I had it nearly memorized. Finally, I enrolled in a history of European philosophy course that summarized all the leading philosophers from Socrates to Sartre. We never dipped into the original texts, but I felt I understood their gist based on an excellent textbook.

Overall, the courses at the Institute were comprehensive and while not as cutthroat as those at Cal, they had their own special challenges. Nevertheless, I managed to earn a B- average that, of course, I couldn't transfer to Berkeley. But as I said, I did receive twenty-six units credit at Cal for my work abroad. So my time had not been wasted. I felt even better when I watched academic disaster engulf many of the regular French students.

About half the first-year students at the University of Aix-Marseille had flunked out. Most had goofed off all year and then tried to cram for the annual exams given in May. In part, they were victims of the French university system, which made no demands on them all year, the year being only seven months. They had no midterms, no semester finals and no exams of any kind until May. No papers were assigned; no specific homework was required other than vague suggestions to read this or that book. The professors didn't care if they showed up for class or not. No one took attendance.

Eventually, there was the reckoning. It was the survival of the fittest. Most of the French Algerian students I knew flunked out. Jean-Michel flunked out among others. Some were philosophical, others pissed. Jean-Michel told me the American system was much better and he wanted to study in the states. "Kansas City! *Cette ville est formidable!*" Jean-Michel had visions of the old West and shootouts on the main streets.

***

Despite my limited finances, I managed to see quite a bit of Europe. Thanksgiving week, I traveled to Heidelberg, Germany to visit Ursula, a big, blue-eyed girl I had met in September at a student hostel in Cap D'Antibe near Cannes. We had gone for a moonlight swim in the Mediterranean and spent most of the warm night on a little rocky beach below the cliffs.

However, as I discovered when I arrived in Heidelberg, she had a boyfriend, Hans, who lurked about. It wasn't a fruitful visit. Billed as an American exchange student, I was invited to lunch to meet her family. Her father, a tall, gray-haired gentleman, was superintendent of schools at Heidelberg and a former SS Captain. He spoke excellent English. We discussed the state of the world, the Kennedy presidency and the Berlin Wall crisis, but avoided any references to World War II. I had the impression that they were very protective of Ursula, their only child and wanted to make sure that she did not have a fling with some flaky American.

Back at the hotel where I was staying, five or six American Air Force Reservists were drowning their sorrows in beer. They were in a foul, bitter mood over being called up by President Kennedy during the Berlin crisis. Even so, they weren't doing much—hanging out in their civvies and drinking beer at the local beer halls. They tried to round up a turkey and have the hotel cook prepare a Thanksgiving dinner, but had to settle for a goose. I was invited to join them. We drank fine Rhine wine and devoured the bird. Even so, it wasn't the same as home. And I think we all felt a little homesick at this point.

On the train trip back to Aix, the French railroad workers went on a twelve-hour strike, and I had to spend a lonely day wandering around Lyon. When I returned to the Institute, I was two days late and I had to answer to the Institute director, Dr. Maza.

"You know Allan, every year, a certain percentage of students drop out of the Institute because they get carried away with the attractions of Europe and what not," explained the good doctor. "Eventually, these students have to go home with no academic credit. Apart from the good times they had, they have nothing to show for their time in Europe. I don't want you to fall into that trap."

I assured him I would not. I said that credit for my academic year was important to me, but at the same time, I did want to see what I could of Europe. That seemed to satisfy him.

All of which illustrated how the Institute "mother-henned" its students, overseeing their every move and trying to make sure there were no *incidents*. I wasn't used to that kind of scrutiny. I was used to the anonymity of Cal where nobody knew or cared what you did. The "mother-henning" was more extreme with the women. All had to live with families, no exceptions. The irony was two women were impregnated by their French boyfriends, anyway. One married her boyfriend; the other went home to her mother.

The recurrent phrase was "Aix is a small town with a network of gossips. Everybody knows who is doing what with whom." It was all because of the landlady's network. My landlady, Mme. Vachyron, was definitely part of that network. I had the feeling she knew my every move, my every visitor, but she was also very pleasant, putting up with my parties and feeding me when I was sick with mono. Thus, I concluded that I was indeed being looked after.

***

My next major outing was to Austria over a long, three-week Christmas break. I packed my ski parka, ski pants and sweaters and then rented skis, boots and poles from a local ski shop in Aix. I took a train to Innsbruck, Austria where I stashed my skis in a locker and spent a day wandering around the mountain town. I sampled the pastries in the coffee shops, drank some beer and discovered a ski lift at the end of one street. The locals marched by with skis over their shoulders apparently on their way to a skiing lunch break. Gee, I thought, the perfect mountain city. I debated spending a few days there, but I had reservations that night at the ski resort town of Ehrwald.

After a two-hour train ride, I arrived in Ehrwald and checked into a dirt-cheap pension that catered to students. The skiing near town turned out to be marginal since it had an elevation of only three thousand feet. The only decent skiing was at the top of the nearby Zugspitze at an elevation nine thousand feet and involved taking a half-hour tram ride. Since I was on a tight budget, I went only a couple of times and though the view was great, the skiing was mediocre. For a $20 lift ticket, all I got were rope tows and T-bars on rutted, icy, ungroomed snow at the top of the mountain. No chairlifts or powder snow in sight. Furthermore, it was impossible to ski down to the bottom because of a lack of snow. Overall, it was nothing like the glorious skiing described by the European students back at the Cal Ski lodge. Despite temperatures being in the teens, no storm was in sight. The locals claimed it was too cold to snow. However, skiing soon became incidental to the trip.

Ehrwald was a classic Alpine village of narrow twisting lanes, chic little shops, quaint cafes, beer cellars and wine stubens. As I soon discovered, it was the central party spot in the area. Our group included six or seven African students from the Ivory Coast, all sons of the elite. Sharp dressers, late risers and always ready for a party, none of them skied. Their idea of a good time was to rise around noon, hang out in the cafes and line up the action for the evening. All were musical, playing a variety of instruments and of course, all could dance. The Austrian blondes loved them and hung on them as if they were royalty.

I also met a character called Diderot. Diderot was a law student in Paris, but by his own account, he spent most of his time traveling. He was stocky and bearded with the lines of a well-traveled face. He said he was the son of a high railway official in France and consequently, he could ride the rails free throughout Europe and Russia. Diderot spoke French, English, German, Russian, Spanish and claimed to have a knowledge of Chinese.

Diderot had a quaint notion of hygiene. He figured as long as his asshole was clean, he was hygienically fit and thus, before going out he would plop his ass into a washbasin and duly soak his hind parts. As Diderot put it, "Look at all these businessmen with their big villas. They shower every day, but they still have dirty assholes."

For New Year's Eve, Diderot, I and a few other students decided to travel to Munich, several hours away, to celebrate. It was there that I came down with a nasty flu. We had been drinking liters and liters of beer in one of the giant beer halls and eating bratwurst and sauerkraut. I threw up in the bathroom and then with my head spinning boarded a late train to return to Ehrwald, where I spent the next several days in bed. I managed to drag my sickly ass back to Aix just in time for classes.

***

Mid-February, we had a weeklong semester break and Bobbie, Joan and I took off for Italy on an overnight train. First, we spent a few days in Rome touring the sights—the amphitheater, the Pantheon, the catacombs and St. Peters, where we spotted the Pope on the balcony. I had never seen so many religious orders, each wearing their own unique vestments. Nor had I ever seen so many sophisticated looking priests, men who looked as if they had denied themselves nothing in life despite their vows. We met a pair of young priests from Chicago while touring the Forum. They talked about their career in the Vatican Diplomatic Service and of the languages they spoke, including Latin on a daily basis. Bobbie and Joan were snowed. "Too bad they are in the priesthood. They're so cute," said Joan.

Then we dipped down to Naples for a look at the ruins of Pompeii and finally up to Florence for its Renaissance art. There, in a café, we met Giuseppe, a young aristocrat who was much taken by Joan. He invited us to his fifteenth century townhouse, showed us his Ruben paintings and invited us to stay the night. After generous libations and some grass, Bobbie and I crashed on a couch. Then Giuseppe disappeared with Joan in some far-off room. I never did find out exactly what happened after that.

Italy, along with Germany, Austria, Greece, Paris and London was the extent of my traveling around. All in all, I had "done" Europe.

***

So how was day-to-day living in Aix? As I wrote in my journal, it could sometimes be monotonous and depressing, especially in winter when the Mistral was blowing:

Jan. 14, 1962

Aix is gray today and the trees are bare. A cold wind scatters the spray of the spurting water in the Rotonde Fountain. The people on the Cours Mirabeau stroll with hunched shoulders in heavy overcoats, bracing against the Mistral whistling down the street. Students sit in cafes, looking out through steamed windows, sipping their drinks and talking.

I walk down a narrow street and turn into a darkened hallway. On the first flight, I fumble to unlock my door in the gloom. I enter the room and gaze at the cluttered table with its beer bottles and papers about. I study the faded yellow wallpaper and then at myself in the mirror – hair too long, pale and a bit too thin. I collapse on the bed, uttering "merde," feeling melancholy but taking pleasure in this feeling. I soon fall asleep, listening to the dark street noises outside.

Jan. 15, 1962

Two slits of gray light slipping through the shutters render objects in my room barely visible. I turn over, rolling to the other side of my great double bed. Peering out of one half-open eye, I can distinguish in the gloom the table in the center of my room. On it is a Munich beer mug with a gooseneck lamp sticking out of it. A small space heater to one side on the floor, and beyond, a dull reflection of the room in the mirror of the armoire. Should I get up? The bed is so soft and warm and the room cold. I pull up the covers and go back to sleep again.

Finally, an hour or so later, I get up, stretch and run my hand through my hair, all the time watching the gray image in the mirror. Then the great question of the day comes to mind, "What's the weather like." I open one shutter and peer up into a ribbon of sky between the buildings of the narrow street below to see if it is blue or not. It's gray today.

After dressing in clothes worn the previous day, I wash and shave at my basin with only cold water. Then I am off, down the stairs and out onto Rue Victory Leydet to buy a couple of rolls at the bakery across the street and a half-liter of milk at the local creamery. When I return to my room, I huddle around my space heater, drink some milk from the carton and eat the brioche and raison.

This morning I have a philosophy class at 11:00. It is now 9:30, so for about an hour-and-a half, I study French. About quarter to eleven, I take off for class with only a notebook, walking through the narrow twisting streets of the old section of the city, dodging cars, ditch-diggers and crates of wine. As I make my way to the Institute, I am overcome by an array of pungent odors wafting out from the various shops – the bakery, the butcher shop, the fish shop and the general stink of dirty wash water and garbage in cans along the street. All of this suffused by centuries of sweat and grim from man and beast emanating from the ancient walls of the old quarter.

I walk through a walled portal to the most ancient part of the city, under the bell tower, whose base was built in Roman times and finally arrive at the Hotel De Ville where my philosophy class is being held. In class, I sit in a half- daze lulled by the dull monotone of the university professor explaining in fractured English one of the finer points of Descartes, taking only sporadic notes.

After class, I walk fast to the student restaurant, the Cité, for my one-franc lunch. While waiting in the line, I greet my French friends, including Jean-Michel, usually ignoring the Americans unless it is Bobbie or Joan. The food, as a rule, is neither good nor bad, but sufficient. The fries are always excellent.

After lunch, I often go with Jean-Michel to have a café at the Deux Garçons. We discuss the usual: women, education and philosophy. About 1:30 PM, I return to my room and study to 4:00. Time for French class. Often poorly prepared, I bluff my way through. The next class is medieval history. This is usually interesting. Smerle has an encyclopedic knowledge of the time.

At 6 PM, I buy some candy or a patisserie to hold me over until dinner. At 7:00, I hike the kilometer to the new Cité for dinner, which is usually cold cuts, fries and salad. Later, I meet more friends at the cafe and check out what is happening for the evening. Most often, it's a movie or a nightclub. Tonight though, I have to write a paper. I leave the café about nine and go back to my room, where I sit at that wretched table and write for a couple of hours and then go to bed. The shutters are once again closed and all is dark. I lay in bed thinking of the monotony of student life in Aix. Then I fall sleep and enter another world.

However, it all wasn't so downbeat. A few days later, on a bright, sunny Sunday when the Mistral decided to take a break, I went for a bike ride in the countryside around Aix:

Jan. 21, 1962

It's mid-afternoon. The winter sun, although bright, is weak. I can scarcely feel it on my back. I bike through narrow, winding roads, admiring the ancient crumbling villas and smelling the cypress. I get off my Velox and hike across a ploughed field, the soft earth crumbling beneath my step. Where the field greets the forest, I spot a man with a hoe. I stop and gaze at this man with a hoe, chopping and working in the sun's filtered rays. He chops and he dig, oblivious to me. I bend down, take a clump of soil and crumble it in my fist into fine sandy mist. It floats to the ground. Quietly muffled in the small valley are the sounds of children playing afar. I climb up a hill, crowned with a cluster of pines and gaze at the scene: the man with the hoe and the villas scattered below, the field of good earth, all misty now with the rays of the setting sun.

A month later in February, on another calm, sunny day, I climbed to the summit of Mont. Saint Victoire, the three thousand foot high hunk of granite that so inspired Cezanne:

February 25, 1962

The heat of the sun is on my back and the pressure of the granite on my chest. I'm poised on a ledge with nothing below. I gaze out over the valley below, a mixture of red, green and yellow. I am engulfed in the presence of nature, the sun, the rock and the dizzying colors beneath. My foot begins to slip and I lunge for a sturdy little pine.

At the summit, I find an earthen chapel, dark, cool and damp inside. Only the altar is lit by the rays of the sun coming through slits in the roof. Outside is a well with a bucket on a chain. I lower it into the depths and bring forth the cold, clear water, splashing over the side of the bucket. I drink long and deep, quenching the thirst of the climb.

On a wide ledge, leaning back against a flat rock, a girl drowses in the warm sun. She is plain but seems so peaceful in that half-slumber that there is a beauty here so simple, so pure. Watching that girl, her smile of contentment. Her eyes opening now and then, squinting into the sun and her black hair flowing in the soft breeze. She stirs, yawns and gazes out into the blue. Then she settles back against the rock changing the position of her head to sun the other side.

So there it was. Europa. The good and the bad. The boring and the sublime. When you added it all up, I felt it was worth it. Now all I had to was re-integrate with the good ol' USA and get on with my student life at Cal.

25. BACK

By the fall of 1962, a lot had changed around Sproul Hall and Sather Gate. The area had undergone a major renovation with the construction of a block-long plaza that ran from Bancroft Avenue to Sather Gate. Across the plaza from Sproul Hall stood a new, five-story student union building that housed a student activities center, student government offices, a luxurious lounge, a bookstore and, in the basement, a beer hall know as the Bears Lair.

Adjacent to the student union was the Commons, a new student cafeteria that offered cheap and tasty food. It also featured an expansive terrace overlooking a sunken plaza where one could sit in the sun and watch the Berkeley world go by.

Sitting on the terrace, I sensed there were more students than ever, all shapes, all sizes, still mostly clean-cut whites, but also many Asians with a sprinkling of Hispanics and blacks. Groups of beatnik looking students lounged about in their beards and sandals. Now and then, a longhaired beauty would come floating by in a clinging flowing gown, obviously braless.

***

Although I had just spent a year living on my own in Aix, I nevertheless decided to return to fraternity life. I initially felt an obligation to the other fraternity brothers to help keep the house afloat with my monthly contribution to room and board and to help recruit new members during rush. The first few weeks went well. The house was about the same, the routines the same, and I was happy to be back. I even hustled during rush, managing to talk two or three freshmen into pledging Alpha Kappa Lambda.

Yet, it was odd being a senior in the house. It was lonely. Gerard, Ken and other friends who were a year or two ahead of me had graduated and moved on. Gerard and Rich had gone to law school, Ken to dental school and Neil to medical school. Bill Singleton went to work for Standard Oil and Jim Dougherty was an officer in the Navy. I didn't have much in common with the current seniors anymore who were busy with their girlfriends, fiancées and career dreams. And the lower classmen seemed so young, so eager, so naïve. They looked up to us seniors, taking their cues on fraternity life—learning how to party, how to be sociable, how to game the University system.

There was talk once again of making me rush chairman, possibly house president—two jobs I did not want. I wanted to concentrate on my studies and possibly raise my grade point average so I could go to law or graduate school. My shitty C average wasn't going to do it. Also, the crowding and lack of privacy in fraternity living soon got on my nerves. Even though I had my own room on the third floor, it was noisy and there was still much screwing around and high jinks. The bathrooms and shower stalls were pits and looked diseased. I got a fungal foot infection from the filthy floors and it took months to get rid of it.

I often gazed longingly out my third floor window at the apartment house next-door and watched the students (mostly graduate students) come and go at will. At night, through their lighted windows, I could see them studying or fixing dinner. All very homey, all very normal. Occasionally, a fair young thing would enter a male student's apartment, laughing, talking and carrying on. Then I would hear music, jazz or some rock and roll. I could imagine what would probably happen after dinner, after the dishes washed (or maybe not washed.) I envied these students. After a few of these sightings, I decided that I absolutely had to move out, rent an apartment and get my own scene going. But I needed a roommate to swing this financially so I was stymied for the moment.

***

The other compelling reason to get out fraternity life was a brawl that left me with a concussion and a black eye. During my eighteen-month absence, the fraternity scene had become more rowdy and in some cases more brutal than before. Generally, parties at AKL were mild affairs. People became tipsy and tried to carry on. Sometimes someone got drunk and passed out, but there had never been any fights or violence fueled by alcohol. But brother Don's fraternity was a different story.

When Don enrolled in Berkeley after leaving the Air Force Academy, he joined Lambda Chi, another Northside fraternity. They had a well-run house and the brothers seemed levelheaded, pragmatic types. Many were studying engineering like Don; others were into business administration. A few of these entrepreneurial types decided to raise money for the house by staging beer parties in their basement with a dollar entrance fee and a quarter for a mug of beer. Don was required to bartend at one of these affairs, and I went over to help him. The party started out low-key enough with a lot of raunchy singing and dancing, but as it wore on, a group of frat rats from a neighboring fraternity became sloppy drunk. Their house was known as one of the worst "animal houses" on campus with a high flunk out rate. They also prided themselves on being a jock house and recruited some of the biggest, toughest individuals they could find for their intramural sports.

One of these characters bellied up to the bar and demanded a beer. I poured him a beer from the tap and pushed it across the counter, all the while checking out his scarred faced and broken nose. He looked more like an ex-convict than a Berkeley fraternity boy.

"That'll be a quarter," I said.

"Huh? Why don't you make it on the house?" he sneered.

"Sorry, can't do that. We are trying to raise money here," I replied.

"Like I said put it on my tab," he said wrapping his meaty paw around the mug.

"No charity here," I responded. "Give it back."

"Like hell," he said taking a big swig.

I grabbed at it and the beer spilled down his front. He sputtered, stared at me, eyes glaring. "Come here, you fucker. Come out from behind that counter."

"Fuck off," I said.

He tried to reach across the counter to grab me, but I stepped back.

"Come on out, you chicken!" he ranted, now really pissed.

My masculine pride injured, I made the foolish mistake of coming out from behind the bar. As I straightened up from ducking under the bar gate, he hit me with a glancing blow on the side of the head. Stunned for a second, I grabbed him by the shirt and pushed him against a stone fireplace. All the time he was beating me on my back and pumping his legs into me. I couldn't get free to slug him. While we were struggling, Don tried to pry us apart, but an even bigger guy from the animal house pulled him aside, saying, "let'em fight." Don turned around and tried to push the dude away, but that was a mistake. Skinny Don was clearly outmatched by the guy who just played with him, finally pushing him through a side door and onto the banks of a little creek that ran through the fraternity grounds. I broke free from my goon and went outside to help Don. Then the fucker grabbed me from behind and pushed me into the creek. All the time this was going on, I could feel my strength ebbing fast. I was still suffering from the after effects of mono. I was no longer the man of iron that I had once been on crew. My muscle mass was gone. I was desperately out of shape after a year of carousing in Europe.

Before I knew it, I was in the creek with my opponent on top of me, pushing my head down into the water and slugging me in the face with a fist that sported a large class ring. I dimly realized that he might kill me, but I seemed to be hovering outside myself, not really caring. I may have been knocked unconscious or not, it was all hazy, but all at once, two of his fraternity brothers grabbed the guy and pulled him off me. I can dimly remember Don being pummeled too nearby on the bank of the creek, but someone was on his assailant's back, hitting and clawing and screaming like a banshee. It was Don's girlfriend, Nancy—a tall, strong girl who was half tomboy. She was screaming for his fraternity brothers to help him. I must say looking back on this incident, the Lambda Chi brothers weren't doing much to help. But Don's attacker, after getting his eyes gouged out by Nancy, did back off. Finally, a Lambda Chi announced he had called the cops. Immediately all the animal house frats split. A few minutes later, two Berkeley police officers arrived and started questioning us. Though we knew which fraternity house the goons had come from, nobody knew any names.

The Berkeley cops took Don and me to the emergency room at Alta Bates, the Berkeley Community Hospital. I received several stitches for a cut over my left eye and was told to watch out for the after effects of a possible concussion. Don had broken a little finger in the scuffle and suffered several cuts and bruises. We were both treated and released with bottles of codeine pills to soothe our pain.

Back at the fraternity house, I slept fitfully the rest of the night. When I woke up in the morning, I threw up in the toilet and then crawled back to bed. Now and then, my frat brothers peeked in and said things, like, "Jeeze Brown. You look like a Mack truck ran over you."

I joked weakly, "You should have seen the other guy."

I moped around the fraternity house for few days, missing my Monday and Tuesday classes. I was too embarrassed to be seen on campus in my battered state, but the following Wednesday, I did go to classes and tried to ignore the stares.

The cops had asked me if I wanted to file charges against a "Mike" whom they did eventually identify and who was a known troublemaker. However, the police did say that based on witnesses, it wasn't clear who started the fight and that it might be futile to pursue. I decided to let it slide and concentrate on my recovery. With 26,000 students on campus, the odds of running into this Mike were slim. In fact, Don told me Mike had flunked out at the end of that semester. So I thought he was long gone, but a year later when I went down to Larry Blake's Rathskeller with some friends for a beer, there he was—an I.D. checker. His face was even more battered and scarred than it had been before. More fights, I guessed. He looked at my I.D., looked up and smiled, "Remember me?"

I remembered. A chill went down my spine, but I didn't react. I didn't say a thing. I took my I.D. back and sat down in a booth. We drank a pitcher of beer, listened to a folk guitarist on the little stage and then left shortly after.

By that time, I realized that it wasn't a kid's game anymore engaging playground brawls. People could get hurt, maybe even killed. Maybe me. Street fights weren't worth the risk. I figured there was always a way to avoid a fight. I was a "lover" not a fighter, I told myself.

***

Two weeks later, my face was presentable and the Berkeley co-eds didn't look away in shock. About this time, I ran into Ana in the library reading room. She had lost her little girl look and was now a well-groomed "Sally." She gave me a slightly embarrassed smile and then asked how I liked Europe.

"Oh, it was great," I replied. "I saw a lot. I received twenty-six units credit, so it wasn't a waste academically, but now it's back to reality. What have you been up to?"

"Oh, I've been really busy," she replied. "I joined Phi Mu and then officially majored in Biology. I'm still Pre-Med. It's hard work, organic chemistry and all, but I like it."

"Sounds good. You must study all the time?"

"Just about."

Unable to think of anything else to say to each other, there was an awkward pause and then sensing that she wanted to get back to her studies, I simply said, "Well, I'll see you around."

"Sure, I'll see you around," she said turning back to her book.

So that was the end to that. As the French say, "If you go away, so does love."

I had heard through the grapevine that she had a boyfriend who was a big wheel in campus politics and destined for a career in law. No doubt, she was balling him.

***

My more pressing woman problem in the fall of 1962 was Bobbie in far-off Chicago. What the hell were we going to do? When I left her in England with Tom and Joan, she was still pining for a lost love that never was. Yet, when I visited her in Chicago right before fall semester, she was all lovey-dovey with me again. Tom was back at Annapolis. Go figure.

I met her mother, her brother and her two sisters. Bobbie's father wasn't around. He lived in downtown Chicago. I was immediately dubbed "Big Al" from California. Her mother had been afraid initially that I was a beatnik, but she soon realized that I was only an overgrown fraternity boy, so I got the nod of approval. For a day or two, we hung out at her house in La Grange Park. It was a low-slung modern brick ranch, sprawled over a half acre of property, which ran down a ravine to a creek on the edge of a forest preserve. The weather was hot and muggy and the house had no air-conditioning, but with a few fans and a lot of open-air exposure, it was tolerable.

Bobbie, Joan and a few other friends were determined to show the "Californian" the glories of Chicago. I hadn't thought much about Chicago one way or the other. Like many Californians, I thought the Midwest was simply a big fly over territory until you landed at New York, which, apart from its own attractions, was the jumping off spot to Europe.

All I knew about Chicago before I met Bobbie was its Carl Sandburg image of stockyards, railroads, steel factories and its mafia image of Al Capone and the rest of the mob gang, a few of whom I had seen at Cal Neva two summers ago.

First, I didn't realize that Chicago was such a waterfront town, sitting as it did on shores of Lake Michigan. A major port in its own right. As I looked out over the lake from the promontory of the Adler Planetarium, it struck me as a giant inland sea. Looking back towards the Loop, the city appeared as if it was floating on the water, a tropical blue body of water in late summer. Sailboats and powerboats cruised in and out of the breakwater at nearby Monroe Street Harbor as if they were sailing the Caribbean. Off in Grant Park, Buckingham fountain shot water high into the air, casting rainbows across the cityscape. Later, riding up and down Lake Shore Drive, we passed mile after mile of beaches full of sun-tanned bodies walking, biking, sunning or playing beach volleyball.

"It looks like the Riviera," I remarked.

"What did you expect?" Bobbie smirked. "We do know how to do summer here."

We toured the standard Chicago sights—Art Institute, Field Museum, Museum of Science and Industry, Adler Planetarium. We walked around the Loop, the downtown area, checking out the architectural gems: the massive brick Monadnock Building, the Carson Pirie Scott Building with its filigree ironwork and wide Chicago windows, the old Reliance Building, one of the first skyscrapers in Chicago and the neo-gothic Tribune Tower. And of course, we prowled the aisles of Marshall Fields, the main department store in the Loop. "Give the lady what she wants," was the store's motto. Marshall Fields made Capwells in Oakland look like a flea market.

From a balcony at the Board of Trade building, we watched the frantic traders buying and selling agriculture futures that in effect set the prices for corn, wheat, soybeans, pork bellies and other commodities. When I asked to see the stockyards, she commented, "Oh, those are mostly gone. You don't want to go down there. It's just a big stench."

I was also introduced to Chicago nightlife. We had a drink at the Playboy Club on Michigan Avenue. Hugh Hefner published his tits and ass magazine right here in Chicago. I teased Bobbie about getting a job as a bunny. "You'd look cute in one of those costumes."

"Oh, stop it. It's so cheap looking," she replied.

"Yeah, but I hear they make a lot of money in tips and so on."

She nudged me in the shoulder. "Never."

Another night, we had a drink at the top of the Prudential Building looking out over Grant Park and the glittering lights of the Loop. Bobbie said it was the tallest building in Chicago, but there were plans for even taller ones. We ate dinner at the Drake Hotel's Cape Cod room. I had a delicious scrod and wondered aloud at how the restaurant managed to have such great seafood miles from the ocean.

"This isn't the boondocks, Allan. All the good restaurants here have fresh seafood flown in daily from either the East Coast or the West Coast."

"Oh."

The following night, we had a great prime rib dinner with a "spinning" salad and a bottle of cabernet sauvignon at Don Roth's Blawkhawk on Wabash Avenue in the Loop. Later, we checked out Old Town, which consisted of a few blocks of historic buildings on North Wells Street undergoing renovation. Then, we attended a production of Second City, a hilarious improvisational group far funnier than the one I had seen in San Francisco called The Committee. Afterward, we went across the street to the Earl of Old Town to have a pitcher of beer and listen to some folk singing.

I was being treated like a royal guest. I wondered where all the money had come from for this. I guessed that Bobbie's parents were footing the bill. However, I did have a few hundred dollars on me too that I had saved up from two months of summer earnings. I paid Bobbie the money I owed her and even bought a dinner and several rounds of drinks.

Overall, Chicago was an impressive city, but, as I flew out of Midway Airport on my way home, I noted the flat landscape that stretched to the horizon. I could not imagine living somewhere without hills, mountains or seashore. Even so, it had been a productive time with Bobbie. We had managed to get away by ourselves to nearby Lake Geneva in southern Wisconsin for one long day where she told me that she would like to visit me over Christmas in the Bay Area. We also discussed the possibility of going into the Peace Corps together. What remained unspoken was whether we would do this as a couple. Other than "Oh, he's at Annapolis now," Bobbie made no further mention of Tom.

26. THE APARTMENT

When I picked my classes for the fall semester, I noticed that with only two more courses I could have a minor in French. I had been given twelve units of French credit for my time in Aix-En-Provence. Now that I was quasi-fluent in the language, I felt ready to take a French literature course and an advanced French grammar course. These courses were designed for French majors and were conducted in French. Students were expected to converse in French and write papers in French. I felt confident that I could handle it.

The nineteenth century French literature course was taught by a Professor T. who had been teaching at Berkeley forever. While his French was technically correct, his accent was horrible despite his many years of spending summers in France. He would have been laughed out of any hip café. His lectures were simplistic. The reading was a joke. We never read an entire book like *Madam Bovary*; we read excerpts in French. We skipped over the nineteenth century like a kid playing hopscotch, landing here and there, but missing a lot. A few chapters by Hugo or Balzac, a verse or two by Baudelaire, Verlaine and Rimbaud and then back to Flaubert or Maupassant. The grade in the course was based on two midterms, a final and three short papers in French. Since I was well versed in the survey of the literature, the tests were no problem. I wrote the first paper in French and then had my fraternity brother Jean-Paul review it and correct it before I turned it in. After one class, Professor T. said he wanted to talk to me.

"Mr. Brown, why did you write your paper in French?"

"Why? Is something wrong with it?"

"No, not at all. Rather well written for a non-French major," he sniffed. "But you know I don't require non-French majors to write in French."

"Oh, I see," I said. "Only French majors get to write in French."

"Yes, that's part of their grade. Look, I'll tell you what I will do. If you want, you can write your paper in French, but I will not grade the French, only the content. However, as I said, you could write in English with no loss in grade."

"I'll think about it."

I wrote one more paper in French and then kissed it off. I suspected Professor T. didn't want to put the effort into a non-French major. In addition, I was probably out-performing a few of his French majors. Already, I knew from class that I spoke better French than most of them. Few had studied in France. Ironically, French majors at Cal were not encouraged to study abroad in France. The French department deemed it more important for French majors to follow their specific French curriculum as undergraduates rather than to pollute their French with café slang and the various other distractions of French living. A year abroad in France was for graduate studies, possibly on a Fulbright.

I received a B in the literature course and then took an advanced grammar course in the spring. Here, I got my comeuppance. I struggled with the esoterica of advanced French. The other advanced French majors breezed through it despite the fact that their spoken French was poor. The instructor, a beat looking chick with gray flecks in her long black hair, wondered what I was doing there.

"Mr. Brown, you really don't need this do you?"

"I want to take it," I insisted. "I need to work on my grammar. It's my minor you know."

"Do you want to teach it?"

"No, I only want to be competent in the language."

"Well, go ahead, but don't expect me to cut you any slack. You have to compete head-to-head with the French majors."

I did compete. Although I had to work hard, I did enjoy the course. Even so, I received only a C for my troubles.

However, I had my little moments of glory. One day I spotted Reginald, my old French teacher, taking his Afgan for a walk on the Northside. A little heavier now, though his hair was still long, Reginald looked as if he had found a home in Berkeley. I said hello in French and carried on a conversation in French. At first, he appeared shocked, but then he smiled and simply said, "See there now, Mr. Brown, I told you, you could do it." Then he walked on.

***

Of course, my spoken French was improving all the time because I was now living with my fraternity brother Jean-Paul in an apartment on the south side of campus. He was a wiry little guy, about 5'3", but he had a big booming voice and a wide smile showing off a broken front tooth that he never bothered to fix. "The girls say it adds character," he claimed.

Jean-Paul was one of the biggest party boys around—drinking, singing loudly and chasing women. Still, he took tough courses— advanced chemistry, biology, German and Latin and he earned all A's and B's. He never seemed to study and always was the first to party. Now he was as tired of fraternity life as I was. And he had just met a be- guiling little girl, Corrine, a miniature Jean Seberg, and he said he needed somewhere to ball in peace.

"Let's get out of here, Al," he said one night over a beer at La Vals. "I found a furnished one-bedroom on Ridge with a brand-new kitchen, a large living room and a great balcony facing south that would be *formi- dable* for sunbathing."

"Sounds intriguing," I said. "What's the rent?"

"Two hundred, but if we split it, it would be about what we pay at the house."

"Yeah, a little more if we include the food."

"Ah, it'll be worth it," he insisted. "Aren't you tired of eating the crap that we do at the fraternity house?"

"Definitely. I'm ready to get out. I can't take the rah-rah anymore. I need some privacy. That year in France spoiled me."

"*Bien sûr.*" And I can help you with your French."

Much to the dismay of our AKL brothers, we gave our notice and moved out within the week. We both promised we would be active in the fraternity, helping out on rush and dropping by now and then for the parties. But it was a promise that was soon forgotten as we immersed ourselves in the Berkeley apartment scene with all its duties and de- lights.

The apartment on Ridge was a block off Telegraph, about five min- utes from campus. The building was a white stucco, boxy-like affair with outdoor walkways and stairs. It was one of the many new apartment buildings springing up on the Southside to accommodate students. We lived on the third floor and from our balcony, we had a view of the Oakland hills. The bedroom had two twin beds and the living room, a daybed, which served as a couch. A large Formica dining table with six chairs filled the dining area. The kitchen opened onto the living room with new appliances, including a dishwasher. The landlord, a theology student, lived downstairs with his wife and never bothered us unless we were late with the rent.

Soon we added some of our own stuff—a portable stereo, two lamps, a small desk in the bedroom and a makeshift bookcase of cinderblocks and boards in the living room. Jean-Paul had a small portable radio that we played now and then. By mutual agreement, we had no television. "Opium for the masses," declared Jean-Paul. Corrine dressed up the place with Cubist and German Expressionist posters.

I adapted immediately to apartment life. After my meager room in Aix and the chaos of fraternity life, this was the lap of luxury. Imagine, a bathroom with a flush toilet and a shower anytime you wanted it! Unlimited electricity, hot water and heating. A full modern kitchen. Space. Space. Space. In addition, I could come and go as I wanted. Eat what I wanted, when I wanted. Study uninterruptedly. No more escaping to the library. I could bring home whom I wanted with no one else the wiser, except Jean-Paul, who couldn't care less. After all, he was busy with Corrine, who, was technically living in her sorority, but had practically moved in with us.

Was I lonely? Hardly ever. Someone was always around. Sometimes, it was great simply to sit in the living room by myself, listening to LP's, staring out through the balcony glass doors at the Oakland hills, sipping coffee or wine. Other times, I lounged on the balcony, drowsy in the late afternoon sun, an unread textbook in my lap. Once in a while, Gerard came over with his girlfriend, Bonnie, and we hung out, fixed dinner and listened to more music.

At the time, Gerard was living with three other law students in an apartment near the Claremont Hotel and was bored. "Studying law is a drag, but living with law students is worse. They're so dull," he often complained.

Once I was settled in my apartment, I fell into a routine. I now had a part-time job in a mailroom at the Engineering College, so I had to get up early, around 6 AM. I would rush down a deserted Telegraph Avenue, past Shakespeare's Bookstore, the Mediterraneum Cafe, Cody's Bookstore, past various bead and knick-knack shops, a couple of banks and Jim's Sporting Goods. I would hustle through a quiet, early morning campus and up to the Engineering College to the mailroom where I sorted mail and delivered it until 10 AM. If I didn't have a 10 AM class, I would retire to the Terrace for a big mid-morning breakfast until my 11 AM class. Usually, I had classes until 3 PM or so, and afterward I would wander back to the apartment to study. Twice a week, I played tennis in a PE class that I was taking, trying to get back into the game that I had neglected for the past three years. Routine dinners at the apartment were a do-it-yourself affair. Usually Corrine fixed something for herself and Jean-Paul, often a steak. I usually cooked a hamburger or a pork chop with frozen vegetables.

Perhaps a word here on how we reduced our food bill. Quite simply, we stole food. Jean-Paul was an expert little shoplifter. He wore his London Fog raincoat to the local supermarket and prowled the aisles, bought a few things and came back to the apartment, his pockets stuffed with four or five strip steaks. I tried it a few times myself. I was initially successful, but being so tall, I invariably attracted attention and one time I was caught red-handed. At first, the store manager threatened to call the police, but then he took pity on me and told me never to enter his store again. That ended my career as a meat shoplifter, but Jean-Paul kept it up and was never caught.

***

Soon we had a French scene going. I was able to speak French with Jean-Paul and other French friends to my hearts content. He was patient and pointed out my many flaws. We read and discussed the most popular French lit of the day: Camus' *L'Étranger, L'Homme Revolté, Le Mythe de Sisyphe;* Jean-Paul Sartre's *La Nausée;* and Alain Robbe Grillet's *La Jalousie.* We also poured over the hip English and American authors: Henry Miller (*Tropic of Cancer*), Lawrence Durrell (*The Alexandrian Quartet*) and J.P. Donleavy (*The Ginger Man*).

We took in the latest foreign films: Fellini's *La Dolce Vita,* Antonioni's *L'Avventura* and *La Notte;* Godard's *Breathless;* Alan Resnais' *Hiroshima Mon Amour* and *Last Year at Marienbad* and Truffaut's *Jules and Jim.* Further, we checked out some of the classics at the Cinema Guild on Telegraph: *Rules of the Game, Treasure of the Sierra Madre* and *Citizen Kane.* We debated and argued the merits of these books and films long into the night.

All this made me want to write like Camus (in English, of course). He seemed so simple, so direct, and so profound. I could feel the heat of sun bouncing off the beaches of Oran. I could understand why Mersault shot the Arab. I knew why revolution was inevitable, yet absurd and possibly futile. And I knew the rock of Sisyphus always rolled back down the hill.

I also had visions of directing a film like Jean-Luc Godard. After all, what did you need? A cheap hand-held 16-mm camera, a portable tape recorder, semi-professional actors, natural street scenes, preferably in Paris, although San Francisco would do. I could find my own Jean Paul Belmondo or Jean Seberg. The Bay Area was full of them. Wing it, ad-lib it, shoot it on the fly and slap it together—jump cuts and all. Voila, you had a New-Wave film.

It was a heady time indeed. Everything was possible. We concocted various schemes for living the good life. Not for us, the nine-to-five corporate world. We would stay in school forever, teach, travel, write, shoot film and screw.

We wanted to pursue an existential life in the face of the Absurd. Our mantra:

Everything is permitted.
You are the sum of your actions.
Only the rebel knows his true limits.
Je baise; donc, je suis.

***

I ball, therefore I am. This was the motto of the French graduate students who hung out at our apartment. Most were enrolled in a one-year program to get a master's degree in engineering from Berkeley. Within weeks of their arrival, many had American girlfriends, usually French majors who wanted to improve their French and maybe their lovemaking skills. I was amazed at how fast the French worked. And at their selection of worthy lovelies. All had the super refined looks to which French men are attracted and all dressed in the French style, even though most were from prosaic places like Vacaville or Fresno. Many had studied in Paris or elsewhere in France and spoke passable French. Others faked it or screwed so good that the French guys didn't care.

We often had big dinners of ten to twelve people, usually robust American fare such as filet mignon or roast courtesy of Jean-Paul. His French pals couldn't get enough of American beef. Sometimes Corrine cooked a French feast under the watchful eye of Jean-Paul. She had learned for him and inspired praise from the others:

"C'est fantastique!"

"Pas mal pour une Américaine."

Of course, the downside to all this French camaraderie was that the engineers left their little American girlfriends at the end of the year. They always returned to France and to their regular French girlfriends or their fiancées. Often the American girls were heartbroken, even though they had been promised nothing up front except a chance to be French for a year. I knew of only one French engineer who married an American. Ali had found a cute little blonde in Marin County who was a hairdresser and, although French born, she had spent most of her life in the Bay Area. For the rest of the American girls, the French interlude was only a bittersweet memory as they went off to marry ex-fraternity boys who became doctors, lawyers and dentists.

27. HISTORIAN?

Amid all this extracurricular activity, I still had to get through an array of history courses to complete my major. One of them was European Diplomatic History taught by Professor S. His course was very popular because he had the ability to make sense out of the complex diplomatic maneuverings of Metternich, Bismarck, Disraeli, Chamberlain, Balfour, Lloyd-George and Churchill—all great men, all affecting the course of European history throughout the late nineteenth and early twentieth centuries.

Professor S. was a nationally known historian. And, as I came to learn, he was also an informal recruiter for the CIA and the State Department. His job was to pinpoint bright students in whom these agencies might be interested.

In November, I went to see Professor S. because I was concerned about a C he had given me on a midterm. I was convinced my test was worth a B or even an A. The question was "In what ways was Napoleon III a tragic figure?" First, I defined what I thought historical tragedy was (rational actions precipitating disastrous outcomes) and then I cited various historical events that illustrated Napoleon III's tragic behavior. I thought I had done a pretty good job on the test, but Professor S. thought otherwise.

"Mr. Brown, good to see you. Sit down," said Professor S. pointing to a leather wingchair. His office was very large and outfitted like a gentlemen's library. A tall, distinguished, gray-haired man, he eyed me for a second and then came right to the point. "What can I do for you?"

"I want to take issue with the grade you gave me on the last mid-term." I said handing my exam booklet over to him.

"Oh really," he said as he put on his reading glasses and flipped through the pages in a fast read.

After reading, he looked up and I continued. "Yes, I feel that I more than answered the question of why Napoleon III was a tragic figure."

"Well let's see..." and then S. went on to say I had left out x, y and z events.

"I was well aware of those events," I responded, "but in my estimation they did not contribute to his tragic character."

"Mr. Brown, that may be true, but at least you should have mentioned them so we would know that you knew. I see you received a B on the first midterm. If you get a B, or better yet, an A on the final that should get you B in the course," he said handing my exam booklet back. "Tell me, Mr. Brown do you plan on going to graduate school in history?"

"No, probably not."

"Well then what do you plan to do?" he asked taking off his reading glasses and rubbing his eyes.

"I'm not sure, possibly law school, journalism or teaching," I said

"All worthwhile endeavors, of course, but have you considered going into government work?" he asked.

"You mean become a bureaucrat?"

"Not at all. I'm thinking State Department or perhaps the Central Intelligence Agency. My son is in the CIA and finds it a rewarding career. The work is fascinating and he is serving his country. Of course, you are aware that ninety-percent of CIA work has nothing to do with covert activity. It's mostly analysis stuff. Perfect for history majors."

"No, I hadn't thought about it one way or the other," I said.

"Well, one of my little projects here at Berkeley is to point out likely candidates to the State Department and the CIA. You seem bright enough and you have a good appearance. Appearance is important, plus the right background. Religion?"

"Protestant."

"Yes, I see. Good. You know these agencies traditionally recruit out of the Ivy League, but now they want to expand their recruitment efforts. So they are eyeing the leading schools here on the West Coast—Berkeley, Stanford and UCLA and the like. If you are interested, I can give you a number. There'll be tests and such, but with my recommendation, that should present no problem. By the way, if accepted, you are exempt from the military draft."

"Thanks, I'll think about it," I said, taking my test back and shaking his hand.

Professor S.'s little conversation stuck with me. Government Service. Overseas. Travel. Cloak and dagger. Draft exempt. Why not? I knew one AKL brother who had gone on to work for the State Department, but the word was he was really working for the CIA. Occasionally, Larry showed up at fraternity functions and regaled us with stories of his overseas postings in the Philippines, Southeast Asia and Indonesia. He was officially an economic attaché at various embassies, but even he admitted he didn't know squat about economics. His major had been political science. His real job was to keep track of communist doings in that region of the world.

It sounded glamorous, but based on my Army ROTC experience, I didn't think I would do well in big governmental organizations. Still, getting out of the draft was tempting. A more likely choice for me was the Peace Corps. It was only a two-year gig, but it too deferred you from the draft. Although only a year old, the Peace Corps was already popular among graduating Berkeley students. As mentioned, it was an option that Bobbie and I had already discussed.

We could teach English somewhere in Africa or the Far East. Maybe do some good. It would be a hoot. Also, I would be able to see my government in action abroad. The State Department, the United States Information Service, the Agency for International Development. Maybe even the spooks. It was something to think about. Meanwhile, I had to get on with my history major.

Inspired by my meeting with Professor S., I studied hard for the rest of the course and managed to get a B.

***

My historical Waterloo that fall was History 101. All Cal history majors had to take History 101, a much-dreaded course that focused on the process of formal historical research. This was a make or break course that determined your future as a historical scholar at Berkeley, which then had the strongest history department on the West Coast.

Most of Cal's history professors had graduated from the Ivy League and had taught at those institutions for years before coming to Berkeley. The attraction for most was instant tenure and a position at the top public university in the nation. A further attraction, as already noted, was the Bay Area itself with its benign weather, myriad of interesting attractions and pleasant, informal living.

The upshot of all of this was these professors had set out to remake Berkeley's history department. They had designed a rigorous curriculum that included historiography, which evolved into a weeder course to separate the bright stars from the also-rans.

Thus it was, one fall morning at the beginning of my senior year, I and twelve other history majors trooped into a temporary classroom behind Dwinelle Hall for History 101. I looked properly historical with my old tweed sport jacket worn over an open dress shirt and khakis. The others were an odd assortment of students—several women—one of whom was a looker, the others homely and shabby in need of a good hair wash. The guys ran from shaggy to fraternity-boy crisp. The teacher, an associate professor, was a heavyset woman with a vaguely German accent. Dr. G. looked harried and unkempt, but she wasted no time getting started:

"This is History 101, a course in historical research and bibliographic methods. As you all know, it is a required course for history majors. It is the most important history course you will take here at Berkeley because it will determine your fitness for graduate school in the discipline at Berkeley or at any other top school in the nation."

A collective gulp from the students. She flashed a tight little smile.

"We will work hard here—researching, studying, writing and discussing various methods of historical research. There will be no tests or finals. Instead you will be graded on class participation, your formal presentations and one major paper on a particular historical problem."

A tentative sigh from the students. No tests, no quizzes and no final. How bad can it be?

Dr. G continued, "We will discuss the paper in more detail later. Suffice to say it will require rigorous research and writing. I will present you with a choice of controversial historical events, noting how they have been interpreted over the years. Your job is to pick one of these events and to research it out as to the facts and the various interpretation of the event. You will critique those interpretations as well as offer your own based on your research. In addition to the standard texts of the event, you will be working with original source materials, newspapers, eyewitness accounts and government records. All of this is on reserve in the main library. You will have special passes to utilize this material."

Hey, this could be interesting, I thought. We get to play junior historians. I was looking forward to working on this paper.

We met once a week for two hours, a minimal time commitment, but it was an intense two hours filled with sharp discussion about various historical problems. We were expected to read several books on the historical method and then bring it to bear on the particular event that we had chosen. Most of the events involved controversial actions by the British and Americans overseas in the 19th and early 20th centuries — the Boer Wars, Dewey in the Philippines, the Opium Wars, the Indian Mutiny, etc.

Even though I plunged into my work and participated in class discussion, it was soon obvious I couldn't match the level or the intensity of the others. Unlike me, all were committed history majors who desperately wanted to go to graduate school. However, I thought I was doing well enough. I took a big picture approach to the various historical problems. I was good on trends and theory but short on facts. One day, I gave a presentation for which I was poorly prepared. I was suffering from serious hangover and so nervous that I kept clicking a ballpoint pen as I tried to make sense of some sketchy note cards while I talked.

After my presentation, Dr. G. confronted me in front of the others.

"Mr. Brown, I do hope you do better on your paper, because this presentation was weak. You seem to be groping for the specific historical facts to support your interpretation. Also, a tip — stop clicking that damn pen when you talk. It so distracting."

Pulling myself together, I countered, "Don't worry Dr. G, my paper will be loaded with facts properly placed in their historical context."

"Well, I hope so. You appear to have much work to do."

"Yes, ma'am."

I had selected the Jamison Raid for my topic. This was an incursion led by Dr. Leander Star Jamison into the Transvaal in South Africa in December of 1895 at the instigation of the great South African imperialist, Cecil Rhodes. Rhodes had his eye on the gold and diamond mines of the Dutch Boer Republics. Jamison and his men had ridden into the Transvaal supposedly to protect the foreign settlers (mainly British nationals) from the "unjust" rule of the Boers. The anticipated uprising by the British settlers never took place and Jamison and his men were captured. The Boers eventually turned them over to the British who tried Jamison and sentenced him to fifteen months in prison. All along, the British government officially denied any advance knowledge of the raid when, in fact, there was much evidence to the contrary. The Boers, however, started organizing for battle and four years later, in 1899, the Second Boer War broke out.

The historical problem was what did the British government know and when did it know it concerning the raid? I dutifully buried myself in the stacks of the library and screened roll after roll of barely readable microfiche of the newspapers of the time. Most accounts were from the British point of view, although there was a scattering of Afrikaans publications that I couldn't read. Fortunately, several books written by Afrikaners about the raid had been translated into English. One author in particular, Jean van der Poel, pointed out that Colonial Secretary, Joseph Chamberlain was well aware that something was brewing, although he probably he didn't know the exact details of the planning and timing of the raid. In any event, Chamberlain was cleared of all complicity by a parliamentary committee inquiry that whitewashed the whole affair.

When I finally sat down to write the paper, I first sketched in the background to the raid by hitting the historical highlights of the British and the Dutch in South Africa. Then I described the actual raid based on contemporary accounts. Next, I delved into the propaganda war, the pros and cons, the charges and counter-charges. Finally, I concluded that the Afrikaners were probably right. Chamberlain was well aware of the planned raid, but preferred "official ignorance" for later deniability. This led to inevitable outcome four years later—the Second Boer War.

When I was done, I thought my thirty-page paper was well written and well documented. However, I had written it in a narrative, journalistic style rather than as a formal historical research paper. And while this made it easy to read, it was to cause me no end of grief from Dr. G.

"This is a rather engaging style, Mr. Brown, but you are light on historical facts and analysis." She said casually glancing over my paper when I first showed it to her

"I thought I documented everything pretty well. Do you have any specific ideas where I could improve it?"

"No, not right now. I would have to spend some time studying it— time I don't have. Suffice to say, stiffen it up a bit."

"I will do my best."

I went back and spent hours retyping the paper on my old Olympia with the flying "f," adding even more facts and footnotes, thinking that would satisfy the bitch.

The big day came when I had to present my paper to the class and defend my thesis. Since I knew the story cold, I thought I gave a rather good presentation. I handed out mimeographed maps of the Transvaal with bordering South Africa, showing the route of the raid. I spoke authoritatively with few notes, but when I was done, Dr. G and a couple of my fellow students were skeptical about my conclusion that Colonial Secretary Chamberlain knew about the raid in advance.

"Where is the evidence that supports this conclusion?" asked Dr. G.

"Despite my best efforts to pin this down, detailed documentation in this area is lacking," I explained. "I had to rely mainly on Afrikaans sources."

"So, Mr. Brown, what we are dealing with here is a one-sided source whose self-interest is being served by assuming a plot by Chamberlain. Correct?" said Dr. G in her snotty, Teutonic manner.

"I suppose," I said lamely.

"See if you can nail that down a bit better in your paper, Mr. Brown."

And so it went. I tried to beef up that part of the paper with more documentation, but time was short, so finally I said *fuck it* and turned the paper in thinking it was good enough for at least a C.

A week later, Dr. G. handed the papers back in sealed envelopes. When I opened mine later, right there on the front page, in bold red ink was a big fat D. That most likely meant a D for the course—the kiss of death for graduate study in history at Berkeley. Although I had no plans to pursue graduate studies in history, I was pissed. I thought I deserved at least a C.

When I went to see Dr. G. a few days later, she was very defensive. First, she pointed out that my two presentations were weak. Then she delivered her opinion on the paper. "It's not up to the standards of historical research for a UC graduate student. And this course is fundamentally about your potential to do serious historical research."

"What do you mean?" I protested. "I spent hours in the library doing research. It's all documented here."

"Yes, you appear to have done the work, but the result is a rather glib and superficial.."

"You mean it's readable," I countered.

"Readability is fine, but not at the expense of serious scholastic presentation. You should have gone much more in-depth into your sources and presented your findings in a more orderly manner. You have written this in the narrative form that precludes systematic historical analysis."

I protested, saying that there was plenty of analysis in it.

She continued, "If you have a problem with this grade, Mr. Brown, you can appeal it to the department head, but I don't think you will have much luck."

I could have murdered the bitch on the spot. But she sensed violence was in the air and immediately got up and left the classroom where we had been meeting and returned to her office. I seriously debated challenging the grade, but she was right. Grades were rarely changed. And with my record of accomplishment at Berkeley, the chance of getting this grade changed was zilch.

"Too bad," they would say. "Not up to snuff. Can't let that type continue in history at Berkeley. Would hurt our reputation. No, better to cut it in the bud right now. Decent chap though. Will probably do well in government or secondary teaching."

Therefore, I let it go. I had other fish to fry. Still, that D looked bad on my transcript. The only D in my major. The ultimate humiliation.

***

However, the next semester my lot in history improved. I took a seminar in history entitled *The Role of the Irrational in Revolutionary Thought*. This was a combination graduate and undergraduate course that would complete my major. The course focused on revolutionary thinkers and intellectual rebels. The professor posed the question: What incited someone to revolutionary violence and anarchism? Was it a rational or irrational impulse? We read Bakunin, Nietzsche, Schopenhauer, Freud, Marcuse, Norman O' Brown, Eric Hofer and came to no clear conclusion. I liked the course because it covered the history of ideas, not so much the names and dates of historical events.

Professor F., a rumpled, slightly seedy man with a scraggly beard and a Gauloise dangling from his lips, spoke as if he spent a lot of time in revolutionary cells. "If you think history is a rational progression of events, forget it," he declared. "Chance and happenstance. What if the assassin had missed when he shot at Archduke Ferdinand in Sarajevo? Would there have been World War I?"

Alternatively: "You may think that great men in history were motivated by reason, but if you dig, you will find the irrational at play in most of their decisions."

Or: "Then there is the question of mass psychology. What motivates the mob? It's certainly not reason. The Nazis recognized this and exploited it to the hilt with the German people. Even today, you can see this irrationality at work in advertising and merchandising."

The students in this seminar were a scruffy, bearded lot. One student in particular, Garvin, fancied himself a Cuban revolutionary. A stocky, pugnacious little guy with a bushy beard and an attitude, Garvin wore army surplus fatigues to class with a Castro cap and dark sunglasses.

"The Cuban revolution is a case study of everything we are talking about," said Garvin. "What has inspired these normally placid people to throw off the chains of oppression of the Batista government? Hope. Hope against all odds. Hope for a better life. Seemingly irrational hope."

The course had no exams and like History 101, we were graded on class participation and a paper at the end of the semester. For my paper, I chose to write on the role of the irrational in history as explored by

Dostoyevsky, Nietzsche, Sartre and Camus. Professor F. liked the idea, but wondered if I taking on too much.

"Whole books have been written on this subject, Mr. Brown."

"Yes, I know, but I plan to skim the highlights to give shape to the bigger picture here. Further, I'm very familiar with most of these authors. I won't be starting from scratch."

"Well, O.K. Give it a shot," he said dubiously. "But don't give me a book. Boil it down to twenty or thirty pages at the most."

I went off and happily buried myself in these literary greats for the next few weeks. The paper I produced pleased him, probably because I regurgitated just about everything he had said in class. I got a B+ on the paper and a B+ in the course. I now felt somewhat redeemed as a history major.

In fact, Professor F. told me upon handing my paper back that I had a feel for intellectual history. "You make this stuff readable and interesting. History needs those who can do that. Are you going on in this area?"

"Ah...I don't think so," I replied. Then I spilled out the whole sorry story about my D in historical bibliography.

"Yeah," he responded. "That course is a killer. The old guard around here runs it. They get carried away. They want everyone to write history as they do. Dry, dusty and unread. That course has discouraged a lot of potential grad students in history. But look, I'll tell you what. If you need a recommendation to go on in the field come to me. There are ways to get around 101."

"Thanks. I'll consider it," I said feeling somewhat vindicated. Maybe further study in history wasn't such a lost cause after all.

28. REVOLUTION I

She: What are you rebelling against?
Brando: What have you got?

The Wild One

In the fall of 1962, the prospect of a full-scale student revolution at Berkeley was mostly a gleam in the collective eyes of a few committed activists. The only real political revolution going on was the Cuban Revolution. Fidel Castro was now in the third year of his regime. He had redistributed land to the peasants and nationalized that nation's major industries. And, increasingly, he had adopted Marxist-Leninist rhetoric in describing his revolution: "The duty of every revolutionary is to make revolution. We know that in America and throughout the world the revolution will be victorious…"

This was music to the ears of those itching for change. The Castro supporters sat in groups on the Terrace in their army camouflage fatigues, Castro caps and sunglasses, drinking coffee and reading to one another from the works of Che Guevara and other revolutionary writers. Garvin from my history seminar was usually among them. The conversations usually went something like this:

"We can use the Cuban revolution as a template here at Berkeley."

"The university administration and the regents are corrupt, dictatorial and blind to the wants and needs of the students."

"Somehow we have to bring this administration down."

Most of the Castro brigade were members of the Young Socialist Alliance and operated the Berkeley chapter of Fair Play For Cuba. All were eager to go to the scene of the action: Cuba. Despite the travel ban, a few did go to observe the new workers' paradise, courtesy of the YSA and came back singing its praises. "Free land, free medical care, improved education—it's a proletariat dream come true."

When the Cuban missile crisis came along in October, those in Fidel fatigues didn't pause a beat. "Serves us right," they said. "We tried to invade Cuba in the Bay of Pigs. The Russians have every right to aim their Cuban missiles at us. We have had nuclear missiles surrounding Russia for years."

The nuclear threat to the U.S. never worried them, but it worried many on campus. On the day of the big showdown, Wednesday, October 24, everyone was sure Soviet missiles would be launched towards the U.S. Berkeley had all but shut down. Most stayed indoors glued to the television. A few students had taken off for Lake Tahoe and the mountains, anywhere out of radioactive reach. There were reports that Nevada residents were threatening to shoot any invading Californian who sought shelter over their border. Local debate centered on whether the Bay Area was a worthy target. Most thought that New York and Washington would be the first to go.

I remember walking around an eerily empty campus, catching only fleeting glimpses of students scurrying here and there. The high overcast day resonated with the psychic cloud that was hanging over all of us. Was the unimaginable about to become reality? Was the first strike on its way? It all seemed so stupid. So unreal. Like two big kids playing chicken. It reminded me of the famous drag race scene in the movie *Rebel Without A Cause*, in which James Dean and his hoodlum rival race their hopped-up cars ever closer to the edge of an ocean cliff and certain oblivion—neither one ready to give in.

Despite the campus gloom and doom, Professor S. didn't cancel his usual morning lecture and the auditorium was packed. The word had gotten out and students who were not even taking his diplomatic history course showed up to hear his steady counsel. Professor S. spent most of the lecture ruminating on the rise and fall of civilizations and the stupid mistakes its leaders often make. However, he was of the opinion that cooler heads would prevail in the missile crisis, which, in fact, they did. The Russians began to dismantle their missiles on Cuba. Later, the U.S. did the same in Turkey. Only decades later would we learn how close we were to real nuclear war, but on that day in October we left Professor S.'s lecture heartened and hopeful that we would not be blown to smithereens.

Meanwhile, the Cuban revolutionaries continued to meet on the Terrace and man the Fair Play For Cuba table next to the student union. They distributed literature touting the glories of the revolution, signed up students to take part in the cause and collected donations to forward to Cuba. Other tables promoted various causes such as abolishing the House Un-American Activities Committee, ending the Speaker Ban on campus and working to end segregation. Posters and leaflets were pasted everywhere on the tables, the chairs and the light poles along Bancroft Avenue. It was a colorful, revolutionary mess. Change was in the air.

At the urging of SLATE and other student groups, the University Board of Regents finally ended mandatory participation in ROTC in the fall of 1962. Henceforth participation in ROTC would be strictly voluntarily. In part, this had come about after a Cal honor student had complained to the University administration that Army ROTC had graded him down on such vagaries as military bearing and comportment as retribution for his anti-ROTC stance. This was great news for most male students at Berkeley, but too late for me. The damage had been done. As noted, my two years of Army ROTC at Cal had effectively sabotaged my grade point average.

SLATE's current battle centered on getting rid of restrictions on who could speak on campus. These sets of restrictions, commonly known as the Speaker Ban, had evolved during the Cold War hysteria of the 1950s. Over the years, the university had banned speakers associated with the Communist Party and other controversial figures such as former Vice President Henry Wallace and more recently, Nation of Islam leader Malcolm X.

Although UC President Clark Kerr had recently liberalized the speaker ban, SLATE was still not satisfied. It sponsored an initiative to get rid of the ban entirely. SLATE received support from Cal student government, many professors and the campus newspaper, *The Daily Californian*. Finally, in spring of 1963, the Regents voted to remove the ban. This was seen as a victory for SLATE and for free speech on campus.

***

One day I spotted Steve running a Civil Rights table on Bancroft, the same Steve with whom I had roomed at Lake Tahoe two summers ago when we both worked at the Cal Neva lodge. He was a nice, middle-class kid back then having a summer lark at the lake. Now he was a straggly, bearded, unkempt Berkeley student in a stinky Army fatigue jacket.

"It's all happening, man. It's all going down at Berkeley. This is where it's at. This is the future," he proclaimed.

Steve had been attending Pomona College in L.A., but after two years there, he had become bored and transferred to Berkeley for some action.

He looked me over. I was in my tweed jacket, dress shirt and khakis — still part of the button-down crowd. "You ought to join SLATE, Al. We have some great parties. Lots of chicks who love to get high when their work is done."

"Nah, I'm beyond that." I said. "I'm graduating this year, and I have to deal with the draft. I'm thinking about joining the Peace Corps."

"Peace Corps is all right," Steve said. "Nice idea, but look at the reality. Many around here think it's a move by Kennedy to co-opt the revolution. Others think it will turn you into a CIA spy."

"Maybe, I said, but it's a two year gig overseas, hopefully somewhere interesting, with paid room and board. Maybe, I can do some good, maybe not, but when it's over, they'll give me a bunch of money, enough for a year or two of graduate school. Then I'll be past twenty-six, past draft age.

"I dig, said Steve nodding. Whatever works for you."

The Civil Rights movement in which Steve was involved was starting to gather steam at Berkeley. It first manifested itself with the Berkeley Fair Housing Ordinance. The Berkeley city council passed an ordinance in January of 1963 prohibiting discrimination based on race in the sale and rental of housing. The few blacks (including international students) attending Cal had long complained about finding a place to rent near campus. At the time, Berkeley was probably as segregated as any city in the South. Caucasians lived in the hills east of Shattuck Avenue and blacks lived west, down on the flats near the freeway.

The white property owners reacted instantaneously to the ordinance. Over ten thousand signed a petition to put the ordinance on the ballot, and it was duly overturned in the April municipal elections. The prevailing attitude among whites was desegregation was all right for the South, but not for Berkeley, supposedly the most liberal city in the Bay Area. The reaction among many student activists was "Berkeley is no better than Birmingham."

Birmingham, Alabama, was a flash point for the civil rights movement. In May of 1963, we saw scenes on television of Bull Conner and his men with water hoses knocking down protesting blacks. We watched as police used snarling dogs and electric prods to quiet the demonstrators who were demanding decent housing and desegregated education. Civil rights leader Martin Luther King Jr. who had organized the protest was thrown into jail where he wrote his famous letter from the Birmingham jail articulating the righteousness of their cause.

However, there was no sense of moral outrage among the general Cal student population. The battles of the South seemed so distant. And despite the flare up over the Berkeley Fair Housing Ordinance, most students felt smug or indifferent, looking down at the racist rednecks in the South. Then, the black author James Baldwin lectured on campus. People talked about it for days afterwards. I was one of the nine thousand in attendance at the Harmon Gym. I had read his *Notes of a Native Son* and *Nobody Knows My Name* in which he described growing up black in America. I was impressed that Baldwin wrote not in anger, but in sorrow with a brooding sense of tragedy. His lecture on race was in the same vein. A small, humble, sad-looking man, yet he still projected strength. He said he was hopeful for a peaceful solution to integration in both the North and the South, but that violence was a probable outcome.

Meanwhile, the civil rights group CORE was stepping up its activities in the Bay Area. It demanded that local employers, especially the giant retailer Montgomery Wards, hire more blacks. After several demonstrations, Wards signed an agreement to do just that. CORE kept the pressure on other local retailers in Oakland and Berkeley and slowly reached agreements with them. A local civil rights group, the Ad Hoc Committee to End Discrimination, temporarily closed down the popular Mel's Drive-In in San Francisco for not hiring enough blacks.

So where was I in all of this? Aside from attending the James Baldwin lecture and sympathizing from afar, I was nowhere. I hardly knew any black students at Cal. The few I did run into were very sharp and well off, the sons and daughters of doctors and lawyers. Hardly products of the ghetto. Except for the color of their skin, they talked and acted like white folks: neat, clean and well dressed in the latest preppy fashions. Indeed, now and then I would see a stunning black chick and wonder.

I flashed back to the summer I had worked on a survey crew in Richmond, north of Berkeley. Driving through the black section of town on an overtime Sunday, we passed by block after block of cheap stucco bungalows with wilted palm trees out front. The paint might be chipping and the stucco dirty, but the bright yellow and pink Cadillacs parked in front were spotless. The local blacks, still clinging to their southern ways, were always dressed up in their Sunday's finest. Broad-brim hats, flower silk shirts and lavender pants with two-tone leather shoes, usually black and white, but sometimes, yellow and brown.

Our crew chief, Coop, drove slowly down the streets, eyeing the young black women strolling or lolling about, sitting on their porches in flowing print dresses with white shoes. Sultry looking women, cat eyes, perfect full lips, stark white teeth, full bodied, breasts that went on forever, a sexy swing in their walk.

"Hey Al," he said to an 18-year-old me, "ever had a piece of black ass?"

No answer.

"Course not. You're too young or scared. You don't know what you're missing. In the Army in the South, we would get us some of that stuff, young and willing. Best ass I ever had. Take my advice and try it sometime, Al. You'll never forget it."

29. REVOLUTION II

The student and civil rights revolution wasn't the only one brewing on the Terrace. From mid-morning to late afternoon, the Terrace was the social center of the campus, a place to greet old friends and meet new ones. It was also ground zero for the sexual revolution at Berkeley and some say for the country. It had become a beehive of hormonal indiscretion. What had changed?

Perhaps it was a budding feminism that empowered women to do what men were already doing—having a career and getting laid. Perhaps they agreed with feminist Betty Freidan that, "no woman gets an orgasm from shining the kitchen floor." Perhaps it was a normal adolescent desire to rebel against their parents. Perhaps it was all of these, but primarily it was the wide availability of the birth control pill in Berkeley through such clinics as Planned Parenthood. Before I left for Europe, hardly anyone was taking the pill because of its restricted distribution. Most sexually advanced women used a diaphragm. However, the pill was now sold widely under the name of Ortho Novum and over two million women in the U.S. were using it. At Berkeley, it seemed everyone was on the pill and hot to trot.

The other factor in all of this was easily obtainable abortion information (at least in Berkeley) even though abortion was still illegal in California except in a few special cases. In 1962, the abortion movement was gaining momentum because of the thalidomide scare. Hundreds of women in the U.S. and Europe had taken the tranquilizer thalidomide during pregnancy and gave birth to children with deformed or missing arms and legs. An Arizona housewife, Sherri Finkbine, who had taken thalidomide, was refused an abortion in her home state. Finkbine flew to Sweden for a safe and legal abortion and returned a national celebrity among abortion rights activists.

Sweden was also a popular option among Berkeley co-eds seeking an abortion. The Cal travel office ran frequent charter flights to Sweden. A cheaper option was to travel down to Tijuana, Mexico to several well-run abortion clinics. A third option was an underground list of Bay Area doctors who would perform abortions.

Jean-Paul's girlfriend, Corrine, was in this predicament when she met Jean-Paul. She had been impregnated by a former boyfriend who had left her to ride his motorcycle across the U.S. Much to Jean-Paul's dismay, he had to make all the abortion arrangements, namely a trip to Tijuana. He managed to locate the boyfriend and shame him into contributing to the cause—about two hundred dollars. Jean-Paul and Corrine scrapped up the rest. Corrine and a girlfriend took the Greyhound to Tijuana for the procedure. Corrine returned several days later, pale and sick. She recuperated at our apartment, lying about on the couch reading, now and then getting up to make tea.

She was obviously very sad about the whole thing. She felt the abortion had been necessary, but was, in fact, grieving for the unborn child.

"You guys think it's so easy," she said once staring out through the picture window at the Oakland hills in the distance.

"What's so easy?" I asked.

"Getting an abortion. You just say, 'knocked up? No problem. Just go off and get an abortion'."

"I don't think Jean-Paul thought it was easy," I replied.

"Well, he wasn't there. How would he know?" she said with a tinge of bitterness. "According to the doctor, it was only a little piece of flesh in the first few weeks. You can't really say it was human. But it was part of me." She stifled a sob.

I said nothing.

The moral of this sad little story to me was to avoid getting somebody pregnant at all costs. Pill or not, I had a six-pack of Trojans in my top desk drawer.

Even so, during this time few worried about the consequences of casual sex or sexually transmitted diseases. The most anybody contracted was the clap or the crabs. Syphilis was rare. And it was all curable. The AIDS breakout was a generation away. No worries mate!

My friend Steve had told me about a couple of wild parties he had been to with his activist friends at a Southside house. As he put it, "Shit what's a little clap if you get to fuck four or five chicks in a night. You just roll on down to the student clinic, get a shot and keep on going. You're only on the scene once in your life, Brown."

"Yeah, it sounds intriguing," I said, "but I heard the women are kind of scaggy, beat out, balling with any jerk."

"Some are. Some aren't. Some are really fine. You just take potluck. Whoever shows up. You might be surprised. Women show up with their boyfriends and husbands. Even a few professors' wives. The guys don't mind if their ol' lady gets screwed because they're looking for action themselves. Lots of bedrooms in this old house. Lot of pot around to loosen things up. If you're really worried about some disease-o, just wear a rubber. No sweat."

I imagined big-titted women roaming around bare-assed, unkempt, hair under their arm and probably smelling a little. Like cavewomen hunting for a mate. I decided to take a pass. There was too much other action around. In fact, the fall was a blur of willing, eager, young bodies. The apartment was the key — having a place to *coucher en paix* as Jean-Paul put it.

***

Amid all this carnality, there was Clarissa — cool, ethereal blonde. Beyond the flesh, but still interesting. Clarissa and I used to hang out on the Terrace, comparing notes on our respective History 101 classes. She would lean forward, elbows on the table, holding her head, smiling her radiant smile, her stark blue eyes twinkling. She always had a perky, quizzical look on her face as I discussed my poor performance in the class.

"Boy, Al, you really did draw a bitch. My professor Mike is a doll. We get away with anything. You should have changed sections, you mo-ron."

"How can you look so young and innocent and be so hip to the ways of history professors at Berkeley?" I asked.

"How come I'm taking this upper-division course in history when I'm only a sophomore?" she replied rhetorically. "Because I'm smart and maybe cute, but mostly smart. That's why I'm in the honors program here and have a hefty scholarship.

Clarissa was a puzzle. I didn't know why she wasted her time with me, a mid-level intellect at this over-achieving school. However, she was also charming and a challenge. She had an off-the-wall wit. She kept her distance physically, but she said she liked my nonchalance and thought I was cute too. I met her through a friend on the Terrace. "This is one different chick you have to meet," he had said.

Clarissa was majoring in both history and philosophy and planned to go to graduate school. We had gone out a few times, but our relationship was platonic. She knew I was seeing other women and that seemed fine with her. Her attitude was screw whomever you want, but save your brain for me. Also, she let it be known she wasn't into flesh yet. "I'm too young, too Catholic," she used to say while offering up a light kiss on the lips.

Clarissa had gone to Catholic school in Rochester, New York. Her father worked for Eastman Kodak there, and he had been transferred to San Jose in Clarissa's junior year of high school.

"I didn't learn anything at that public school," she told me. "It was supposed to be good, but the teachers were too indulgent with the spoiled brats that went there. Whatever brains I have, I attribute to the nuns in Rochester."

A year after moving to California, Clarissa's father was laid off and had to work odd sales jobs on the Peninsula. As a result, there was no money for Clarissa to attend a private school like Stanford. Clarissa settled on Cal because it was cheap and she had a scholarship.

One Friday night, we went to see *Last Year at Marienbad* by Alain Resnais. I had seen it once before, but Clarissa had not.

"I liked the idea of the film, but the characters were cold," she remarked. "The woman was a stone mannequin. Still, it was intriguing with its play on memory and reality — like a hall of mirrors."

I nodded as she expanded her analysis, all the while watching her eyes sparkle in the streetlights as we walked along.

At the door of her boarding house, a light kiss on the lips.

"You know, Clarissa, we should get more involved," I said.

She smiled enigmatically as she withdrew through the doorway. "Maybe," she replied.

So pure, so blonde, my own Grace Kelly.

Still, I was horny. What to do? Where to go? Hey! I realized I was only a few short blocks from Joyce's place. Joyce was a sexy little number my French class that I had gone out with. She lived in a large house with several other roommates. The door was wide open. There had apparently been a party, but the revelers had gone off somewhere. Wine and beer bottles littered the floor. I walked up the creaky stairs to Joyce's bedroom. There she was, sleeping soundly. I took off my clothes and slid in beside her. She was startled at first, then seeing it was only me, smiled, cuddled and was soon underway. All the time I was thinking about Clarissa and how we had a commonality of spirit

30. BOBBIE

How did I rationalize all this screwing around in relation to Bobbie? Of course, she was far away in Chicago plugging through her senior year at Lake Forest College. At the beginning of the fall semester, we wrote weekly letters and telephoned every other week. At first, I missed her terribly. I kept having flash images of her at the summit of Mont St. Victoire. After a long dirty climb, we took one Sunday, I wrote in my journal:

> *You jingle in the crisp, clear mountain air.*
> *What a mess you were, hair hanging down.*
> *Squashed blouse covered by a filthy suede jacket.*
> *Completely unconscious of the people around.*
> *Smiling as you shivered in the wind and sun.*

However, as we both became more involved in school, the letters and calls became more infrequent. Originally, Bobbie had planned to come to the Bay Area over Christmas vacation, but then due to family obligations, she decided at the last minute, to stay in Chicago. I sensed there was something more to it than that. I had been counting on her visit. I had big plans to show her around Berkeley, the Bay Area and to take her skiing. Furthermore, when I brought up the Peace Corps, she grew increasingly vague.

So Christmas came and went. I was discovering that carrying on a long distant relationship was a lot of work and anxiety. As the French say, "distance is the enemy of love." Also, there were too many other female distractions at Berkeley. If I were committed to Bobbie, why was I chasing around here? Was I that serious about her? Did I really want to get married and go off with her in the Peace Corps? I didn't know and increasingly, I didn't care. Then, just as I had given up hope that she would ever come to Berkeley, I got an urgent phone call.

"O.K. I'm coming out, Allan," Bobbie announced. "I found a cheap airfare. I really want to see you and San Francisco over semester break. Can we eat at Fisherman's Wharf and do all the tourist stuff?"

"Sure, sure. I'm still here waiting for you," I responded, half happy, half bewildered, half disappointed. I had been planning to go skiing over the break, but now I had to abandon those plans.

***

One rainy morning, a few days later, I picked up Bobbie up at San Francisco Airport. She came bounding down the gangway and jumped into my waiting arms. She smelled so fresh, so full of the Chicago lakefront air, her cheeks flushed, her reddish blonde hair glistening under her little tartan cap. She had lost a few pounds since I last saw her. "I can't stand the food at Lake Forest College," she explained.

She was stunning in her Scottish plaid skirt, green cashmere sweater and knee socks with cute black buckle loafers. She was fresh, unsullied with her big wide Midwestern smile. Light-years apart from the second-day pastry that I had been sampling at Berkeley. I felt a pang of guilt.

I lugged her suitcase over to the parking lot and then drove to San Francisco through a heavy downpour.

"You sure you want to see San Francisco today?" I asked. "It's so wet."

"Of course I want to see it, rainy or not. Can we have lunch at Fisherman's Wharf?" she said, tugging at my sleeve.

"Sure. Why not," I responded driving on.

I took her on the standard tour along the 17-Mile Drive. First through Golden Gate Park, all green, lush and wet with dripping eucalyptus trees. Then out to Ocean Beach with its nasty gray sand and roiling dirty waves. We got out for a minute and stood in the rain. Bobbie was transfixed by the Pacific and did her little jingle, a fake shiver that she picked up from Peter Pan's Tinker Bell. At the nearby Cliff House, we tried to spot the seals on the rocks, but not even the big tourist telescopes on the deck could bring them into focus through the mist.

Back in the car, I drove by the stately Palace of The Legion Of Honor with its neoclassic splendor. Bobbie was eager to spend some time here, but as I explained, time was short and noted that its art collection paled in comparison to that of the Art Institute in Chicago.

"That may be true, but I still want to see it, if not today then later," said Bobbie who was an art history major. "I read somewhere they had acquired an El Greco."

"Do say," I said. "But it boils down to lunch at Fisherman's Wharf or spending time here."

She thought for a moment and then answered, "Lunch with a lot of seafood."

On the way, we drove through Sea Cliff, the ritziest residential section of San Francisco, which featured mansions perched on oceanfront cliffs with magnificent, if sodden views, of the Pacific and the Golden Gate. Finally, I drove up Russian Hill for more views of the city. All the time Bobbie was remarking on the pastel colors of the buildings.

"Oh, that's so cute. All those greens, yellows and pinks. Imagine. It looks like a toy town. Is it for real?" she teased.

"Yes, it's real," I responded, slightly amazed at her remark. I had always taken the pastel colors of the buildings for granted.

We parked the car on the top of Russian Hill and hopped on a cable car heading down Hyde Street. At the bottom, we walked over to Fisherman's Wharf, past the tourist shops, the fish markets and the boiling crab pots. Bobbie's eyes were all a glitter. "Wow. I've never seen so much seafood."

"What about the old port of Marseille?" I said. "Remember the times we had bouillabaisse on the waterfront?"

"Oh, yes, but this is San Francisco and as you know, I'm a fish face."

"I didn't forget," I said stopping in front of Alioto's, a huge three-story eating factory right on the waterfront. "This may look like a warehouse, but the seafood is great here."

Without batting an eye, Bobbie marched right up to the first floor dining room where we were seated and dined on calamari, shrimp, crab, sole and a lot of pasta. All of this washed down with a bottle of Chenin Blanc. As we were eating and simultaneously depleting my ski fund, Bobbie looked out the picture window, gazing at the harbor, the bay and the Golden Gate Bridge beyond, now visible in the clearing skies. She positively glowed, happy with her seafood, happy with San Francisco and maybe, happy with me.

After lunch, stuffed and a little tipsy, we retrieved the car and drove along the Embarcadero, past the clock tower of the Ferry Building, which Bobbie thought was quaint. We got back on the on-ramp to the Bay Bridge and drove to Oakland en route to Martinez. Once through the Caldecott Tunnel, Bobbie marveled at the rolling green hills of Contra

Costa County, now glistening after the big rain. Finally, we came to the outskirts of Martinez and soon pulled up to my house.

My mother had been working nonstop to spruce the house up for her Chicago guest. As mothers often do, she sensed something was going on. I had brought home a few girls before, but I had always let her know that it was nothing serious. Bobbie was obviously different. In addition, she would be the only one who had slept at our house.

Bobbie slept in Kenny's room. Kenny slept in Don's bed in my room. Don was off skiing. We were all on our best behavior. My mother thought Bobbie was a darling. My father just smiled, taken by her beauty and bubbly personality. Twelve-year-old Kenny was besotted. We messed around Martinez for a day and a night and then I announced that we had to get back to Berkeley to sightsee and go to a party. Taking me aside, Bobbie wondered why we couldn't do that yet remain in Martinez. She liked it here. She liked my parents. She liked her room. She wasn't at all sure that she wanted to stay over in my apartment.

"Don't worry," I said. "It's all kosher. You can sleep in one of the twin beds. I can sleep on the daybed in the living room. My roommate Jean-Paul isn't there. He went home for semester break."

So, with not a lot enthusiasm, she agreed.

By the time we got to Berkeley, Bobbie had perked up. As we drove by, she marveled at the Claremont hotel, the big white chateau hotel up on a hill. Half-joking, she asked if she could stay there.

"Sure, why not. They have honeymoon suites," I kidded.

She nudged me on the shoulder. "You're only thinking about one thing. Getting me alone."

"Well, why not?"

"I don't know. This isn't Europe, Allan. You're on your home turf. It isn't fair."

"Fair is fair," I muttered and then I shut up, wondering how this was going to turn out.

Whatever, Bobbie was still excited at seeing Telegraph Avenue with its bookstores and shops. She was amazed at all the weird looking types wandering up and down the avenue. I pulled into the apartment parking lot and lugged her suitcase upstairs. I had cleaned up the place. It was now spic-and-span. She nodded in approval at the kitchen, the living room, the back balcony and even the bedroom, all nice and tidy.

"Oh, it's just like a home," she exclaimed. "You're lucky you can live in an apartment and fix your own food. This might be fun. We can play house."

"Yeah, sure. House."

"I guess you can sleep in one of the twins," she said after checking out the bedroom. "After all, we did share rooms in Europe."

"Yes, we sure did," I answered.

Embarrassed silence. We kissed and then she pulled away, saying she wanted to see the campus. So we hiked up Telegraph and walked through campus. Only a few students were about. Still, Bobbie was impressed with the buildings, the grounds, Sather gate, the Campanile and the library. After a quick look around, we walked back down Telegraph and had an espresso at the Mediterannum Café where she checked out the beat crowd.

"It's just like you said, Allan. I half expect to see Jack Kerouac anytime."

We browsed at Cody's Bookstore and then we went to the supermarket a few blocks away where I had once shoplifted meat. The manager gave me the eye as we walked in, but said nothing. I dutifully shopped and paid for steak, potatoes and vegetables. I was planning an Allan Brown feast, knowing that Jean-Paul had an excellent bottle of wine stashed away.

We returned to the apartment, put on some music and had a sip of wine. It was dark now, lights glittering outside. Bobbie felt at home, more at ease. A little tipsy, she started dancing around while I cooked. She later made a salad and we sat down to a candlelight dinner with Eddie Piaf in the background. She dove into the steak, remarking that it wasn't bad for a "guy" steak.

"Here we are, like an old married couple," I said.

"Yes, so it would seem, Allan. Cheers"

We clinked glasses.

It promised to be a warm night in the middle of the California winter.

***

The next morning, a guilt trip.

"Oh, I shouldn't have done that!" she said sitting bolt upright in bed, the covers slipping down.

"Done what?" I mumbled, still buried in the covers.

"You know."

"What?"

It was the same old story. Bobbie couldn't admit to herself that she was a creature of the flesh. She still had this starry-eyed vision of herself as a virgin bride in a white gown in a big cathedral with many kids.

Eventually, we got up, dressed and went over to the Terrace for breakfast. Later, we drove around Berkeley and up into the hills to Tilden Park, where we hiked through the eucalyptus groves and strolled around Lake Anza on what was now a warm spring-like day. Bobbie kept marveling at the weather.

"How can this be? In the low seventies in the middle of winter."

"It's just the Bay Area. Mild year round," I explained

"And to think it's about twenty-degrees now in Chicago. Maybe zero, with the wind chill."

"No kidding."

Later that afternoon, we cleaned up and visited Gerard at his apartment near the Claremont Hotel. This was a cool, ultramodern three-bedroom place with floor to ceiling windows, sort of a Bauhaus style. He was there was his girlfriend Bonnie, a tall, blonde Jew from Bel Aire. We had a beer and then decided to head over to San Francisco for dinner and some nightlife. Bobbie was eager to have another meal at Fisherman's Wharf, but we settled on Italian in North Beach.

"Who knows, we may run into Ginsberg or Kerouac," I remarked.

"Really?" said Bobbie, wide-eyed. She was a fan of *On The Road* despite being a self-admitted Midwestern square.

"Oh, yeah," I said.

"Hey, Al," interjected Gerard. "Why don't we check out City Lights Bookstore first? The beats hang out there."

So late afternoon, we set off for the City, crossing the Bay Bridge riding into the glare of the sun now sinking behind a fog bank on the Golden Gate. We found a parking spot on a Chinatown side street and checked out the tourist junk shops along Grant Street. We walked over to Columbus and Broadway where we ducked into Ferlinghetti's City Lights Bookstore.

The place was jammed with beards and sandals, tweeds and pipes and long black hair in long black dresses with pancake make up. Bobbie was taken aback. Later, she said it was the weirdest bookstore she had ever been in. In addition to the predictable poetry and literature sections, there was one whole section devoted to the exotic sexual practices of various cultures, including works on the Karma Sutra. There was also section for homosexuals, proudly featuring John Rechy's *City of Night* and Gore Vidal's *The City and the Pillar*—cult hits among the queers.

After an hour of browsing, we trudged along Columbus Avenue to Washington Square, where we found a cheap, little Italian joint. We dined on lasagna and fettuccini. Bobbie still had her seafood, a delicious calamari. We downed it all with a liter of local Pisano red. Later, we retired to Enrico's outdoor café on Broadway where we had a liquor-laden coffee. Enrico's was one of the newer hip hangouts, which prided itself on its diverse clientele: lawyers, politicians, beats, actors, students, prostitutes, transvestites and guys with broken noses and strange Brooklyn accents.

Following Enrico's, we strolled up and down Broadway listening to the jazz emanating from the various nightclubs, one of which featured Gerry Mulligan jamming on his sax with some group. We finished the night off with a Black Russian at the "Top of the Mark" at the Mark Hopkins Hotel. We managed to find a seat near a window in the lavish Art Deco bar with its glittering views of the City and the Bay Area. Bobbie was impressed. "Much better than the Pru," she declared.

After this San Francisco outing, my ski fund was entirely depleted.

***

The next night we went to a party that Gerard had arranged at his apartment in honor of Bobbie. Many frat brothers and their dates, fiancées and wives were there, intrigued that a Chicago girl would travel all the way to the Bay Area for the likes of "Brown" as they put it. "She must be some chick!" said Rich Petrillo.

We sang old fraternity drinking songs, drank beer and hard liquor, and in general carried on. Bobbie put on a charm show that snowed everybody. She sat cross-legged on the living room rug in her little black dress and sang several Irish ditties, in a clear, sweet, perfectly pitched voice. A born performer the brothers later said. Later I heard things like, "So Brown finally got hooked." "Think he'll tie the knot?" "Dunno." "She's the best he'll ever find."

***

The following day, Bobbie's last full day in California, we beat it out of the Bay Area. Bobbie had been bugging me to see where gold had been discovered. I dutifully drove to Sacramento and up Highway 50 until we hit the turnoff to Colma, the scene of the discovery that set off the largest gold rush in the history of the planet. The town was now a well-restored tourist trap and featured a replica of the mill where a workman under James Marshall had stumbled across some gold nuggets in 1848. Bobbie was duly impressed, but surprised to learn that John Sutter, who owned the mill, never profited from the gold rush and died broke.

"Despite everything, it's a dream that never dies in California," I said. "This is still the land of riches."

"Yes, I've heard," she replied. "I know a couple from my neighborhood who married and settled here in Sacramento. John runs a bowling alley. Susan claims they're doing well and they have bought a house. Both are only high school graduates."

"Well, you have to start somewhere, don't you?" I responded.

"I suppose," she said looking off into the green foothills of the Sierras.

Back on Highway 50, I suggested we drive to South Shore on Lake Tahoe. "Do a bit of gambling on the Nevada side and check out one of the twenty-four-hour wedding chapels," I casually remarked.

"Wedding chapel?" She blinked.

"Yes, the famous ten-minute wedding ceremony. I know a lot of friends who have tied the knot that way."

"What are you saying, Allan?"

"Well, maybe we should end all this indecision about the Peace Corps and get hitched so we can go in together."

"Hitched?"

"Like married," I said.

"Oh."

Then as if she hadn't heard the marriage part, she said, "Well it would be interesting to see Lake Tahoe. I've never been in a gambling casino. I've always wanted to play roulette and watch that little ball go around and around."

I could sense her defenses were down. I wasn't sure if I wanted to go through with this, but I felt compelled to push it to the limit to see what there really was between her and me.

I was now speeding east on Highway 50 up into the mountains with snow banks lining the road. As we traveled along, we talked about the Peace Corps. We both wanted to go to a French speaking African country and teach English. The former British colonies weren't for us. Too stuffy, too rigid. The French, on the other hand, had instilled French culture into their colonies and mixed it up with the natives.

By the time we reached the mountain town of Twin Pines, Bobbie realized that I was serious. It wasn't a lark. She started having second thoughts.

"You know, Allan, I'm flattered. But as I told you many times I want a Catholic wedding at Holy Name Cathedral in Chicago with all my family and friends around."

"Think of all the money your dad would save if we simply ran off," I said sarcastically. "Or he could give us the cash instead."

Hesitation. She looked out the window at the snow banks and the pines flashing by. Finally, she said, "Allan, this is nuts. We can't do this."

"Why not?" I responded. "Let's get it over with. Let's get it done. And then we can plan our lives. Two years in the Peace Corps. Two years in Europe going to school. Then back in the U.S. where I might launch a career or go to law school."

She freaked. "Allan, turn this car around! I can't run off to Nevada and get married like some crazy California girl. I want to be married in Holy Name Cathedral and I want my kids to be Catholic, raised in the Midwest."

Silence. I didn't answer.

There it was. So stark. So futile. It was the same song that she had sung in Europe. And what was I to her? Just a traveling companion for Europe. A convenience. A flaky California boy who dreamed of running off to some faraway country.

She glanced over, looking contrite. I said nothing.

I drove for a couple more miles then pulled into a roadside gas station/grocery store where I bought some cokes. We leaned up against the car drinking the cokes in the warm afternoon sun, the rays bouncing off the surrounding fields of snow. The scent of resin was in the air; a bird chirped now and then; a gentle wind whispered in the pines. A lone truck roared down Highway 50. After a while, we got back in the car and headed back to Berkeley.

***

Back at the apartment, Bobbie packed for her flight back to Chicago the next day, and I slept on the couch. On the drive over to the airport, Bobbie was quiet, maybe feeling guilty, maybe having second thoughts. Finally, she said, "I had a wonderful time out here, Allan. I'm sorry to have hurt your feelings about Tahoe. I have to think about all of this. I'll phone you tomorrow and I promise to take a look at the Peace Corps application."

The next day, no phone call. The following day, no phone call. The third day—ring. "I been meaning to phone," she said, "but I've been so busy getting reorganized for school. Also, I wanted time to think."

"So what do you think?" I asked.

"I still don't know about the Peace Corps, Allan. It's pointless to fill out the application unless we go in together, and I'm not ready to commit. I've always planned to work after I graduate. I need a little career in Chicago. It's always been a dream of mine to work downtown and have my own place. I don't know."

Well I knew. The Peace Corps dream was dead. If I went, I went in alone. She had also mentioned that Tom was back in town. He had dropped out of the Naval Academy was now going to Northwestern University.

"Tom and I are only friends," she insisted. "He came over to the house once over Christmas. I still care for you Allan, and I had a great time in the Bay Area."

"Yeah, it was good, wasn't it?" I said.

She never did fill out that Peach Corps application. However, after a lot of indecision, I did.

31. OPTIONS

The Peace Corps application that I had picked up at the Student Union was a handsome blue and white booklet with an embossed American eagle. Inside it had a photo of President Kennedy and a quote from his 1961 Inaugural Address: "Ask not what your country can do for you; ask what you can do for your country." On the opposite page was a photo of Peace Corps Director Sargent Shriver with a much longer message about the glories of serving our country in far-away places.

I had just attended a Peace Corps recruiting session in the auditorium at the Student Union. The recruiter told the packed audience that Berkeley supplied most of the Peace Corps volunteers from the West Coast. He said the sky was the limit as to where you wanted to go and what you wanted to do. Volunteers were serving in Africa, Asia, Latin America and the Caribbean. All majors were welcome. Of course, if you had some specific skills such as teaching, farming or construction, that was even better. If you spoke a foreign language, great. That might determine where you served. However, if you didn't, no problem. The Peace Corps would teach you one. He finished with the final inducements that got everybody's pulse racing:

"First, all you men who join will receive an automatic deferment from the military while you are in the Peace Corps. Second, all volunteers will receive two thousand dollars in severance pay for their service—money no doubt many of you could use for graduate school. And third, if you want to work for another government agency such as the State Department, Central Intelligence Agency or the Agency for International Development, you most likely will get preferential treatment as a former Peace Corps volunteer. So what are you waiting for? Fill out that application," he said, snapping shut his briefcase. "Questions?"

The application was daunting. Twenty pages of questions to answer. In addition to my personal and educational background and my work history, they wanted to know if I had ever served with an intelligence agency or if I had ever been convicted of a felony. They wanted several letters of recommendations. In addition, I had to write an essay on why I wanted to join the Peace Corps. I also had to indicate where I wanted to serve—Africa, Latin America, Asia, etc. Further, the recruiter had mentioned that all applicants had to be willing to undergo an extensive background check by the FBI. I had to ask myself if I was willing to go through all this application hassle to join up. Was I willing to bury myself in some exotic, overseas jungle for two years? Was I willing to do this alone since Bobbie had skipped out? I had to think.

***

Thus it was one afternoon, I sat down at the dining room table with a yellow legal pad to review my options. First, I wrote down what I positively did not want to do. Number one was to go out into the cold cruel world and get a corporate job. I shuddered at the thought.

Yet jobs were plentiful. Just about any male college graduate who wanted to work in corporate America could do so. In fact, many of my fraternity brothers had already lined up jobs as trainees at IBM, Standard Oil and Bank of America. A couple had even taken a job at Capwells. Most planned to escape the draft by joining the National Guard or the Army Reserves. Many were marrying their college sweetheart right after graduation. All very orderly. All very predictable. All straight out of the pages of William Whyte's *Organization Man*.

***

Number two on my list of the things that I didn't want to do was go into the Army. Army ROTC taught me that military service wasn't for me. It was bad enough to be drafted when there was no war in sight, but in the spring of 1963, the U.S. was becoming increasingly involved in Southeast Asia. There were news reports of military "advisors" being sent to help the South Vietnamese Army fight the Communist Viet Cong, who were trying to take over the south. U.S. Army helicopter pilots were also being sent over there to ferry the South Vietnamese troops to various battlegrounds.

I recalled the night I was riding the Broadway bus in Oakland after seeing a movie at the Paramount Theater. There was only one other passenger on board. He was a scruffy looking guy in jeans and a ratty windbreaker. He had a scarred face and a ragged crew cut that was in the process of growing out. After a block, he got up from his seat and slipped into a seat behind me. I could smell his whiskey breath as he leaned forward. I wasn't sure if he was going to rob me or kiss me.

"Hey, buddy, you want to see some medals?" he rasped.

"Bug off," I said scooting away.

He leaned closer. "Hey, don't be afraid. I'm on the up and up. I'm Special Forces, U.S. Army. I know I don't look like it. I'm out of uniform. Here, look at my medals." He shoved a handful of ribbons and medals over to me. I picked through them. They didn't make any sense to me except to verify that he probably was a soldier.

"Hey, buddy," he said again, still talking in my ear. "Stay cool. I know a lot of shit about what's going on in Southeast Asia."

Now interested, I asked, "What shit is that?"

"Do you know where Laos is?"

"Somewhere near South Vietnam," I answered.

"Yeah right, just to the west of it. It's a little landlocked shit hole, but it runs right along the border of South Vietnam for hundreds of klicks (kilometers). Very important spot. We are in there up to our eyeballs."

"How come you know so much about this?" I asked.

"I was a radioman up-country in Laos, part of a Special Forces team. We worked with the CIA. We worked with the Hmong guerrillas—a pretty brutal bunch. The communist Pathet Lao want to take over Laos. Nobody here in the U.S. knows a thing about it. All top secret."

"No kidding," I said skeptically. "So why are you telling me this?"

"I've got to tell someone man. I can't tell friends or family for security reasons, so I'm telling you, a total stranger."

"No shit."

"Yeah, I've seen stuff that no man ought to see. These people, both sides are real savages. Cut off balls and dicks in mouths. Severed heads on pikes. Poison punji sticks. You can die an ugly death from them. You name it, these fuckers will do it. All of it encouraged by the CIA. The CIA has its own fuckin' airline to ship arms and opium. *Air America*, they call it."

"Air America?"

"Yeah, right."

The guy was silent for a minute, staring out the window and then he got up abruptly and lurched out the door of bus at the next stop, shouting, "See ya around, buddy."

I didn't know whether to believe this dude or not. Maybe he was making it up. Maybe he wasn't ever in the U.S. Special Forces. Maybe he bought his medals from an Army Surplus store. Nonetheless, I had a forbidding sense the U.S. Army was finding its war.

***

Number three on my list of options was law school; a practical option that I wasn't too enthused about. Still, I knew law school would prepare me for a profession that was in demand and at the same time give me a student deferment. Although I had done rather mediocre on the law school test (all those symbolic logic symbols threw me off), my score was still good enough to enroll at Hastings Law School in San Francisco in the fall. This was no big feat. Hastings took any Berkeley graduate. It was the default law school for Berkeley graduates who couldn't get into the more competitive Boalt Law School on campus. However, once admitted, you had to deal with a cutthroat environment in which the school tried to weed out as many students as possible.

Gerard was going to Hastings and he said it was a bitch. He was hanging on by his fingertips. He showed me his law books — thick, dense tomes of one thousand years of jurisprudence — British and American case law. Then Gerard showed me his briefs written on yellow legal pads, page after page of dull legal rhetoric.

"Five or six hours a night of intensive studying, plus three hours of classes over in the City. I'm stressed," he said.

"Wow."

"Yeah, it's a bitch, Al. I don't know how much longer I can last. I didn't do too well on my last test."

"Well, keep slugging away," I encouraged.

"Yeah, that's what Bonnie keeps saying. This is all her idea. I'm not sure I want to be a lawyer. But you know L.A. Jews. They have to marry either a doctor or a lawyer."

"Well, what do you want to do?" I said, sensing that Gerard wasn't thinking clearly, his head too full of Jewish pussy.

"Right now, I'm thinking if this doesn't work out, I'd like to go to France for a year and become certified to teach French like my old man. He said he would foot the bill. Bonnie thinks it's a dumb idea. She says I'll be throwing my life away, making a pittance."

"Maybe," I said. "But what about the draft?"

"Dad's already checked it out. He says the Martinez draft board gives student deferments to study abroad."

"Sounds like you're set to go."

"Yeah, well, we'll see," said Gerard turning back to his law books.

Gerard was lucky—twenty-four years old, still in school and still being supported by his parents. An only child.

My father, on the other hand, had already served notice that once I graduated the money spigot would be turned off. "You are on your own, Allan," he had said. "We supported you for four years at Berkeley and a year abroad. I think we have done our bit, don't you? Time to get a job."

"Sure, Dad," I said. "I don't expect anything more. Although, you know I'm considering law school."

"That's nice," he responded. "But as I said, you're going to have to make that on your own. Get a part-time job or something. Stretch law school out to four years so you can work. Maybe go to night school. I know many Martinez lawyers who did that. Maybe Hastings has night school."

"I don't know about that. I'll have to check it out," I said. At the same time, I was thinking that my father had no problem supporting Don while he took a fifth year in Engineering at Berkeley. But that was different. Don was in a serious curriculum—mechanical engineering. When he got out, he would get a good job. I, on the other hand, had only a history degree.

***

So, without the money or perhaps enough motivation to go to law school, I settled on the Peace Corps. I felt it offered the most tantalizing opportunity: two years abroad, fun and adventure in some underdeveloped country. I had read Joseph Conrad's *Heart of Darkness*. I wanted to go upriver, look for Kurtz and get fashionably ill with malaria (but not too ill). I wanted to see the look of enlightenment on the faces of the happy natives as I unveiled some piece of Western wisdom in an open-air classroom in the jungle. I wanted to hang out with old colonials at their club and hear how it used to be when they ran things. I wanted to have fun with the sons of the new rulers who knew how to party.

Then there was that draft deferment for two years. No fuss, no muss. By the end of my Peace Corps service, I would be twenty-five. All I had to do was spend a year in graduate school financed by my two grand severance pay and I would be over the hump. I would be past the magic age of twenty-six. No longer draftable. Finally free from the clutches of the military. I dutifully filled out the twenty-page Peace Corps application, indicating I wanted to go to French speaking Africa.

By this time, I knew something about Africa. I was taking a course called the "Politics of Sub-Saharan Africa" taught by a Professor Y. Many African nations had already become, or were in the process of becoming, independent: Nigeria, Kenya, Ivory Coast, Senegal, Ghana, Belgian Congo, etc. It was a heady time. Hopes were high for a united democratic Africa. Its leaders had all been educated at the finest universities in Britain, France and America. Presumably, all had been inculcated in the values of democracy. Constitutions had been written, many modeled on the American constitution. Legislatures were set up; the electoral process had been established. There were just a few problems.

Britain, France, Belgium and Germany had paid little attention to tribal loyalties when drawing up the borders of their new African domains. Many tribes were deadly rivals. Even after independence, there was no let up in the commercial exploitation by the former colonial powers. These countries might have been politically independent, but they were still economically dependent on the West.

While U.S. commercial exploitation was minimal compared to Europe's, our influence was strongly felt. The U.S. was active in the propaganda war, trying to convince Africans that capitalism was the way to go instead of socialism or communism. During this time, some of the new African leaders were entertaining thoughts of socialist style governments, saying that it was a more natural fit to their tribal traditions of sharing. Delegations of Soviets began to show up more frequently along with generous foreign aid.

According to Professor Y, the Peace Corps was part of the propaganda war to win the hearts and minds of the Africans. The Kennedy administration thought that the sight of healthy, smart, dedicated young Americans helping Africans live a better life would be an inspiration to emulate America.

"So you see, ladies and gentlemen, it's an open question as to how these countries will proceed. The democratic trappings are there, but those shallow imitations of Western democracy are no guarantee of a free society," concluded Professor Y. at the end of his course. "The Chinese have an ancient saying that might apply to Africa: *May you live in interesting times.* In case you didn't know, that saying is a Chinese curse."

***

A few weeks later, a knock at our apartment door. Jean-Paul was studying at the dining room table. I was half-asleep in the bedroom trying to take a nap. Jean-Paul had no idea I was home. He muttered "*merde*" and answered the door.

"Yes?"

Jean-Paul was confronted by a man in a dark suit with sunglasses who identified himself as a FBI agent. "Sorry to disturb you, but we are doing a background check on Allan Brown. Are you his roommate?"

"Ah, yes," Jean-Paul responded warily.

"As you may know, Mr. Brown has applied to the Peace Corps, and we are required to do this background check. May I come in and ask you a few questions?"

"Ah, I guess," said Jean-Paul, letting the agent in. After he offered the agent a seat on the couch, the interview began.

"How long have you known Allan Brown?"

"Oh, a few years? We were fraternity brothers."

"Would you say he was a person of good character?"

"Ah, sure. I mean he works hard at his studies. He surveys in the summer for money for school. He seems to be a good guy."

"What about his student associates here at Berkeley? Is he active in campus politics or any radical off-campus organizations like SLATE?"

"Oh no. He is very apolitical. I don't think he has ever joined any student group."

"Do you think he is sincere in wanting to join the Peace Corps? A lot of males apply only to get out of the Army."

"But of course, he is sincere. Allan has spent time in Europe. He studied in France. He speaks decent French for an American. And he has talked about going into the Peace Corps for months. He has talked about how he wants to help these countries if he can," said Jean-Paul convincingly.

The interview went on for another fifteen minutes. I could tell Jean-Paul was growing tired of bullshitting the agent. I owed him a great bottle of wine. Finally, the agent wrapped up his interview and left.

I got up and went into the living room. "Thanks pal," I said.

Jean-Paul gave a start. "*Mon Dieu*, you're here! If I had known that, I would have dragged you out of the bedroom to deal with that guy."

"Well, he would have only come back when you were alone to conduct the interview," I replied.

"Maybe, but I don't like talking to the FBI. They'll probably wonder what you are doing here living with a Frenchman. Maybe wonder if you and I are communists or something. Also, they might look into my immigrant status and maybe revoke my green card," said Jean-Paul, irritated.

"Don't worry about it, Jean-Paul. He won't be back."

Despite my making light of the encounter, I had a feeling of unease. The FBI knew all about me. My home in Martinez, my high school, my major at college, my work history. They probably checked me out with the American Institute in France, trying to determine what I did over there. Big Brother was indeed alive and well.

***

A month later, I received a letter from the Peace Corps offering me an assignment in Nigeria, possibly teaching French. A three-month training period would begin early June and would consist of one month in Puerto Rico for jungle survival training and two months at Columbia University in New York for academic training. Would I please reply soonest?

Nigeria? I didn't want to go to Nigeria. I wanted a French speaking country such as Senegal or the Ivory Coast where I could teach English or history and converse in French daily. There was a phone number where I could speak with a Peace Corps representative in Washington DC if I had any questions. I phoned the Peace Corps office and eventually got through to some official connected with the Nigeria program.

"Well of course, Mr. Brown. You do not have accept this assignment. Other assignments, possibly to French-speaking Africa do come up, but I'm afraid this is the main one for Africa this summer. You will be part of a large contingent of volunteers going to Nigeria. The Nigerian government has requested an unprecedented number this year. So it's up to you. You can take advantage of this unique opportunity or wait until your preferred choice comes along. Good day, Mr. Brown."

I thanked him and hung up. Then I reassessed things. If I waited several months or possibly a year for another assignment, I would be a ripe target for the draft. The Martinez draft board had already inquired as to my graduation date and my plans for further schooling. I had told them I was planning on going into the Peace Corps immediately after graduating. I got a letter back telling me that the Peace Corps was a noble thing to do and that they should be notified when I actually entered Peace Corps service. They were waiting. I had no choice. If I was going into the Peace Corps, I had to take this assignment. I checked the acceptance box on the Peace Corps invitation letter and sent it off to Washington.

After that, I had a big slug of Scotch that I rarely touched. I was now a wine person. It burned going down and within a few minutes, I was feeling at peace with the world. I had made a decision. There was order in my universe. There was structure in my life. I would be spending the next two years in Nigeria. It was now early April. I would be leaving in two months for Peace Corps training. Bobbie was out. I would be going in alone. It was a done deal. I was free and clear. Or almost free and clear. I still had to deal with Darrah.

32. DARRAH

A week or so after Bobbie left, I was browsing through the Cal Bookstore, minding my own business when I was confronted by a tall, dark, curly haired girl with a crooked grin.

"Hello, Allan, how are you doing?"

"Doing great," I said, trying to remember who she was.

"Maybe you don't remember me," she said as she stuck her hand out. "I'm Darrah, Ana's friend from the dorm days."

"Oh yeah," I did remember a Darrah from a few years ago. She had been part of a group that hung out with Ana. All had gone on to join sororities.

I looked at her and smiled. She was very different from the Darrah I remembered.

Ana had introduced me to Darrah at the Strawberry Canyon swimming pool. She was about twenty pounds lighter then—very sleek and shapely in a black bathing suit. The Darrah I was looking at now was not only bordering on fat, she had pale, blotched skin with a fair amount of acne.

"So what have you been up to," I asked trying to be polite.

"I just returned from six months in Italy on a work-study program. But I'm afraid I spent too much time eating pasta," she joked.

"Yeah, that Italian cuisine can be a killer," I answered. "I did a year myself in the South of France, Aix-En-Provance."

"Yes, I know, Ana told me. I see her now and then. How's your brother, Don?"

"Don?" Then I remembered that Don had taken Darrah out several times and had remarked, "She had good hands."

"Yes, you know the taller of the Brown brothers."

"Don is engaged to a Chi Omega."

"Engaged! Well what a surprise," she said feigning shock. "Snagged by some little Sally I suppose"

"Nancy is a very nice girl," I replied thinking what a goof my brother was to let himself get caught so early.

We chatted on for a while. Darrah told me that she was majoring in English and worked on the Daily Cal. She wanted to go into journalism. I told her I was trying to finish my history major and was considering the Peace Corps.

"Really? One of my roommates is thinking about the Peace Corps next year when she graduates. Maybe she can talk to you. Do you have a number where she can reach you?"

"Sure," I said and we exchanged numbers. Then, I excused myself saying I had a class, which I didn't. Darrah wasn't my type. Too big, too pushy, too obviously desperate.

Two weeks later, I got a call at my apartment. It wasn't the room-mate. It was Darrah.

"Hey, Allan, this is Darrah. We're going to have a party at our place tomorrow night. Why don't you come over and bring some friends?"

Darrah was sharing an apartment with two classmates from L.A. — a three-bedroom affair down near Shattuck Avenue. I couldn't think what to say, so I said, "Yeah, sure," not knowing if I would go. However, for lack of anything else to do, I did go, thinking that perhaps Darrah had some cute friends.

Darrah answered the door about five-pounds lighter. Her hair was glossy and straight, her complexion clear, her chest swelled nicely under her cashmere sweater. She was mellow and charming as she sat on the couch, petting a cat. Only a few people had shown up, including the two long-term boyfriends of her roommates. We danced a little, talked a lot, drank wine and ate some middle-eastern type snacks.

Darrah called her setup "Yidville North." "I hate being around L.A. Jews," she said after a few glasses of wine. "They're so noisy, so pushy. You'd think they still lived in the ghetto."

"Really?" I said stroking her cat.

"Yes, Allan. Cal is so calm and quiet compared to UCLA or USC and of course so intellectually superior. And it's cheap. That's why I'm here. My roommates, Suzy and Peggy live in Beverley Hills. Their fathers could afford to send them anywhere, but they like it here too. It's still California, but far enough away from home."

I enjoyed listening to Darrah. She was unlike any Jewish girl I had ever met. Bold, straightforward and at times slightly devious. She reminded me of a guy in some respects. And, as I said, she was becoming increasingly attractive.

I mentioned that I was living with a Frenchman and that we had an interesting scene going at our apartment too.

"I'd love to meet Jean-Paul and Corrine and all his French friends. When's the next big dinner?"

"Ah, maybe next week. I'll give you a call," I answered.

"Great. Don't forget."

I did forget, but Darrah didn't and she phoned me. "Hey, Allan, is this dinner on or not?"

Not knowing what else to say, I said, "Sure. Saturday. See you at six."

Darrah arrived, another five pounds lighter joking she hadn't eaten since I saw her last. She was wearing a tight black sweater with a red scarf, black skirt and boots. She was indeed striking, and I could feel the animal heat coming off her.

As it turned out, there were only four of us for dinner—Jean-Paul and Corrine, Darrah and me. After a dinner of French onion soup, prime rib and fresh vegetables washed down by two bottles of Cabernet Sauvignon, we sat around and talked about Camus, Sartre and the new French movies just out. Darrah was immediately entranced by Jean-Paul as he made erudite cracks about this and that, smiling, showing off his jagged front tooth. During the meal, I got barely a nod from Darrah except a squeeze of the hand under the table.

By and by, we put on a Ravi Shankar raga, dimmed the lights and lit a joint. Soon, Jean-Paul disappeared into the bedroom with Corrine. Darrah and I were left to our own devices. After a few preliminaries, I unbuckled her bra. Darrah didn't resist. She had firm breasts and smooth skin. She did indeed have wandering hands as Don had mentioned. I began to wonder how far he had gone with her. Further, I wondered how far I wanted to go with her.

Sensing my hesitation, Darrah pulled away, put herself back together and then remarked, "I noticed a pair of skis in the hallway. Are they yours?"

"Yeah, I'm going up to Truckee next weekend and ski at Squaw. A fraternity brother belongs to a ski club lodge up there."

"You know, Allan, I love to ski. I haven't been skiing for a couple of years. One thing I hated about coming home from Italy right after Christmas was not skiing in the Alps. Why don't we go up together? Maybe you can give me some pointers. It'll be fun."

I was thinking that this was practically an open invitation. Was it worth it? Was it worth getting involved? Worse yet, was it worth sacrificing a ski weekend with some novice skier? But the image of her bare body in front of a roaring fire inspired me to say yes.

The next weekend, we were ensconced in a tiny lodge that was only an overgrown cabin with dormitory bunk beds and not much heat. There wasn't even a fireplace. It was a dreary place. Our group was the only one staying there.

Darrah and I had spent the day skiing at Squaw. It had been overcast, occasionally snowing slush. The skiing was lousy and, as I suspected, Darrah could barely ski at all. I stayed with her in the morning, giving her a few tips and then suggested she take a lesson. Then I went off on my own. Later a storm had moved in and the upper levels of Squaw were whited out. We quit early, and after a few hot wines at the Squaw Lodge, we drove back to the cabin, where Darrah fixed an excellent spaghetti dinner. As it turned, out she was the only female on this trip, but she was a good sport about being the housemother for us — feeding me and four other frat brothers. One of them managed to get a wood-burning stove going, which filled the cabin with some cheery heat.

Bedtime was early. The brothers, sensing we might want to be alone, drifted off to the boys' dorm room with a fifth of Jack Daniels and a deck of cards. Darrah and I cleaned up and sat in front of the stove. As the fire died down, a chill began to creep into the cabin. Wordlessly, we went into the woman's dorm and piled a bunch of blankets on Darrah's bed. We slipped into bed together with our clothes still on, but later they were on the floor. She had lost another five pound as was approaching her former sleekness. When I pressed for an ending, she pulled away saying that she was a virgin.

"A virgin? Six months in Italy! How can you be a virgin?" I said, surprised.

"Well, there was someone in Switzerland. We came close but never really did it. "

"Really?" I said.

***

A few days later, back in Berkeley, we went to see *Phaedra* with Melina Mercouri and Anthony Perkins. Darrah seemed to have made her mind up about us. She invited me to her apartment. Her roommates were gone. Moments after we arrived, Darrah excused herself and a few minutes later came out in a flimsy gown. We didn't waste any time. We picked up where we had left off at the ski cabin. A half hour later, Darrah was no longer a virgin. She was smiling, purring like a big cat. "You know, I always heard it could be so relaxing, especially afterwards. Here, you want a brownie? I have to study, but you can stay the night if you want."

"I have to get back," I said. "I have to get up early for my mailroom job tomorrow."

Actually, I wanted some time to think, to recalibrate so to speak. Actually, Darrah was a great lay. Her now tight, taut body drew upon some wellspring of sensuality in her that set her apart from others. The phrase, "horny Jew" was no exaggeration.

We saw each other three or four times a week after that, mostly in the late afternoon at my apartment. Darrah remarked it was a perfect setup. The afternoons for balling and the nights for studying. Nary a word was uttered about love or commitment. This was about lust, pure and simple. I was mainly the instrument through which Darrah explored her sensual possibilities. Jean-Paul told me years later that sometimes when we were noisily going at in the bedroom, he would remark to Corrine in the living room, "The elephants are mating."

Darrah thought that with Jean-Paul and Corrine we comprised a classic foursome. "Two are tiny, two are tall." Jean-Paul provided the intellectual stimulation and I the physical stimulation. Corrine cooked the food and kept things humming in the apartment and Darrah just soaked it all up.

Her attitude annoyed me sometimes, but I didn't care because our days were numbered, so it wasn't worth getting upset about. She was well aware that at the end of the school year I was going into the Peace Corps. She would return to L.A. for summer school at UCLA. So we relaxed, screwed, ate well and had a good time until early May when hints of anxiety crept in.

One day beside the pool at her apartment, she began to complain, "You know, Allan, we're spending too much time together. I have to study. I have to make straight A's if I want to get into a good graduate school."

"Darrah, chill out," I said. "You have another year to go, you'll make it."

"I'm not so sure," she replied. "I want to go to the Columbia Graduate School of Journalism, the best in the country."

"My, such ambition," I said.

"Yes, I come from rather modest circumstances in Los Angeles. Not all Jews are rich, you know."

"Yes, I know."

"My mother and father are in rental real estate. Nobody gets rich renting real estate. Jeeze, we even have to rent out the top floor of our house. The big money is in sales. I have to have a career. I can't stay home and be a good little housewife. I want to do something interesting in journalism. Everybody says I'm a great writer."

"And so you are," I said. Darrah had once looked over a history paper I had written and with a few deft strokes had done an editing job that improved it greatly.

"What about you? Why are you going into the Peace Corps?" she asked.

"Mainly to get out of the draft, but also I want to see Africa." I responded. "Maybe teach English or French."

"I think you're unfocused, Allan," she said. "Don't waste your time with the Peace Corps. You should go to law school or get a teaching degree."

"Maybe down the road, but not yet," I responded.

And so it went. It was hot in the sun. Darrah was now tan and glistening with sweat and suntan oil. We had a beer and went inside for lunch. Soon we were in the bedroom going at it. All the while she was gently hitting me on the chest saying, "This is what I mean, wasting my time with you, but oh God how I love it, I do love getting fucked. I must be a nymphomaniac."

"N...n...not at all, Darrah," I stammered. "Nymphos can't climax. That's not you at all, unless you're faking it."

"Faking it! You shit! I love it! I'm always coming all over the place. It's like I'm on fire," she said on top of me, riding up and down like on a horse, sweating, smelling of lotion and come, rolling around, with a crooked dreamy smile on her face.

***

It all came to an abrupt halt after I completed my finals. I took Darrah for a little walk. I had been scheduled to leave for the Peace Corps the first of June, but since I was done with my finals a week early, I made arrangements to stop off in Chicago to see Bobbie for a few days. Darrah had seen a photo of Bobbie and noted her blonde hair and cute Midwestern looks.

"I might have known it, a Midwestern blonde," she said scornfully. "That's what you're all about, Allan. Despite your European pretensions, you're just a frat boy at heart. You want some blonde bitch that will give you three or four brats and make a good little wifey."

"Not at all. It's over with Bobbie and me. I'm only going to visit. Also, I like Chicago. It's a great town," I explained as we walked down Telegraph Avenue.

"I thought we might have these last few days together, with no distractions, no study pressure," Darrah said sadly.

"Look, I'm sorry, Darrah, but as you yourself said, this can't go on. You have big plans. I don't fit in. You say I'm not ambitious, that I'm unfocused. Well, Mr. Unfocused is going off to the Peace Corps. Maybe I'll have some focus when I get back."

She said nothing because she knew it was true. She turned to walk down to her apartment, but before she did, I noticed tears in her eyes.

33. GRADUATION

Imagine the scene. The Class of 1963. Some three to four thousand seniors with parents, siblings and friends. Twenty to twenty-five thousand people seated in Memorial Stadium — all beaming proudly as the graduating seniors strutted about in their blue and gold gowns. It was always beautiful weather in Berkeley in early June. Clear blue skies, a mild wind with a hint of eucalyptus blowing down from Strawberry Canyon.

One by one, the seniors would file by the Chancellor, receive their diploma, flip their tassel and head on back to their seat. The whole process took about five seconds per graduate. Still, for the entire graduating class, it took over two and a half hours.

Cynics compared the proceedings to an assembly line out of the Charlie Chaplin film, *Modern Times.* Maybe, but I wouldn't know because wasn't there. I never attended my graduation ceremony. All spiffy and preppy in my new, tropical weight seersucker suit, I was winging my way to New York, via Chicago, on an American Airlines jetliner. Drinks were free and the stewardesses cute and friendly with their slim asses swaying at eye level as they moved up and down the aisle.

***

Skipping the graduation ceremony had been a major point of contention with my parents.

Father: "Here you are, the first college graduate in our family and you ditch the ceremony. I don't understand it. Let us get a little satisfaction at seeing you receive that diploma."

Mother: "You are so inconsiderate, Allan. We made a real financial sacrifice to send you to Berkeley and Europe. At the very least, we should be able see you in your cap and gown with diploma in hand. I would love to take a picture of that."

Me: "I'm sorry. But you saw the schedule. I have to be in New York a few days before graduation. What's the big deal? A lot of graduating seniors don't go to the ceremony. It's just a big cattle call. I can pick the diploma up later."

Father: "That may be, but it's your cattle call."

***

Missing my graduation ceremony was of no concern to me. However, as I strolled through campus a week earlier, I was struck by the realization that I would never again be attending classes at Cal. I would never again sit in a five-hundred-seat lecture hall and listen to some Cal professor drone on. I would never again sit around a seminar table and feel obliged to say something profound or insightful. I would never again have to sweat a Berkeley bluebook final or argue for a grade. I was done, done, done. My mediocre C average saw to that.

"We did our best for you, Mr. Brown," the administrative ghosts whispered. "You made it. Not spectacular, but good enough to graduate. Good luck with your future endeavors and don't let the door hit you on the ass on your way out."

Running through my mind was a passage that I had written in my journal that summarized how I felt after time at Berkeley:

> *Que sais-je? The question implies a suspicion that I know little or nothing at all. Socrates felt he was the wisest man in the world because he alone knew he knew nothing. Kant says we can describe a thing, but can never know the thing in itself. Camus answers that while we can never know a thing, we must try even if the effort is absurd.*

***

Back at the apartment on Ridge Avenue, more mundane matters awaited, namely, packing up and getting out of there. Jean-Paul and I had paid rent until the end of May. Jean-Paul was graduating too. He had made it through Berkeley in three years, instead of the usual four. At one point, he was taking eighteen units a semester — six courses at least. He was hell-bent on going to medical school in France next fall. He had waltzed through all his premed courses: organic chemistry, biology, physics and aced his MCAT, all the while taking German and various esoteric literature courses.

"*Médecin*," he said. "That's the ticket. It's interesting work. You help people. You are paid well. Nice house, nice car."

"Why can't you do that here in the U.S.?" I asked.

"Because it is too expensive, Al. I can't afford the tuition at these overpriced medical schools. In France, if you qualify to get in, they are free. Also I want to return to my country."

Corrine was in despair over Jean-Paul's plans to depart. She had been practically living at the apartment. She had tried to convince Jean-Paul to stay over the summer at least and to keep the apartment. She even offered to help put him through medical school.

"I'll work. I'll get a job as a secretary," she pleaded. "You know, I'm good at shorthand. My mother forced me to take it in high school. She said it would come in handy. The Cal Placement office has a lot of on campus jobs for secretaries."

Jean-Paul was unmoved. He didn't want any further entanglement with Corrine. She was madly in love with him, but Jean-Paul would not commit. As he would tell me now and then, "*Mon Dieu*, I don't know what to do with her. She is great, but I cannot marry. I cannot take her to France. It would be absurd. She doesn't understand that."

Corrine wasn't stupid. Eventually, she understood, and though devastated, she put on a good face and resigned herself to letting him go for the time being. She later told me that she thought Jean-Paul would not stay in France for long. "He's too Americanized. Also, he loves playing the role of the expatriate Frenchman here. He's used to being the biggest brain around. He'll have none of that in France. He'll just be another little Frenchman."

Corrine didn't want to return home to Sacramento to her parents. Instead, she said goodbye to Jean-Paul and moved in with another girlfriend who had also decided to hang out at Berkeley for the summer and work.

Before he drove off to his home in San Mateo in his beat-up old Chrysler, Jean- Paul shot me a hangdog look and muttered, "*L'amour, c'est dur*."

***

Corrine and Jean-Paul weren't the only ones breaking up. Gerard had decided to quit law school and to go to France for a year. This move prompted his girlfriend Bonnie to say goodbye. She couldn't conceive of being married to a future French teacher. Gerard didn't appear too upset. As he put it, "It's amazing how that Jewish pussy can cloud your mind."

"I know what you mean," I replied.

"Now, I'm free. Now, I can do what I want, which is to go to France, learn the language better and enjoy the *juenes filles*."

"Right on," I said. And we proceeded to smoke a joint at his apartment and then get drunk on Scotch while listening to Georges Brassens records.

Later that night, as I wandered through the streets of Berkeley, higher than a kite, fragmented images and words flashed through my mind:

A plateau rising 500 feet out the Midi, sunny blue and granite.

***

Fog drifting across the Necker, as the ferry docks in Heidelberg.
"Ein Mark, bitte."

***

A tall, blonde girl in smooth, slim stretch pants,
walking across the Pont Du Gard.

***

The smell of uncured wool.
The smell of other warm Aegean nights

***

The splash and gurgle of the fountains,
rising above the sun-baked roofs,
and lost in the silence of the
black Provençal skies.

***

The winds come off the beach late at night.
She turns and cries, a sweet sadness fills her knowing that what
is now will never be again.

***

Suntan lotion and hot sweat in a tiny bedroom.
The elephants and the minnows going at it.

***

A black swarm of mosquitoes.
Slow moving chocolate rivers.
Thatched huts full of laughing children

***

We speak English
Nous parlons français

***

The heartbeat of history pulsating in the air
I — an eyewitness to these times

Let's see where it goes, I thought, as I stumbled back to my apartment.

FIN

www.ingramcontent.com/pod-product-compliance
Lightning Source LLC
Chambersburg PA
CBHW031243090426

42742CB00007B/301